CW01187712

BAROQUE TRICKS

The Voicers and the Experts in Holland, August 1950 (see Chapter Seven). Left to right: Thomas Austin, Fred. Howe (Harrison & Harrison), Agnes Downes, Dr. M.A. Vente, Walter Shewring, Ralph Downes and Walter Goodey (J.W. Walker & Sons).

BAROQUE TRICKS

Adventures with the Organ Builders

by

RALPH DOWNES

POSITIF PRESS · OXFORD

© Ralph Downes and Positif Press, 1983.

Photoset in Trump Mediaeval and Printed by Parchment (Oxford) Ltd.

Designed and produced by John Brennan at the Positif Press, Oxford. All rights reserved. No part of this publication may be reproduced, stored in a retrieval system, or transmitted, in any form or by any means, electronic, mechanical, photo-copying, recording or otherwise, without the prior permission of the Publishers.

Positif Press, 130 Southfield Road, Oxford OX4 1PA, (0865) 243220

ISBN 0 906894 08 5

CONTENTS

DEDICATION	6
PREFACE	7
ACKNOWLEDGEMENTS AND CREDITS	9
CHAPTER ONE Antecedents, Early Glimmers	11
CHAPTER TWO Development	39
CHAPTER THREE Crisis of Trial and Error	67
CHAPTER FOUR Portentous Interlude	77
CHAPTER FIVE The Study of Pipe-scales (1): More Ill-fated Empiricism	99
CHAPTER SIX Illumination	109
CHAPTER SEVEN The Voicers: Study of Pipe-scales (2)	135
CHAPTER EIGHT The Study of Pipe-scales (3): An Acoustical Somersault	144
CHAPTER NINE Operation Phoenix	152
CHAPTER TEN In the Doldrums (Royal Festival Hall)	164
CHAPTER ELEVEN Fruition and an Assessment	172
CHAPTER TWELVE The Way Forward	212
NOTES	224
APPENDICES	227
INDEX	239

TO

Arthur, Chester, Dennis, Ernesto, Fred,
Harry, John, Keith, Michael, "Mike",
Philip, Reginald, Stephen, Vince, Walter,
and other esteemed friends in the
Organ-Building Craft;

and to Her

whose devotion, pertinacity, and sensitive
musical expertise sustained me on course
for half a century.

PREFACE

Some years ago, two of my friends urged me to write about my experiences during the planning and building of the then very controversial organ in the Royal Festival Hall, London; but time could never be found for such an undertaking. In any case these experiences were only part of a long evolution of ideas, emotional responses and actual practice as a performing musician, and subsequently as critic and overseer of organ design and its realisation. I venture now to hope that a full account of this development may be of some interest to the outside world. Professional colleagues have occasionally said to me, "I know what I like in an organ, but I have not much of an idea of what goes on under the bonnet". Well, there need not be any mystery about that: fortunately the laws of sound, the natural laws of acoustics, aerodynamics and mechanics on this planet do not change.

The modern sophisticated attitude towards natural laws may tend to defy rather than conform: but the older traditional conformity (even when wedded to skilful circumvention) typified, for instance, in Michael Praetorius's famous expression of gratitude to the Creator[1], is still a valid standpoint for the accomplished craftsman. It is still to be proven that the Space Age, as such, will make any notable contribution to the Arts and Humanities, or indeed to human happiness, enriching them in any way whatever.

As a 'natural' musician, I am strongly attracted to basic, even primitive phenomena: the voice of the Siamese cat charms me no less than that of its polite Anglo-Saxon cousin; equally seductive to my ear are the raucous commentary of the blackbird, close at hand, and the subtle distant notes of nightingales. I am still excited to recall the first impact of a Lewis Trumpet in a small Full Great (1915)[2], or of *Father Willis*'s Full Swell at St. Paul's (1916), or a Hill Double Trumpet and wooden Trombone speaking their *natural* tones (1918)[3], or the Exeter Father Willis.'Great to 15th' backed by an ethereal Swell Organ whose fiery trumpets were based on a slender Contra *Hautboy* (not Fagotto) (1920) — all sounds which possessed a healthy lack of inhibition; while I can still recall revelling in softer luscious combinations of 'primary colours' which completed the tonal spectrum.

Vivid contrasts such as these can be a most fruitful ingredient of music-making, whereas an unrelieved refinement, "freedom from harshness", (as one distinguished organ-builder, with an air of moralising, has expressed his objective) can in practice mean only unrelieved boredom and artistic sterility. That music-making should have to exhibit this refinement in order to become socially acceptable is indeed most curious: yet we admire fluty sopranos, deficient in real 'chest-register', and our national predilection for the disembodied falsetto hooting of some Cathedral choirboys is well known — in both instances, word-projection goes by the board. We like our grand piano hammers thickly felted to produce an infallibly 'beautiful' tone. Were they leathered, or the voices used naturally as in speech, what artistry would then be needed to control them, but how worthwhile! What aesthetic riches would be made available! Those of us who have heard Paul Badura-Skoda's Beethoven, or Paderewski's Liszt or Chopin, or Michael Howard's or Allan Wicks' choristers, can testify: truly, 'safety' in musical instruments or music-making is only for fools or cowards!

British, and in its own way, American organ-building went through just such a phase of monotonous unmusicality during the first four decades of this century. The following account, necessarily largely autobiographical, represents a kind of musical pilgrimage towards a Light which was constantly sensed rather than seen clearly. The attendant discoveries and the accumulation of practical conclusions reached in the course of that journey have been constantly assisted by the friendly and often enthusiastic co-operation of expert practitioners in the organ-building craft, to many of whom — some now no longer with us — I have presumed to dedicate this volume. I have been emboldened to do this by the sincere and sometimes touching messages of appreciation, both verbal and written, which I have often received from them at the conclusion of a successful project; evidence surely that our concerted quest, even though occasionally beset by mistakes or disagreements *en route*, had not been a vain one.

Being somewhat at a loss for a title, I recalled a chance encounter with Mr. Cecil Clutton about the time of the rebuilding of the organ in St. Albans Cathedral: "Hello", he said, "up to your baroque tricks again!" This seems to me such a felicitous expression of the views of one part of the Establishment, that I have not scrupled to make use of it — without permission.

London
February 1981

ACKNOWLEDGEMENTS AND CREDITS

Grateful thanks are due to Mr. Frederick H. Scheer (Clerk of Session) and Mrs. Guy (Edna) Atwood (sometime Organist) of the First Presbyterian Church, Plainsboro (near Princeton), New Jersey, for confirmation of the specification of the Möller organ there: also to Mr. Rodney Tomkins, BA FRCO, of Derby, for checking details of former organs in that city, in collaboration with Mr. E. R. Stow (Queen's Hall Methodist Mission), the present possessor of the Scotchbrook Notebook — an invaluable source of information. I am also grateful to the Chief Executive of Cardiff City Council for permission to publish details of the organ being built for the new St. David's Hall (Director, Robert Corder); to the following for supplying photographs and/or granting permission for their reproduction: Mrs. Margaret Mallender (Cathedral Archivist) and Dr. Eric Leigh (Assistant Organist) of Derby Cathedral (photographs of the former organ there): the view of the former organ at Brompton Oratory, and of the old Boston Music Hall organ (now rebuilt at Methuen, Massachusetts) are reproduced by permission of the Editor of *The Organ*, Dr. Bryan Hesford. The original plate of the late Gilbert Benham's photograph of the present organ at the Oratory was kindly loaned by Mr. Colin Langman (Librarian) from the collection deposited in the Organ Club Library (Royal College of Organists). Photographs of the organs in Paisley Abbey (by George Edward Russell, FRSA) and St. Mary's Church, Chigwell, Essex (by Charles K. Bowers of Isleworth) were released by Messrs J. W. Walker & Sons, who also gave permission to copy or summarise working drawings of the Paisley and Buckfast Abbey instruments. A like permission was granted by Mr. Peter Jones, FRIBA, Acting Director of Architecture, Greater London Council, for reproduction of sketches and plans; and Mr. Nicholas Boyle, Publicity Manager of the Royal Festival Hall, who supplied the general photograph of the organ there.

I am also indebted to Mr Mark Venning, Managing Director of Harrison & Harrison Ltd. for reading the draft manuscript, and for permission to reproduce the large Elevation drawn by Mr. Bob Wood for the Royal Festival Hall organ, and the photograph of the small-scale model executed by the firm about 1950-51.

Credit must also be accorded to M. C. von Haven (Copenhagen) for his photograph of the Marcussen organ in the concert hall of the Danish State Radio complex. The photograph of the organ in the Old Church, Amsterdam, is an old one whose origin cannot now be traced; that of the rebuilt organ in Gloucester Cathedral is included by permission of Gerald Pates.

The majority of these were re-photographed by my son, Professor Kerry Downes of Reading University, who also gave me invaluable advice, and read the printer's proofs as a gratuitous and highly esteemed contribution to the project. I also acknowledge gratefully the legal advice given by Mr. T. J. L. Cox (Oswald Hickson, Collier & Co.), and my old friend, Charles Higgins (formerly with Birkbeck Montagu's), who read the first draft entire; to the publisher I am indebted for essential processing of diagrams and tracings. Finally, for the preparation of the final typescript by Miss Marion Smith, an expert in that field, I must express particular indebtedness.

CHAPTER ONE

Antecedents, Early Glimmers

Although I had played the piano, with occasional bouts of amateur tuition, from the age of seven, the organ only began to attract me with a compulsive fascination about two years later. Derby, where I was born in 1904, possessed several moderate-sized 3-manual organs of good character, and the first at hand was the fine Lewis instrument built in 1888 in St. Alkmund's Church (where I was baptised). The building was a decent essay in Victorian gothic (Stevens, 1846, replacing a mediaeval building), spacious for its size, though marred by cumbersome galleries over both aisles (Plate I). When the latter were removed, about 1912 or 1913, followed by a cleaning of the organ by the local organ-builder, J. H. Adkins, the acoustics of the church

PLATE I *St. Alkmund's Church, Derby, c1900.*

were vastly improved, and this enhanced the organ's nobility of effect: from that moment came the desire to *imitate* its sound on the piano, and, distantly, to play on it. The specification was:

GREAT		SWELL	
Bordun	16	Lieblich Bordun	16
Large Open Diapason	8	Geigen Diapason	8
Small Open Diapason	8	Rohr Flöte	8
Hohl Flöte	8	Viole de Gambe	8
Octave	4	Voix Céleste	8
Wald Flöte	4	Geigen Principal	4
Superoctave	2	Mixture 3 rks	2
Mixture 2 rks	1⅓	Horn	8
Trumpet	8	Oboe	8
		Vox Humana	8
CHOIR (open)		Clarion	4
Salicional	8	Tremulant	
Lieblich Gedackt	8		
Dulciana	8	PEDAL	
Flauto Traverso	4	Great Bass	16
Piccolo Harmonique	2	Violon	16
Clarinet (enclosed)	8	Sub Bass	16
		Bass Flute	8

Mechanical action for everything except the Pedals, which were pneumatic. Six mechanical composition pedals, balanced Swell pedal. Five unison couplers (no Choir to Great). Hand-blown, pressure probably 3½ inches (Water Gauge).

This organ was outstandingly good, even though the key-actions were on the heavy side: most of the pipework was of spotted metal, and the Principals had brilliance and drive, especially the 4-foot pitch, as was characteristic of Lewis's best work. The three string-toned stops were particularly fine, the Violon almost giving to the Pedal the sound of a soft reed, from its open position on the north aisle front. The Full Great was most impressive for its size, due to the rich voicing of all its components. (*This* organ no longer exists, and the church itself was razed to the ground in the late 1960s.) Not a little of the organ's excellence of effect was due to the performance of the organist, F. Isherwood Plummer, ARCM ARCO, who had travelled weekly to the RCM from his home in Southport, Lancs, to study with W. S. Hoyte, subsequently (after graduation) becoming organist of the Cathedral at Fredericton, NB, before finally settling in Derby.

In the other organs I shall mention as instruments of character, even *personality*, this impression was again largely due to the performance of their incumbents, who were proud of and jealously wedded to them, displaying in their skilful control a virtuosity and musical involvement potentially quite equal to today's standards. If there were deficiencies, these were in the realm of repertoire and sometimes of taste. In this provincial Midland town, only the most popular Bach works were heard: movements of Mendelssohn, Widor and Rheinberger; W. T. Best's remarkable transcriptions (invaluable at a time when orchestral or chamber concerts were rare, and broadcasting non-existent): the more 'immediate' works of the French school — Dubois, Lefébure-Wély, Guilmant, Grison, Salomé, Saint-Saëns, Batiste even; English works by Henry Smart, S. S. Wesley, Stanford, Parry, even John Ireland, and the popular blind organists, Hollins and Wolstenholme. Of Franck or Reger, practically nothing ever, and absolutely nothing pre-Bach. Professional organists needed to spend many hours of the day teaching the piano in order to supplement the meagre salaries paid by their church appointments — on average about £50 to £60 per year. But if their repertoire seemed unenterprising or over-popularly orientated, their better performances did attract an audience — in church; for unlike Nottingham, Sheffield or Birmingham, Derby had no large public hall. Concerts by the local Choral Union (and Orchestral Society) were given in the railway-station-like Drill Hall of the Notts and Derby Regiment, where stood my Exhibit No. 2 — a large and memorable 3-manual Bevington, which had appeared in one of the exhibitions, possibly 1868[4], and had been purchased for a song afterwards.

Standing in glorious isolation between high banks of chorus seating, it looked impressive with its array of long painted front pipes. It was but rarely played, apart from oratorio accompaniments, but it had an agreeably old-fashioned mellow sound, to which a Bell Diapason contributed a peculiar quality. The flue-work predominated, the reeds being somewhat crude but not very loud, the upperwork rather fluty: the names of all four Pedal stops (including a reed 16-feet) were prefixed by 'Grand', which summed up their effect. It was quite undeserving of its eventual neglect and destruction, and the sight and sound of it always thrilled me much in the way that I remembered the much larger old Gray & Davison organ in the Crystal Palace in 1911 at the Festival of Empire.

Then there was All Saints' Church — now altered and called The Cathedral. This was a plain rectangular, mainly barrel-vaulted building by James Gibbs (1725), resembling his design for St Martin's-in-the-Fields, London, but loftier and plainer, without side galleries: thus it was acoustically perfect for music, even when full (Plate II). Here stood proudly in a west gallery a splendidly outspoken old organ built by Elliott in 1807, in an earlier case attributed to Father Smith by some. Its four heavily-corniced towers gave it a majestic appearance which was quite in character with its voice (Plate III). It was enlarged, with full-compass Pedal stops, by Stringer in 1879, and, I think, renovated somewhat by Hill around the turn of the century [5]. The specification in 1917[6] was:

GREAT		SWELL	
Double Diapason (st)	16	Bourdon	16
Open Diapason (front)	8	Open Diapason	8
Open Diapason	8	Stopped Diapason	8
Clarabella	8	Keraulophon	8
Keraulophon	8	Vox Angelica (tc)	8
Stopped Diapason	8	Principal	4
Principal	4	Wald Flute	4
Flute	4	Flageolet	2
Twelfth	2⅔	Mixture	III or IV
Fifteenth	2	Contra Fagotto	16
Mixture	IV	Cornopean	8
Trumpet	8	Oboe	8
		Clarion	4
CHOIR		(No tremulant)	
Open Diapason	8		
Gedact	8	PEDAL	
Dulciana	8	Open Diapason (w)	16
Bell Gamba	8	Bourdon	16
Flute	4	Violoncello (ext)	8
Piccolo	2	Bass Flute (ext)	8
Clarionet	8	Trombone	16
		Trumpet (ext)	8

Six unison couplers. Six or seven mechanical composition-pedals. Lever swell-pedal. Manual actions, tracker. Pedal action, pneumatic. Hand-blown: pressure probably between 2½ and 3 inches.

At that period this organ was played with distinction by T. H. Bennett, a highly successful local choral conductor, who understood and identified completely with its striking qualities. Staccato chords on Full Great with its snappy tracker-action had the pungency of *chamade* trumpets! The fluework had charm, sweetness and warmth, but was substantial enough to almost completely mask the closed Full Swell: the transformation when the box was opened sent cold shivers

PLATE II *All Saints' Church, Derby.*

down the spine! The Full Organ, especially if heard while entering at the west door, resembled a brass band, the Pedal reeds having pungency and drive without actually being very loud, silhouetted, as it were, against the warm tone of the Open Woods. Bottom G of the Trombone had a slight 'back-curve' in the tongue, which gave a gratuitous 32-foot beat when it was held with the Full Organ: this I adored! From its position in the gallery this organ could give a firm lead to capacity congregations on Sunday nights, singing really heartily: and before Evensong began they listened attentively to a half-hour recital in which the varied resources of the organ were fully exploited. At the age of 14 I was for a time Deputy Organist [*sic*] and knew the instrument well, trying (albeit with quite insufficient technique) to copy Bennett's brilliant style of playing, which had a profound and lasting effect on my attitude to the organ. When he was removed from the post, and I had left Derby, his successors failed to appreciate the instrument; it was neglected and finally destroyed *in toto* about 1940. A contributory factor was the change in worship from very 'low' evangelical to a 'broad-church' Cathedral service, demanding niceties of musical expression which the incumbents were unable to extract from the instrument; also, its west-end position was deemed a serious handicap for choir accompaniment. Yet in the days of Bennett's tenure the choir sang anthems, and his competence was such that ensemble

PLATE III *All Saints' Church, Derby, casework by Bernard Smith, c1703.*

presented no problems as he accompanied them, perhaps sixty feet away.

To continue this review of formative influences in my developing organ-aesthetic: at the opposite end of the scale was the large 'urbane' 4-manual organ on which I had my first real organ lessons: Ingram, rebuilt by Henry Willis II, in St. Werburgh's broad modern gothic church. Its *size* made it impressive, even though it was somewhat buried in a large north-east chamber. Here again, a fine player — Norman Hibbert, Mus Bac, one of Dr. Keeton's famous Peterborough brood — invested the organ with added personality: but apart from appreciation of his masterly performance, which even included transcriptions of Beethoven symphony movements, and once, a completely successful accompaniment of the Finale of Franck's Sonata for Violin and Piano (!), I was never greatly moved by the organ itself, even though I could admire its excellent Solo division (which included Tubas 8- and 4-feet, superb Orchestral Oboe and Clarionet, and liquid Harmonic Flutes) situated behind a north aisle front, and next to Pedal Trombones and Posaunes which had a telling effect in the nave. In summarised form the specification was:

GREAT
16 8 8 8 8 8 4 4 2⅔ 2 III 8
SWELL
16 8 8(Hohl) 8/8 4 2 III 16 8 8 4 Trem
CHOIR
8 8 8 8 4 4 2 8 (Cl)
SOLO (encl) (open)
8 4 8 8 8(Vox h) Trem   8 4
PEDAL
32(st) 16 16 16 10⅔ 8 8 16 8

Action: tubular pneumatic. Various pressures

Three other excellent local organs made their impact on my imagination, each of about 30 speaking stops: the Temperance Hall (Binns), a good substantial sound with fiery Swell reeds which made a tonal blaze with added octave-couplers; King Street Wesleyan Church (reputedly by Booth of Wakefield)[7], which was rather an aristocrat, with 16-foot Double Diapason front in a fine 3-towered classical case of polished walnut or mahogany, and a lifelike Pedal Contra Fagotto 16-feet; Green Hill Wesleyan Church (Peter Conacher) with finely brash (?French) Swell reeds 8 8; and lastly St Andrew's, of which more anon: this was said to be by Forster & Andrews of Hull[8]. It stood in an open south-easterly position in a broad, lofty Victorian gothic church, had a charmingly reticent but brilliant flue chorus and free-toned reeds including a Pedal Double Trumpet 16-feet. All these organs were well sited, and occasioned me many thrilling experiences in the years 1915-19, both at first and second hand.

Two other arrivals in Derby had a permanent influence on my thinking. The first was a magnificent *Orgue Mustel*, installed about 1913-14 in a local 'super cinema': with a highly proficient player this provided an exciting foretaste of French organ-sonorities. It was an instrument of great versatility and power (even though literally a 'glorified harmonium'[9]). Little did I dream that in a few years I should be playing it professionally myself! The other was Pattman's famous travelling organ, built by Harrison of Durham. (An account of this instrument appears in *The Harrison Story* by Laurence Elvin.) What Elvin does *not* say is that after a two-week run at the London Coliseum in November 1916, the organ paused for a few days at the Hippodrome (variety theatre), Derby. There, in response to a cordial invitation (sought from the great man himself) I arrived as a 12-year-old Boy Scout on the Saturday morning to try out the instrument. It was my first contact with Harrisons' voicing, and I duly noted the fine string-tones, limpid flutes, solid diapasons, 'leathery' Tubas, and especially the phenomenal 6-stop Swell with a Double Trumpet 16-feet as the *only* reed[10].

In the appalling acoustical conditions of a variety theatre stage, this organ was one hundred per cent effective! I also noted, for future reference, as it turned out, the terribly stiff balanced swell-pedals which were connected from the detached moveable console to the boxes by means of Bowden cables! Pattman had strong ankles, as his virtuoso improvised pedal-cadenzas in the 'show' amply demonstrated: but I could scarcely move the swells at all, with short legs into the bargain. Of course, being directly mechanical, they *worked*, instantly, and were skilfully employed in *sforzandi* in pieces like Grieg's *Peer Gynt Suite*, or the accompaniment of '*Mon coeur s'ouvre à ta voix*' from Saint-Saëns' *Samson et Dalila*!

The Derby organs were tuned and maintained efficiently by the local organ-builder, Adkins, mentioned earlier, who had imagination and was a competent organist. I spent many an hour sitting by his voicing machine, subconsciously imbibing information while he worked on the pipes of various reeds and string-tones; and got his views on many topics. Being used to rather 'open' reed tone, I was fascinated by the 'close' sound of a trumpet whose spring had been knocked down too far, making the tongue too short for the resonator: this was the first of several corrupt influences — the 'smooth reed'; (but this was due to *my* preference, not Mr Adkins', who did not approve). The second was the 'big diapason'. Here he *was* the culprit; but first I will recall being taken to Evensong on a weekday in the lovely Lichfield Cathedral in 1916, and listening ecstatically to John B. Lott, Mus Bac, accompanying the psalms (to *very* Victorian chants), and adding Great Diapasons No 3, 2 and 1, in that order, for each Gloria Patri — sometimes playing the tune *8va bassa* on the Tuba of the splendid Hill organ of that date. The sum total, architectural and musical, was to my mind Heaven itself. Said Mr Adkins, "You would enjoy hearing the new big diapason I have just put into St Andrew's organ". (See above: this was in 1920). "Of course the organ is old Forster & Andrews — the old diapasons just *breathe*, they are charming but not really adequate. I've just taken ****" (a local musical worthy) "to hear it: as we walked into the church the organist brought it on. **** gripped my arm and said, 'WHATEVER'S *THAT*?!! ...'" I was all agog, and soon found an opportunity to bother the Vicar to let me try it, spending a whole afternoon revelling in the warm blanket of tone in which it enveloped the rest of the organ. He rather kindly but firmly refused to let me repeat the performance a day or two later.

These impressions were soon to bear fruit. Under the threat of non-renewal of parental subsidy for music, I was constrained to find a job, having left school at exactly 16. I became 'Pianist-Organist' (solo) at the Trent Bridge Pavilion, Nottingham, which was running as a cinema theatre. The 'Organist' part consisted of an Interval Piece, billed 'By Request', to be played on a miserable 'American Organ' (reed, suction-operated) which had Pedals and a fake array of pipes. Wind was supplied manually, by the Manager! I even attempted to skate through the then popular Overture to *Raymond* by Ambroise Thomas, and other comparable 'light classics', but it was a wretched experience, and occasioned my first essay in the field of organ-design. With the Manager's approval I sent to Mr. Adkins for an estimate for massive improvements. As I recall, the project was for a new 2-manual detached console, one manual to work the existing reed-organ, and the other to control a new extension-chest with a large Diapason and Tuba, with upward and downward ranges — and of course a new pedal-board and electric blowing! Surprisingly at the time, it was Adkins who 'downed' the venture: "It wouldn't work, my boy: the pipes would never be in tune with the free-reeds". Meek acceptance of this reproof was the only course open to me; there was no money available anyway. Of course it was a crazy, enthusiastic idea, which had taken its rise out of the *predecessor* of Pattman's organ — the one which set Pattman thinking, in fact — billed throughout the provinces as "Max Erard and his 4-ton Cathedral Organ". Of course I had heard it: made up of a largely dummy console, with many pistons and stops which popped in and out without changing the sound (the latter being produced by a Mustel Organ as a foundation, supplemented by a few real pipes — a big diapason and a Tuba, of course) it went the round of the variety theatres for a year or two, until Pattman's put an end to pretence.

I can recall another significant conversation with Adkins, slightly previously, probably while returning from a small tuning operation at All Saints' after the repair and reinstatement of the front pipes one of which had collapsed into the nave pews. He was complaining about the old organ in general, and in particular the inadequacy of the 'old-fashioned' voicing, and I pressed him for further elucidation: how did modern voicing differ from this? These old diapasons, he said, (in fact, the whole organ) kept to one level of loudness from bass to treble — the latter, if anything, tended to fall off in strength. Modern voicing, which he saw as desirable and correct, gave more drive to the treble, making it melodic and more prominent. Here was food for reflection: though it was odd that going from All Saints' back to the Geigenprincipal-dominated Lewis Swell at St. Alkmund's, I always thought the latter sounded rather thin and miserable in comparison. I decided that perhaps the acoustics of the smaller church were to blame: of this, more anon.

The necessity of moving to Nottingham in mid-1921 brought me into direct touch with modern methods. First, I had lessons on the new Walker organ in St. Mary's church: built in 1915-16, its specification in summarised form was:

GREAT
16 $\underline{8}$ $\underline{8}$ $\underline{8}$ 8(clarab) 4 4(hfl) 2 8(Tpt)
SWELL
16(st) 8 8 8/8 4 4(w) III 16(fag) 8 8 8(Vox h) Trem
CHOIR
8 8(VdO) 8/8(flat) 4 4(hohl) Trem
SOLO (encl)   (unencl)
8 8(OOb) 8(Cl)   8(Tuba)   Trem to encl.
PEDAL
Sub 32(ext) 16 16(gamb) 16 8(ext) 8(ext) 8(ext) 32 16(ext) 8(ext)

Octave and Sub for Swell and Solo. Tubular pneumatic detached console. Wind pressures, about 4¾ inches flue, 7½ inches reed.

I was much impressed by its bland, massive ensemble as heard from the chancel arch: there was undoubted nobility in the sound of the all-open Great with its full-toned Trumpet on heavy wind; the 16-foot reed-dominated Full Swell; the colourful Choir stops and Solo division; the rich, imposing Pedal section. Backing on to the eastern side of traceried arches in the east wall of the south transept (which arches were completely blocked by huge Pedal pipes and the back of the swell-box), it could only speak eastwards into a new chapel flanking the chancel and connected therewith by two high arches. Thus, although the voicing sounded very loud and 'hard' at the console, it failed to penetrate effectively beyond the crossing and into the large and spacious nave. One prominent feature was the so-called Contra Trombone 32-feet, the first I had ever met at first hand: making an excited first trial of this stop I was astounded at its literally *thunderous* effect, so much as to lack credibility. What was there of 'trombone' about a sound which merely threatened (it seemed) to wreck the organ gallery? It was only after I had inherited its younger brother at Brompton Oratory, fifteen years later, that I could appreciate how this stop had been conceived and *why* it was basically so wrong.

A second experience in Nottingham had something in common with the first: I saw the building of the large Elite cinema with a 4-manual organ by Henry Willis III, finished in 1921. By then I was playing in a small chamber orchestra in a neighbouring cinema, and had the temerity to apply for the job of organist. I had not a hope, but I did gain *entrée* to scrutinize the new organ, which was quite large. The Great (unenclosed) and Pedal divisions were behind the rather over-substantial cinema screen; the Swell and Solo were in chambers prominently placed to each side, over Exit doors; the Echo, or Celestial, was above a pierced rosette in the ceiling. As could be imagined now, with hindsight, the balances were all wrong: the Great was muffled, the Swell and Solo too loud in relation to it; the Celestial, which sounded very pretty in the Grand Circle or the top Gallery, was almost inaudible in the Stalls. I remember witnessing a rather stupefied assemblage of Management, Organist, Musical Director and Mr Willis himself, discussing solutions, no doubt; but I never heard what they decided, for I was soon back in Derby. However, it was basically a good organ, as I was enabled to confirm some thirty years later when I was surprised to find myself performing on it in the Brangwyn Hall, Swansea, whither it had been moved into a more favourable location, which made all the difference to its effect.

In 1922, after a brief spell as Mustel Organist (as mentioned earlier), when I mastered the difficult blowing-technique, and became a star performer, I soon had to prepare for entrance to the RCM, and everything else was dropped for the time being. Once settled there as a student, I began to receive impressions of a different kind from visits to, and shortly afterwards, my appointment as assistant organist at, Southwark Cathedral, London Bridge (1923-25). This organ was widely regarded as Lewis's masterpiece. It had the recognisable 'trade marks' remembered from St. Alkmund's — the strong 4-foot Principal tone, the characteristic string sonorities — but included a thrilling Great flue-chorus (16(Viola), 16(Bdn), 8, 8, 8(Hfl), 8, 4, 4(Hfl), 2⅔, 2, IV, III-V(Cornet), 8(Trpt)) to which the reed contributed only its special 'tang'. As a stroke of genius, Lewis based this not only on an impressive flue Pedal (32, 32(Violon), 16(ext), 16(ext), 16, 16, 8(ext), 8(ext), 4(ext)), but also wooden Posaunes 32- and 16-feet (extended) and a real French Bombarde 16-feet with 8-foot Trumpet extension. The whole of this was voiced on a moderate and uniform wind-pressure (3½ inches) and had a splendidly uninhibited sound. This organ was supposed to be Lewis's public affirmation of a vital principle at a time when the leading organ-builders were all introducing higher wind-pressures, with resulting distortion of pipe-speech and loss of musical quality and tonal balance[11].

As a momentary digression I must add that at first hearing I found the Great Mixtures unbelievably strident and cacophonous: the organist, E. T. Cook, played the Bach A minor Fugue after Sunday evensong, and the effect of the final three chords on Full Great baffled description: all the 'fifth' ranks stood out boldly in the dominant key! Of course this was 'Schulze' style; and in accordance with provincial practice, I had never heard or used Mixtures without the reeds before this time. The young Marcel Dupré took London by storm in 1922-23 when he played Bach fugues on exposed Mixtures: it was the talk of the town. I myself heard this at Westminster Cathedral on the beginnings of the new organ, and I found the experience interesting but not endurable indefinitely. I am sure that such registration was not usually envisaged by the organ-builders who made the Mixtures for Full Organ only.

However, I got used to the "Southwark sound" and there was no denying the grandeur of the Full Organ or the beauty of the individual stops, even though through bad placement in a chamber, much was lost in the nave. The 32-foot Posaune spoke promptly, and although not overloud (and rather 'rattling' when played *solo*), it imparted added majesty to the French Bombarde. (Musically here was some affinity with Father Willis's 32-foot Posaunes, at the Royal Albert Hall (prior to 1924), at St. Paul's (prior to 1925), and even Salisbury Cathedral (prior to 1930): all were rather 'light-weight' but clearly audible as a sub-harmonic of the powerful 16-foot pitch of the main reed foundation, and musically highly satisfactory.)[12]

Southwark had two Solo reeds on a heavier pressure — 12 inches — enclosed with the other, light-winded, Solo stops. Tunks, who had been Lewis's head voicer, and still tuned the organ in 1925, showed me a pipe from the Trompette Harmonique, and demonstrated how the addition of a small felt 'load' on the free end of the tongue could remove all the marvellous brilliance of the tone, leaving only a dull 'horny' sound — another indelible impression! The very light felt weights actually on the bass tongues of the Bombarde, however, seemed harmless enough: the tongues might well have rattled excessively without this 'crutch': this also will be discussed later at an appropriate point.

But even living in close relationship with the Southwark organ was of itself no guarantee of exclusive personal conversion to its underlying philosophy at that time: the Big Diapason, the Heavy Pressure Reed and the Detached Console were all in vogue and in the air; their provision was considered to be the first essential requirement in any rebuild. Where there were only three manuals, the Heavy Pressure Reed was made playable on both Great and Choir manuals, so that fugue-subjects could be played (even 'thumbed out') on the Choir Tuba or Tromba, especially in the tenor register. Another typical example of contemporary use of the device could be seen in William Walond's Voluntary in G, as published under the title *Introduction and Toccata*: the added staccato quaver chords for the left hand, played upon the heavy reed, do bear some resemblance to exciting trombone chords in the modern orchestra. I myself made great sport with this technical 'gimmick' in playing Bach's B minor Prelude, transferring the quaver left-hand chords to the Choir Tuba (with octave coupler), on my new Rushworth organ at Keble College, Oxford, where I had become Organ Scholar in 1925 — until a monumental 'demonstration' in true organ style by William Minay, during a friendly visit, brought me abruptly to my senses! From that moment I began to play my Bach much slower, too.

Even so, the Big Diapason remained a corrupting influence: there was (and still is) at Keble an example allegedly copied from the Schulze organ at St. Mary's, Tyne Dock, and contributed at an earlier stage to this organ by the Revd. Noel Bonavia Hunt. I heard and admired the phenomenal large example by Hill at King's College, Cambridge, in 1926, "the best thing in the organ", the rest of which was admittedly disappointing. About the Harrison high-pressure, heavily leathered one at the Royal Albert Hall (1924) and the Willis III specimen with double-languids on heavy wind at Westminster Cathedral (1923), I was less sure — were they not too blanket-like, too enormous to be really musical?

The violent reaction against 'orchestralised Bach' mentioned above brought me back to a genuine interest in true organ-architecture. There were three Great diapasons on the Keble organ — mine for the time being — why not transpose No 3 as a Quint 5⅓ foot? This I did, and was delighted with the enriched sonority; though all had to be reinstated before the tuner's next visit — not, however, before receiving the enthusiastic approbation of a Manchester antiquarian who gleefully informed me of the survival of a 5⅓ foot Quint in the old Jardine organ at Holy Trinity church, Hulme.

My severe, almost Schweitzerian, Bach style soon gave place to a new interest in French and Belgian music, which I played in what was then understood as 'French style', with much use of octave couplers on reeds and mixtures, and in softer combinations, the blending of keen-toned 'strings' with flutes and diapasons! About 1927 I was playing some of Louis Vierne's recent compositions, and was fascinated by the Nazard registration he sometimes specified: there were no examples of this stop to hand, but experimental transposition of flutes to 2⅔ foot pitch demonstrated the charmingly colourful effect. When my opinion was asked regarding details of a projected rebuilding of the Father Willis organ in St. Peter's Oxford, I boldly suggested inserting a Nazard in the Choir Organ in place of some redundant stop. "Where did you get those ideas?" asked, suspiciously, Mr Willis (III), to whom I was introduced: "From French music," I replied. I did not know then, but was soon to learn, that Willis was just beginning to introduce this kind of mutation-stop into his new organs; the first one I actually met was in the Sheldonian Theatre in Oxford, where he rebuilt in 1928 a most interesting *multum-in-parvo* 3-manual organ by his grand-father. This organ was not highly esteemed, probably because of its high pitch: I believe the 3rd manual was a 5-stop Solo Organ containing a Tuba Mirabilis!

One Sunday morning I was summoned with a neighbouring Organ Scholar to the Sheldonian, where Dr. (later, Sir William) Harris and Sir Hugh Allen (Heather Professor of Music) were to meet Henry Willis III. Sir Hugh had asked the latter to produce a specification for a reedless, 2-manual, all-diapason organ to be used mainly for *continuo* and choral accompaniment for the Bach Choir in Oxford. This scheme was shown to me, and as I recall, each manual contained the octave and fifth harmonic series from 16-foot to 1-foot pitch, some of them doubled and all drawing as separate stops: Pedals to match. It looked exciting on paper, though perhaps lacking in credibility in those days: one could not assess the effect with any certainty. Evidently Sir Hugh felt this, for he was in a querulous mood that morning, and rather disposed to argue about the improbability of the University's being induced to allow electric current to be brought into the building — the Father Willis organ was hand-blown. Our hearts sank: the scheme was running on the rocks! Finally Sir Hugh got up to go, throwing the specification at the rest of us, and saying, "Here, you do something about this". Dr. Harris's face lit up at this prospect: "Do let's have a Tuba" was his first remark. Later, in 1928, when I asked Mr. Willis about this, he said, "There will be a Mixture in the Swell which will be as good as a Tuba". This was exciting news indeed: I had heard of 'resultant' tones being produced from ranks of flue-pipes tuned to the pure harmonic series so as to sound like reeds, but knew of no example; that such a phenomenon could achieve Tuba power would be remarkable.

The console arrived, and there, instead of a reed stop in the Swell, was the knob engraved, "Armonica Clausa VI ranks". But alas, when the pipes arrived in place, they sounded short of wind, rather 'oily' in sonority, and out of tune — probably due to the conflict of tempered and untempered thirds — and all rather weak. What a disappointment! (With hindsight, one might think that something like the baroque 'Grand Cornet' had been the objective: but more of that in a later chapter). However, the new-style flue mutations, Nazard and Tierce, were there, as were the old Tuba and Ophicleide, revoiced; and all in all the organ sounded well: I spent many pleasurable hours practising on its novel all-American console: Mr. Willis had exchanged ideas with Ernest M. Skinner during a visit to the USA the previous year. So, the Nazard and Tierce had come to stay — *vive Vierne*!

During my last year at Oxford I had had various discussions — not least notably with C. H. Trevor — on the ensemble of the Keble College organ, which, though a gem colouristically, and set in a most helpful acoustic, lacked real character in its Full organ. The 'tame' effect seemed to stem from the Great Mixture, *vis-à-vis* the Large Diapason. Trevor described its sound as like "rattling a bunch of keys". Asked for his idea of a good recipe for mixtures, Trevor replied, "Willis's: small-scale pipes, blown hard". Oddly enough, the Keble stop had a similar composition to those of Father Willis, beginning 17 19 22 at bottom C. I discussed this further with a visiting Fellow of the College who had some experience of voicing organ-pipes, and together we decided that the chief offender was the Principal 4-feet, the treble of which was too fluty. We worked on this, loudening the treble in a gradual crescendo, and as it seemed to succeed, we gave similar treatment to other trebles including the (Great) Choir Tuba. (The organ had been built by Hill in 1876, then seriously altered — not for the better — on the advice of a former Organ Scholar, Aubyn Raymar, by a north of England firm; lastly resuscitated, almost miraculously, by Llewelyn Simon (of Rushworth & Dreaper) and Dr. Henry G. Ley.) Truly, I had embraced the 'modern' heresy!

Shortly before leaving Oxford I received the specification of the brand new organ by the Skinner Organ Company for Princeton University, NJ, whither I departed in August 1928 to become the first Organist and Director of Music in the great new gothic chapel.

As a 'paper specification' this seemed to have everything one could desire, excepting, perhaps, the large amount of borrowing of stops in the Pedal division: that was generally accepted as a necessary evil at that time. But when at last I arrived and actually tried it out, I was *bitterly* disappointed. Magnificently constructed as it was, it completely lacked the tonal balance which could have brought such a scheme to life, musically speaking. This was due to two things: the location and planning of the various divisions; and the fact (as I was soon to discover) that there had already been serious tampering with the natural acoustics of this fine building — large areas of apparent stonework were in fact composed of acoustic tiling, mainly for absorption of high-frequency reverberation!

As to planning, this large organ was crammed into two chambers, facing one another across the Memorial Choir. At the back of the deeper one (south) was a huge shutter-frame enclosing the Swell, and below it, the Choir Organ, which included some Great stops and the Pedal Fagotto extension, 32-16-feet. In front of this was the Great

GREAT (unenclosed)		SWELL		PEDAL	
Quintatön (tc)	32	Bourdon	16	Diapason (ext)	32
Diapason	16	Diapason	8	Diapason (wood)	16
Bourdon (Pedal ext)	16	Geigen Diapason	8	Diapason (m Great)	16
1st Diapason	8	Rohrfloete	8	Contrabass (wood)	16
2nd Diapason	8	Flauto Dolce	8	Bourdon	16
3rd Diapason	8	Flute Celeste	8	Gamba (Choir)	16
Principal Flute	8	Gamba	8	Echo Lieblich (Sw)	16
Quint	5⅓	Gamba Celeste	8	Quint (fr Bourdon)	10⅔
Octave	4	Salicional	8	Principal (ext Cbass)	8
Principal	4	Voix Celeste	8	Octave (wood ext)	8
Tenth	3⅕	Octave	4	Gedeckt (ext)	8
Twelfth	2⅔	Flute triangulaire	4	Still gedeckt (ext)	8
Fifteenth	2	Piccolo	2	Twelfth (fr Brdn)	5⅓
Harmonics	V	Chorus Mixture	V	Flute (ext)	4
(15, 17, 19, 21, 22)		Cornet V:		Harmonics	V
(enclosed with Choir):-		Cor de Nuit	8	(15, 17, 19, 21, 22)	
Doppel Flute	8	Fugara	4	Bombarde (w ext)	32
Flute (harmonic)	4	Nazard	2⅓	Fagotto (ext Choir)	32
Plein Jeu	III-VI	Flautino	2	Trombone (metal)	16
Contra Tromba	16	Tierce	1⅗	Tuba (Solo)	16
Tromba	8	Posaune	16	Fagotto (Choir)	16
Octave Tromba	4	French Trumpet	8	Quint Trombone	
		Cornopean	8	(Great)	10⅔
CHOIR (enclosed)		Oboe	8	Trombone (ext)	8
Gamba	16	Vox Humana	8	Clarion (ext)	4
Diapason	8	Clarion	4		
Concert Flute	8	Tremolo		SOLO (enclosed)	
Viol d'orchestre	8			Stentorphone	8
Viol Celeste	8			Flauto Mirabilis	8
Dulciana	8			Gamba	8
Dulciana Celeste	8			Gamba Celeste	8
Quintadena (comb)	8			Octave	4
Harmonic Flute	4			Orchestral Flute	4
Violina	4			Mixture	V
Nazard	2⅔			French Horn	8
Piccolo	2			English Horn	8
Tierce	1⅗			Tremolo	
Septième	1⅐			Tuba	16
Fagotto	16			Tuba	8
Corno di bassetto	8	Full array of couplers		Tuba Mirabilis	8
Orchestral Oboe	8	(tablets). Electro-		Clarion	4
Trumpet	8	pneumatic, "pitman"			
Tremolo		actions (see Note 15).			

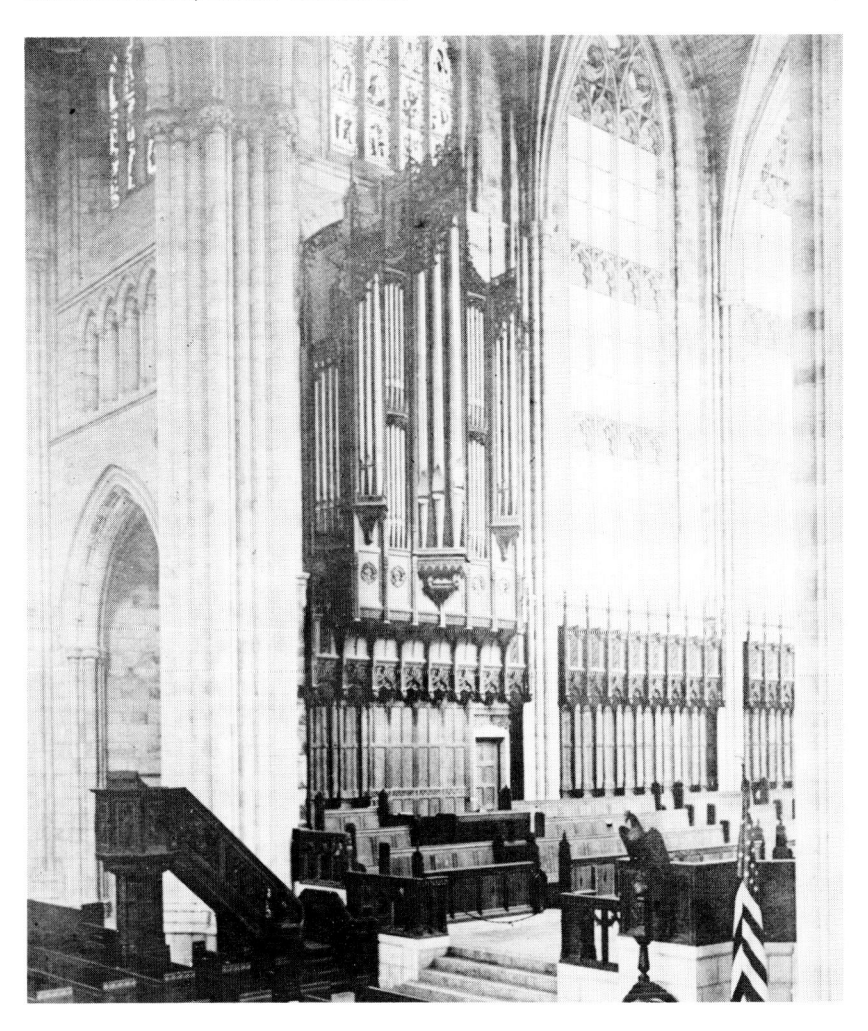

PLATE IV *Princeton University Chapel, NJ, north chamber organ case.*

Organ, its basses being on an upper storey with the Pedal 'trebles'; the largest Pedal basses stood on unit-chests at the sides, east and west. Again, in front of all this was a massive steel frame supporting a façade of huge metal dummy pipes and a solid oak carved 'case' [*sic*]. The only other openings were three or four small triforium-style lancets giving into the south transept at the top of the chamber, which was roofed in with undoubtedly absorbent wall-board. The north chamber contained only the Solo Organ, built on three levels, almost entirely within the thickness of the main Choir wall. (See Plate IV).

The product of this arrangement was a fairly solid Great flue division, behind which the Great reeds and Plein Jeu were almost inaudible even when the Choir box was open; a reasonably prominent Swell Organ: but the whole Choir division, even though charming, was far too remote. The Pedal was ponderous but unclear: its 'chorus' amounted to nothing, but the Bombarde's lowest notes were a direct assault on the *solar plexus* for anyone sitting in the south transept. Only the Solo Organ sounded clear and uninhibited; but even with closed shutters it was 'big' and thus of limited use. The wind-pressures were uniformly high — something like 6¾ inches for the main Great (reeds, flutes and Plein Jeu on 12 inches): Swell about 9½ inches: Choir about 8½ inches: Solo flues and English Horn 7½ inches: Tuba chorus and French Horn 15 inches: Tuba Mirabilis 25 inches: Pedal flues at least 6 inches: reeds 25 inches. All the large reeds had massive *wooden* basses, and all the metal of the major pipework was thick and heavy. It could not be denied that exquisite effects and tone-colours could be found; and with the aid of the very responsive 'pitman' actions and plentiful supply of combination-pistons (all instantly adjustable), it was possible to give brilliant sensational performances of all kinds of modern and Romantic music, and some major Bach works. The main defects only became seriously obvious when accompanying voices — the University Choir, for instance. The acoustic treatment of the building made it generally unfavourable for voices — their sound did not carry well; but owing to the high wind-pressures, the unenclosed parts of the organ carried too well, and were, at a distance, too loud for any choral singing. The more remote enclosed portions, though in balance at a distance, were inaudible to the singers. This situation was exacerbated by the fact that the (student) Choir consisted of tenors and basses only, facing across the chancel like a cathedral choir. There was nothing for it but to give them exclusively *a capella* music to sing, and reserve the organ for congregational singing and solo pieces.

Things could have been worse, for this was the first Skinner organ in which the Englishman, G. Donald Harrison (ex Willis) had any say; though it only amounted to the replacement of some undulants (Gemshorn and Celeste) planned for the Great Organ, by the 32-foot Quintatön and the Quint and Tenth; but these were relatively too weak to make much impact. He may also have brightened up the Swell Chorus Mixture, in English style: "How jolly!" said the great George Cunningham (of Birmingham Town Hall) at his Princeton recital in 1929; (most American mixtures were weak, fluty and too low in pitch). But the Swell Cornet Décomposé was specially disappointing: it was so weak and thin, even when all five ranks were speaking, that there was absolutely no point in being able to draw them separately. The little stopped rank, 'Cor de Nuit', had an Old World charm but was inferior in quality and output to its neighbour, the Rohrfloete, which it more or less duplicated.

ANTECEDENTS, EARLY GLIMMERS

More will be said later on all these topics: at the time I was much too busily engaged with other musical work to be able to plan changes in the organ, even had money and support been available. It had been a gift, and all concerned were very proud of it. Only after about four years, when maintenance and tuning had passed into other hands, did I see a chance of improving the arrangement of the flutes, bringing out the Great Doppelflute (stopped) from its buried position, and exchanging it with the Flauto Mirabilis in the Solo. The brothers Bartholemay, of Philadelphia, who did this for me, had good reason to complain about the swap on spatial grounds; and the Mirabilis did not like being jumped up to 12 inches pressure: but I stuck to my point, and they made a good job of it. I now had a decent accompanimental stop in the Solo; it also combined better with the wooden-harmonic 4-foot Orchestral Flute than had the Mirabilis which always sounded out of tune with it.

About this time (1933-34) a Swiss architect on the University Faculty designed a new Presbyterian church in the vicinity, and called me in as organ consultant. There was little money for an organ, and it had to be placed in two upper-storey chambers above and behind an apsidal semi-dome made of fabric stretched on a frame. (Fifteen years later I was to reject absolutely any such location for an organ at the Royal Festival Hall, but these were early days.) Continuing mentally from the old cinema days, and considering the money to be saved by borrowing and extension, I produced the following extraordinary specification, which, for my taste, contained everything a self-respecting organ should have, especially a Pedal reed 16-feet:

GREAT (enclosed)		SWELL (enclosed)	
Diapason	8	Viola da gamba	8
Flauto mirabilis	8	Gedeckt	8
Dulciana	8	Gambette (ext)	4
Octave (ext)	4	Gedeckt (ext)	4
Dulciana (ext)	4	Nazard (ext Gedeckt)	2⅔
Flute (ext)	4	Flautina (ext)	2
Quint (ext Dulciana)	2⅔	Tromba	8
Dulciana 15th (ext)	2	Tremolo	
Chimes			
Tremolo		PEDAL (enclosed in both)	
		Contrabass (ext Gt Diap)	16
Full array of couplers and pistons, all instantly adjustable.		Bourdon	16
		Lieblich gedeckt (Swell)	16
		Flute (ext)	8
General Crescendo pedal.		Gedeckt (Swell)	8
Electro-pneumatic.		Tromba (ext Swell)	16

The firm of M. P. Möller, whose organs had impressed me as efficient and musically voiced, was chosen to build it, having just acquired the English Richard Whitelegg as tonal director; and he made the most of these sparse resources, even exchanging the Gamba (which turned out to be too foundational) for a narrower scaled stop of greater contrasting character, to suit my wishes. There was no doubt about the organ's success, and the opening recital, which I gave, included works of contrasted periods and styles. The only complaints came from some of the 'new purists' on the staff of the Westminster Choir College, newly arrived from Dayton, Ohio, and housed in a fine new building in Princeton. Carl Weinrich (pupil of the great Lynnwood Farnam) headed the organ department, and was aware of the neo-classical 'Organ Reform' just started in Germany. An organ was commissioned from the Skinner Company, to Carl Weinrich's specification, containing German-style chorus development: in his occasional performances on the University organ he had exemplified this trend by using Mixture-stops in a very exposed way — more satisfying to the player than the listener — as, for example, in the obbligato of the Benedictus of Bach's Mass in B minor, played on the harsh Chorus Mixture of the Solo Organ rather than on a flute combination! When the first mock-up of the College organ arrived, it was displeasing to the ear: everything very hard and unsympathetic; but neither Weinrich nor I could at that stage diagnose the precise reason. The sequel, which will be mentioned later, was illuminating for us both.

It is necessary here to digress in order to record an experience of great significance for me: my visit, in about 1932, to the old Boston Music Hall organ originally completed there in 1863 by E. F. Walcker of Ludwigsburg but later ousted and re-erected by E. R. Searles in 1909 in a hall built on his estate specially to house it[13]. After Searles' death the fate of the organ became precarious, and at the time of my visit with the well-known New England connoisseur, William King Covell, there was considerable anxiety over its possible demolition. A sympathetic caretaker and Covell himself had kept it in reasonably good tune, even though we went in winter and the hall was thus unheated. Searles had effected a very conservative rebuild, and many of the old soundboards and all the pipes were intact, except for a semitone increase in scale due to two changes in the pitch. (Plate V.)

Examined stop by stop, this organ had a quaint 19th-century flavour: wind-pressures were low; there were a number of free-reeds (harmonium type), and the other reeds mostly emitted a soft buzzing sound, except for a Cornettino 2-feet on the Pedals, which was a loud 'perky' Clarinet. The mixtures were rather fluty, but not feeble at all. There was, in addition to a real 32-foot Principalbass and a free-reed Bombardon, a synthetic 32-feet called Grand Bourdon, composed of four ranks of wooden pipes tuned to the harmonic series: this was most impressive.

PLATE V *Boston Music Hall organ by E.F. Walcker of Ludwigsburg, 1863.*

But the big surprise came when King Covell played the opening bars of the Bach Fantasia and Fugue in C minor: bottom C on the Pedal, the first note, sounded a *magnificent* chord of C major (the mixtures contained tierce ranks), but thereafter, when the polyphony began, the texture of the music was amazingly clear. It was an utterly unaccustomed sound — one was not conscious of Mixtures as such, but only of the astounding clarity of the musical line[14]. On my return to Princeton I realised for the first time how far the University organ lacked a really musical chorus: the Mixtures sounded miserably thin, the main foundation stops hard and unsympathetic. *Something* needed to be done — but what? One could not say, yet. In any case, any thought of rebuilding the organ was not even to be considered, and I had other heavy responsibilities in connection with the Choir and the embryonic Department of Music.

In due course an opportunity for experiment came with the migration to Princeton of Chester A. Raymond, organ-builder, who took over the maintenance of the organs in the town, and eventually the University organ also. The extent of his enthusiastic co-operation is shown by the following incident.

I had been hearing a great deal from my American colleagues about German researches into re-discovered Silbermann organs, as well as their notions on improvement of tonal design — this was at the very beginning of the American 'Organ Reform'. One theory was that the 4-foot Principal was the most important ingredient in the Great Organ chorus, and that its pipes should be of a larger scale (ie, diameter) than the 8-foot. As will be noted in a later chapter, a pipe of larger scale but *equal power* produces a broader, more foundational sonority with less overtone development, than a pipe of narrower scale. It was therefore obvious that a wider scaled 4-foot Principal added to a narrower 8-foot would give a fine blend, the broader 4-foot seeming to amplify the 8-foot unison tone.

Increasingly dissatisfied with the Princeton choruses, I decided to replan the Great division, moving up the (now neglected) First Diapason to 4-foot pitch, keeping the Third Diapason as the main unison, with the Second as a Quint or so! Chester Raymond, always genuinely co-operative, began to move down the enormous, heavy 8-foot bass pipes of the bottom octave of the First Diapason to the floor of the loft 15 feet below, and we set up a chord, c, c′, e′, g′, c′′, as a mock-up of the new chorus. When I tried it that night it sounded so atrocious that in a fit of panic I telephoned Donald Harrison, who was now Technical Director of the newly constituted Aeolian-Skinner Company, to ask his opinion on what I had done. He appreciated my reasoning but was friendly enough to advise me that I was risking disaster. I agreed, and reluctantly Chester Raymond was persuaded to restore the *status quo*!

However, change was now in the air, and I decided to tackle the inhuman power-scale of the organ, especially now that the University Choir had attained some excellence and occasionally needed to sing accompanied works: I also had access to a limited amount of money for improvements.

We decided to begin a reduction of wind-pressures. This could only be done within narrow limits because the cut-up (height) of the mouths of the flue pipes was high, and too great a reduction would cause 'gasping' and unsteady tone. But some improvement was realised at once in the Great division, reduced to 5 inches for the open section, and 10⅞ inches for the enclosed — less would have made the Great reeds slow in speech. More developments were soon to follow.

Returning to the scene of Westminster College, Weinrich had persuaded Donald Harrison personally to take over the amendment and completion of the unsatisfactory organ project; and almost simultaneously Harrison invited me to go and see some of his recent work in New England. He explained that he had largely abandoned his company's former use of heavy thick pipe-metal in favour of lighter construction in 'spotted metal', a 50/50 alloy of tin and lead: pipe-scales for some stops were also reduced somewhat — all of this encouraging a more transparent, singing quality of sound with greater overtone development. In addition, much more attention was being given to the relative positions of stops on the soundboards and of soundboards in the organ. Theoretically, the stops on a sliderless 'pitman'[15] chest could be arranged in almost any order since the basses were on their own independent wind: but now, care was being taken to plant the Principal ranks in the best position for their sound in the building, and then to back them up with a logical arrangement of the chorus and other stops. In the partly experimental, incomplete new west-end organ of the church of St. Mary the Virgin, New York, these measures were proved effective in embryo, even though the pressures were still a little too high and the sound therefore uncomfortably aggressive — the Great was an all-flue division, very prominently placed, rather like Lewis's Great at Southwark, but more foundational.

I saw two organs during our trip: Trinity College, Hartford, Connecticut, and All Saints' Church, Worcester, Massachusetts. Trinity was transitional — a 4-manual organ, much of it in the old solid, hard style; but the Swell and Choir divisions had excellent features, the former containing a scintillating Cavaillé-Coll type Plein Jeu VI ranks with excellent blending qualities; the Choir mutations were rich and pleasing, and there was at least one Trompette with quite a new character, penetrating but musically very easy on the ear, and excellent in solo use or combination. Donald told me that his ideal was taking shape along Cavaillé lines: two good flue divisions, Great and Choir, each with a chorus structure, and a large colourful Swell with French chorus reeds: Pedal to match, although the latter still tended to what the Americans called "augmentation" (actually, diminution), much of it borrowed or extended.

At Worcester, things had moved a step further. Don spoke enthusiastically of his current revival of the Flûte Conique — another Cavaillé idea — sometimes as a Swell 16-feet, whence it was borrowed on to the Pedal, but here for the mutations, especially the Tierces. The conical pipe could sound conveniently fluty (for mutational blend) but on account of its shape it stressed the Octave harmonic (for lightness and soft brilliance). The flue-choruses of Great and (enclosed) Choir were as follows:

GREAT
16 16 8(Pr) 8(Fl harm) 8(Bdn) 8(Gem) 5⅓ 4 4(Rohr) $3^{1}/_{5}$ 2⅔ 2 $1^{3}/_{5}$ $1^{1}/_{7}$ IV III
CHOIR
16(Viol) 8(Pr) 8(Viol) 8(Ged) 8(Dulc) 8(Unda) 4 4(Fl) 2⅔(Naz) 2(Pic) $1^{3}/_{5}$ 1⅓ 1 V

The Swell and the Bombarde (Solo) also had good chorus structure: all the reeds were of modified French type, including a very fine Trompette in the Choir. But the greatest advance was in the Pedal division, where, as he gleefully explained, he had been able for the first time to install a neat little 32-note soundboard in the bottom of the organ, with 'all-straight' pipework, at a cost to the Company of scarcely more than that of the usual ponderous extended 'augmented' arrangement. There was no doubt as to the musically satisfactory effect of a Bach Prelude and Fugue (actually the G major, BWV 541) played by William Self, the organist, without using any Pedal coupler. It was as clear as a bell and clean as a whistle: a different kind of clarity, however, from that of the old Boston Walcker; more 'Mixture orientated', more English, perhaps — in the Lewis sense, but less strident than his Geigenprincipals tended to be. Wind-pressures were, of course, lower than formerly; which meant lower cut-up of mouths, quicker steadier speech, a more singing tone. Here the reeds also were consistently better than at Hartford: the tang of the French trompettes, though lively, was refined and most musical.

PEDAL organ flue chorus
(omitting three stops borrowed from the manuals)
32(st) 16(Cb) 16(Sub) 10⅔(Qu) 8 8 $6^{2}/_{5}$ 5⅓ 4 4 2 V — all "trebles" on the small soundboard, big basses planted out separately.

Of course there was some opposition to these developments, though I *never* heard the word 'baroque' mentioned! Donald Harrison later floored his critics by the musical blend of his many-mixtured Great Organ at Groton School: they would not believe that so many ranks were sounding! This was in a sense a major break-through. The secret, as he explained to me, was the use of wide scales with low-cut mouths. We have already noted the advantages of a broad-toned 4-foot pitch: if the 2⅔, 2, or 1⅓ foot, etc, were also wide, the 'resultants' cast down upon the 8-foot fundamental would be quite powerful, solidifying the latter (which could be of narrower scale accordingly, and thus more 'singing' in character). His mixtures broke like the Silbermann examples, one rank at a time ("quint-repetition", as the Germans say), though his Plein Jeu resembled that of Cavaillé rather than the classical French. The Westminster College organ, though smaller, was finished on these lines.

Meantime, at the University, Chester Raymond had made an interesting proposal: his father-in-law, Anton Gottfried, the well-known organ-voicer, was coming on a visit to Princeton and would be disposed (for the good of the cause) to help me improve the organ. Gottfried, I soon learnt, had been apprenticed to Walcker in Ludwigsburg as a young man. When he sat at the console and began work on the Great stops, I began to learn truths that were so simple that one could wonder why one had not thought of them before. I listened with rapt attention as he took the C's of each foundation stop, carefully balancing each with the others for equality of impact and output. Once this was done, and only then, the intervening pipes were brought into line, throughout each octave of the compass. Thus a weak tenor register was re-vivified, a strident treble softened; and each stop became musical and also polyphonically clear. Naturally, the now reduced wind-pressure imposed limitations, so that the optimum level had to be found for the speech of the C pipes, with enough margin allowed to take care of any 'rebels'.

Having got as far as the 2-foot, the musical effect was noticeably improved; then the 2⅔ foot was set so as just to fit comfortably between it and the 4-foot below — not too loud! the next stop was the Harmonics, V ranks: Gottfried said, "What is the use of Harmonics if they don't harmonise, or Mixtures if they don't mix?" All the ranks were weighed against the fundamental and also within themselves — C against c, and so on — and the resulting chorus was an undeniable improvement, less 'mixtury' in tone-colour, less cutting, but musically clear and harmonious. The Plein Jeu (now reduced to 10⅞ inch pressure) in the Choir-box was very strident as heard against this new background, and also had very prominent 'octave-breaks' which 'reversed the music'. Gottfried decided to arch the mouths of the pipes, thus softening the speech-impact without cutting the lips too high for a steady note. The result was a jewel-like shimmer of brilliance: and when I had softened the three Trombas (by sharpening at the tongue and closing the slots cut at the top of the resonators), an excellent blend was obtained. Don Harrison looked in one day during this operation, and I regarded his comment as high praise: "I guess you've got something there!"

After Mr Gottfried's short stay, Raymond and I continued similarly with the rest of the organ, including some transposition of stops which will be noted later. We came to the Swell Cornet, V ranks. I knew instinctively that it was all wrong as it stood: it ought to equal the output of, say, the Chorus Mixture. "This stopped rank, 8-feet, middle c — make it much louder," I called out from the console: Raymond, from inside the Swell-box, replied doubtfully, but persevered; and the sound was much improved; we balanced it eventually through all the C's, and likewise all the other ranks. I had never heard a real Cornet-stop, and working on, empirically, I was convinced that we were getting somewhere: when the 2-foot rank and the Tierce (not loudened very much) were completed, the tone-picture was most exciting, and when tuned it became a lovely full-toned solo-stop. Of course the rather narrow pipes of the 4-foot rank had to have their mouths raised, and there were odd 'rebels' which needed special attention, but eventually it was finished and sounded very well.

Owing to the improvement in the 8-foot Cor de Nuit, the Rohrfloete 8-feet became redundant: we therefore moved the pipes (from tenor c up) to the enclosed Great, exchanging with the 4-foot open Flute from that department; and the latter then became a most useful Harmonic Flute 8-feet for the Swell. Similarly the rather useless and characterless Principal Flute 8-feet was exchanged from tenor c with the small Principal 4-feet, which (joined to the Principal Flute bass) made an excellent Geigen principal 8-feet; while the Principal Flute became a telling extra 4-foot for the Great; now there were three varieties, Octave, Principal Flute and Lieblich Flöte, all of which blended excellently with the other stops in the Great. The First Diapason, previously throttled down before the wind-pressure was reduced, was now uselessly 'woolly'; but Gottfried set to work on it before he left, and it became a new 8-foot stop of some nobility, speaking on a more copious supply of wind, by means of the enlargement of the footholes it recovered its 'life' and character.

We continued with the Solo division, taking the sting and 'scrape' out of the big Gambas, seeking a rich, horny sonority; but the wind-pressures and the Tubas had to be left as they were. During our work on the Swell and Solo chorus Mixtures, we had the problem of 'covering the breaks', i.e, the *reprises* in the ascending scale, where lower-pitched pipes came in to replace high ones which faded out for lack of practicable length. Some of these breaks were rather abrupt, the pitch jumping a whole octave from one note to the next; and this was disturbing to the musical melodic line. It became clear to me then, for the first time, that when a 22nd pipe (1-foot pitch) dropped out, the only way to avoid a gap was to make sure that the 2-foot rank continued 1-foot pitch over the break, *as a 1st harmonic*. Looking in the reverse direction, the 1-foot rank must be slightly softer than the 2-foot, all through. (In the Mixtures as we found them, all pipes were of equal strength and all rather forced — for 'brilliance' no doubt). Working on this principle it was obvious that the further removed any harmonic overtone was from its fundamental, the softer it ought to be — this was surely Nature. It meant a good deal of work for Raymond, who had to put hundreds of small pipes on their speech after softening; but we carried it through.

The quint ranks were equally difficult, and I had seen how Gottfried had softened them in the Harmonics stop. (Trade organ-men *always* made them too loud!) By making the quint fit just comfortably between the octaves (thus becoming much softer and even very slightly fluty — a fluty Principal tone), we again got a good blend and a clear contrapuntal line from the whole Mixture when added to unison and octave stops. The entire organ took on a more musical character even though it was softer and might have lost a little of its 'punch'. Gottfried came back later to put thinner tongues into some of the Swell reed-stops, which the reduction in wind-pressure had made slow in speech: and we all felt conscious of great success, the musical blend everywhere was vastly improved, and the dynamic scale of the whole was more related to the human voice, so that choral accompaniment became a more practical possibility. The stop-lists of the Great, Swell and Solo divisions were now as follows: those of the Choir and Pedal had to remain unchanged[16]. The pressures for the Tubas, French Horn and Solo flues could not be dropped, nor could the main Pedal stops, but the Bombarde-Trombone-Tromba-Clarion unit came down 5 inches to 20 inches — a practical limit, but still musically worthwhile.

GREAT
(unenclosed, reduced to 5 inches wind:
enclosed reduced to 10⅞ inches)

Quintaton (tenor c)	32	Lieblich Flute (enclosed)	4
Diapason	16	Tenth	3⅕
Bourdon	16	Twelfth	2⅔
First Diapason	8	Fifteenth	2
Second Diapason	8	Harmonics	V
Third Diapason	8	(15, 17, 19, 21, 22)	
Geigen Diapason	8	Plein Jeu (enclosed)	III-VI
Flauto Mirabilis (enclosed)	8	Contra Tromba	16
Quint (stopped metal)	5⅓	(enclosed)	
Octave	4	Tromba (enclosed)	8
Principal Flute	4	Octave Tromba (enclosed)	4

SWELL		SOLO	
(reduced to 8¾ inches)		(enclosed: flues and English Horn, 7½ inches, Tubas and French Horn, 15 inches, Tuba Mirabilis, 25 inches)	
Bourdon	16		
Diapason	8		
Principal Flute	8		
(Geigen re-voiced)		Stentorphone	8
Gamba	8	Doppel Flute (stopped)	8
Gamba Celeste	8	Gamba	8
Harmonic Flute	8	Gamba Celeste	8
Cor de Nuit (Cornet No 1)	8	Orchestral Flute	4
Salicional	8	(wood, harmonic)	
Voix Celeste	8	Octave	4
Flauto Dolce (conical)	8	Mixture	V
Flute Celeste	8	French Horn	8
Principal	4	English Horn	8
Flute Triangulaire	4	Tuba	16
Fugara (Cornet No 2)	4	Tuba	8
Nazard (Cornet No 3)	2⅔	Tuba Clarion	4
Flautino (Cornet No 4)	2	Tuba Mirabilis	8
Piccolo	2	Tremolo to light wind	
Tierce (Cornet No 5)	$1^{3}/_{5}$		
(Cornet — all ranks	V)		
Mixture	V		
Posaune	16		
Trumpet	8		
Cornopean	8		
Oboe	8		
Vox Humana	8		
Clarion	4		
Tremolo			

CHAPTER TWO

Development

My move to Brompton Oratory at the beginning of 1936 abruptly terminated all organ-building adventures for the time being. The organ which I now inherited, originally built in 1858 by Bishop & Starr (and at that time the second largest in London) had been enlarged on its transplant from the old to the new church (1884) to the following specification: Surely a splendid classical design!

GREAT		SWELL		CHOIR	
Sub Open Diapason	16	Double Diap (st)	16	Bourdon bass	16
Open Diapason	8	Open Diapason	8	(12 pipes)	
Gamba	8	Salicional	8	Sub Dulciana treble	16
(or Bell Diapason)		Stopped Clarionette		Open Diapason (tc)	8
Clarabella	8	Flute	8	Viol di Gamba (tc)	8
Harmonic Flute (g)	8	Voix celeste	8	Dulciana	8
Stopped Diapason	8	Principal	4	Metallic Flute (w) (tc)	8
Principal	4	Fifteenth	2	Stopped Diap bass	8
Wald Flute	4	Sesquialtera	III	Geigenprincipal	4
Twelfth	2⅔	Mixture	III	Hohlflute	4
Fifteenth	2	Contra Fagotto	16	Flauto traverso (tc)	4
Blockflute (w)	2	Cornopean	8	Piccolo (w)	2
Sesquialtera	IV	Hautboy	8	Fifteenth	2
Mixture	III	Clarion	4	Dulciana Mixture	III
Posaune	8	Tremulant		Bassoon bass	8
Clarion	4			(12 pipes)	
				Bassoon treble (tc)	8
PEDAL				Cremona (tc)	8
Contra Open					
Diapason (w)	32	Fifteenth	4	SOLO	
Open Diapason (w)	16	Sesquialtera	III	Flûte harmonique	8
Open Diapason (m)	16	Mixture	III	Lieblich Gedact	8
Violone (w)	16	Bombardon	16	Vox humana (encl)	8
Bourdon	16	Clarion	8	Tuba Mirabilis (case)	8
Principal	8	Octave coupler for		Tuba Clarion (case)	4
Stopped Flute	8	certain stops		Tremulant	

Pneumatic lever for Great and couplers; later to Swell.
Reversed console with 'long action' [sic].
Wind-pressures: Great and Choir, 3 inches; Swell ± 3½ inches;
Solo, 6 inches; Pedal flues, 3 inches, reeds, 5 inches.

But having been moved by the successors of the original builder, this old organ went through various vicissitudes, firstly owing to the difficulty of adapting it in the new church to a prescribed withdrawn cramped position (in a choir *gallery* under a low domed ceiling above a south-eastern aisle-chapel off the nave — there were many complaints and grievances on both sides): secondly, as a result of the emergence and influence of the then new 'orchestral transcriptionist' school of thought, during the incumbency of Edward D'Evry, organist from 1893 to 1935, who, especially after the Papal *'Motu Proprio'* ban on orchestras in church (1903), built up a reputation for clever 'one-man band' accompaniments of Viennese masses — a reputation which I as his successor was expected to uphold and continue. Thus, whereas much of the old pipework continued to charm by purity and reticence, some of the essential chorus-work (including most of the Pedal) was taken out and replaced over the years by totally incongruous material, supplied by Walker, who after a final break with the old firm took over the instrument in 1904.

The new additions, which stood side by side with the old material, were: (1) an enclosed Echo [sic] division, played from the Choir keys, and containing a loud modern 'Viole d'Orchestre', an Orchestral Oboe, and the existing Cremona (tenor c) removed from its soundboard; plus Octave couplers, all put on a heavy wind-pressure of 7 inches; (2) an 8-foot Tuba, replacing the old Solo reeds, built out in front of the organ with resonators hooded to project the tone into the nave, (Plate VI) and also heavily winded on 10½ inches pressure; and (3) a thunderous 32-foot Contra Trombone [sic] like the one I met years before at St. Mary's, Nottingham — this a downward extension of a Walker 16-foot Trombone, also on 10½ inches pressure. Other minor but significant changes had included removal of a Great Sesquialtera in favour of a modern 'capped' Double Trumpet. Whatever good practical reasons there may have been for these changes, the eventual result was that (as the late C. H. Trevor remarked to me in 1936) in the Full Organ, only (1), (2) and (3) were audible — all the rest was submerged! An advantage arising from the 'withdrawn' character of the older stops was that quite large amounts of organ could be used for choir accompaniment without fear of drowning the voices. Of course the Walker additions were of a piece with what I had met at Nottingham— the vivid Orchestral Oboe, the super-keen-toned Viole, the rather 'leathery' Tuba: given the superb acoustics of the Oratory, it was

DEVELOPMENT

PLATE VI *Brompton Oratory, the organ c1936.*

possible to hash up various quasi-orchestral and even pseudo-Continental ensembles with the help of the Echo stops and their independent octave couplers and Tremulant, and even my passion for French romantic music was temporarily and partially satisfied thereby.

The Oratory (Roman) traditions relegated the organ to a secondary, mainly accompanimental role at that time: moreover, my French leanings were viewed with dismay by the clergy, though my Musical Director (Henry Washington), who had secretly adored old Vierne's improvisations at Notre-Dame, Paris, listened with me to some recordings of these in an atmosphere of covetous delight. However, business was business, and the actual organ at the Oratory in 1936 was a Fact of Life: and here I only shared the lot of countless colleagues who ideally desired better instruments but had to make do: the more intelligent ones employing various ingenious subterfuges to obtain clarity and balance.

My own last years at Princeton had been given to intensive revision of a keyboard technique based on the teachings of Widor, Dupré and Germani in the 'grand legato' style: included also was a more detailed regard for precise registration, in the sense of discovering exactly what combination of stops was appropriate for a particular work or section of a work, first ideally, and then in terms of the particular organ being played. (Tempo and articulation were inextricably bound up with this.) Clarity, the supreme desideratum, would include *clean playing* (as exemplified then in the Bach performances of Dupré, G. D. Cunningham or C. H. Trevor, for instance), achieved by absolute keyboard-control: but this could be almost unavailing if the stops of the organ were not balanced musically within their range, both as to power and quality of speech. On the whole, in England at this period, the larger 8-foot and 4-foot stops (flue and reed) spoke stridently in the treble range, with indistinct tenor and muffled ponderous bass. The 2-foot stops and mixtures were voiced louder in the bass, and in the best organs this achieved a *kind* of tonal balance with the 8-foot stops, but a faulty one when it came to using smaller combinations.

The kind of subterfuge employed by the more discerning players could be cited as (1) omission of the 4-foot Principal in a *forte* registration, using 8-foot and 2-foot Principal-tones only; or (2) playing on the 4-foot Principal one octave lower where the music allowed this: thus profiting from the less forced tonality of the bass range; or again, and especially in contrapuntal music involving the Pedals, playing everything on the manuals one octave higher, using the 16-foot Diapason as the unison, thereby removing the tenor range from the region where it would be obscured by the bass if a Pedal coupler were needed. The unmusical effect of the soprano-biassed voicing was greatly aggravated by the universal adoption of higher wind-pressures — 4½ inches being a common average (even for unenclosed pipes) and anything from 7 inches upwards for the reeds. At the Oratory, these pressures were slightly lower — about 3¼ inches for the Great flue stops, and 4¼ inches for the reeds, but the top-heavy sound was still there in the basic treatment at the time.

Since the playing of a Bach fugue with 'normal registration', including the use of the Great to Pedal coupler (that notorious destroyer of the tenor-part) often came out as a loud soprano melody with occasional bursts of alto and various mumblings below, which might just as well have been an 'Oom-pah' accompaniment, subterfuge (2) was often applied in a more or less vain attempt to right matters, namely, the reservation of one manual exclusively for coupling to the meagre but often too bulky Pedal. (At the Oratory, where the Pedal division now amounted only to 32, 16, 16, 16, 16(Sw), 8, 8(ext), 32, 16(ext), the Solo flutes and Echo stops had to fulfil this function.) Few people seemed at all upset by this grotesque phenomenon, and as organ-builders increasingly regarded this kind of tonal imbalance as desirable, so were non-organist musicians repelled by the instrument, and little music of any lasting value was written for it. French and German composers *were* active, and the same kind of subterfuges had to be employed to make their work effective, or moderately so, on English modern organs. The use of octave couplers on reeds and mixtures was deemed sufficiently 'flashy' treatment to do justice to the French style — with hindsight one could exclaim, "How very mistaken!" A more attractive method of delineating German works consisted in the use of 8-foot and 2-foot flutes alone — a form of registration popularised successfully (against much local prejudice) by Susi Hock (later, Jeans) from Vienna in the very early 1930s: this was ungenerously labelled 'bubble and squeak' by the entrenched opposition. At least it was 'easier on the ear' than the conventional combinations!

My only actual attempt to institute any change in the Oratory organ in 1936 was an enquiry as to the feasibility of moving the mild-toned Voix Celeste (Salicional-type) from the Swell (where it paired very poorly with a new Walker keen-toned Echo Gamba) into the Choir, to match up with the Dulciana — a Cavaillé-type arrangement. An estimate was given, but nothing was done, though the transaction occasioned a personal contact with Reginald Walker, the Managing Director of the firm, whom I myself regarded instinctively as 'entrenched Establishment': as one of my sympathetic colleagues said to me, "Talking to him is like talking to a brick wall!" (Only after his sudden and premature death in 1951 did I fully realise how mistaken I had been — as will appear presently in this account). But change was 'in the air' already, as the following two incidents will doubtless show.

The first was a Press report (with portrait) in the London *Evening News*, 17 January 1936, headed "OLD CHURCH ORGANS ARE 'NEW' AGAIN", and continuing:

> Mr Ralph Downes ... organist at Brompton Oratory, thinks that the old-fashioned organ of the 18th century will soon become the 'fashion' in our churches. There is a trend in this direction already in some countries, notably in America. ... "Generally speaking, the organ is an unpopular instrument at the moment ... has lost its true character because there has been an attempt on the part of the builder to reproduce the effects of an orchestra. Now there are signs that the instrument which produced the music of the 18th century is coming back. I for one hope the music of the old organ will come back soon."

I soon learned that these remarks had been greeted with raised eyebrows, and wry or ribald comments 'on the shop-floor' of at least one organ-factory: "Ha! We're going back to Father Smith, I suppose?" None of us at that time had any idea how attitudes would change within the next fifteen years!

The other was a different kind of conference, but one which constituted a kind of break-through for me, enabling me to see certain essential facts more clearly. My friend, William Strickland, noted American organist and conductor, was coming over on his first trip to Europe; and through the good offices of another friend (and superb catalyst), Aubrey Thompson-Allen, of the Willis firm, Henry Willis III, with his most gracious hospitality took him and me to see and play his newly rebuilt organ at the Alexandra Palace. It was a fine reconstruction from every point of view, and Mr. Willis was very proud of his new, pungently-toned Contrabass 16-feet in the Pedal division. Privately, I did not like the sound of this organ, which incidentally had retained Father Willis's plentiful array of Mixtures, and was further enriched now with solo-mutations, Nazard, Tierce and Solo Nazard as well as others in the Principal class. Asked for my opinion during tea on the terrace afterwards, I found myself saying that I found the mutation series too differentiated in power from the mixture chorus — too soft. "I see what you mean, my boy," said Mr. Willis, "you are quite right." In another connection, he said, "The Pedal is big enough: you can hear it quite clearly," to which I replied, "Yes, as to *weight*, but not so clearly as to *pitch*."

When we discussed this later, Strickland said he was impressed with what I had said. In fact, it was a self-revelation for me — something going back into my Princeton days but not previously formulated. It was the beginning of the idea of an organ in which all stops had a certain equality so that *all* pulled their weight in the full ensemble; as opposed to the contemporary practice of making *loud* and *soft* stops, the former blotting out the latter in the ensemble. This idea of equality was actually quite traditional, and exemplified in early organs by Father Willis, J. W. Walker, Gray & Davison, Lewis and others, before the advent of raised wind-pressures. For the time being, in the 1930s, it had gone by the board in all large organs — of over, say, 15 or 20 speaking-stops! Yet it alone made 'musical sense': this I felt in my bones. In a demonstration of the organ at the London Royal Festival Hall in 1954, I coined the title, "It all began from the music": and this had certainly been true for Donald Harrison in his complete reverence for the musical score, and aided and abetted by a few distinguished young organists, some of them pupils of Widor and Dupré, and including Ernest White, Edward Gammons and Clarence Watters — the latter a real perfectionist. I hoped it was true of me.

A number of incidents in 1937 had a fundamental influence on my thought and practice. The first was my first actual contact with the work of Cavaillé-Coll:[17] a visit to his small organ in the church of Notre-Dame de France, Leicester Square, London. In summarised form its specification was:

GREAT
16(Bdn) 8 8(Gamb) 8(Flh) 8(Sal) 8(Cor.d.n) 4 2 PjIII-VI
16(Bs) 8(Tr) 4(Cl)
SWELL
8(Flt) 8/8(gb) 4(Fl) 2(Fl) 8(Tp) 8(Hb) 8(Vh) Trem
PEDAL
16(Cb) 16(Bdn) 16(Bom) 8(Tr)
Coup Unis and Oct

The organist, Bernard Page, played Franck's 3rd Choral and some of the Final in B flat: I was astounded at the effect of this organ's sonority on this music: it was a perfect marriage; the loud passages were dramatised as never before, due especially to the trenchant character of the reeds in general, but particularly those of the Pedal division, which spoke out with commanding authority and not a vestige of hesitancy. The rich composite tone of the 8-foot flue ensemble was warm but clear, a perfect blend: especially did I notice the plump, easy speech of the basses whose pipes were on the front — those of the Montre and Flûte Harmonique — probably containing a high percentage of tin, as was Cavaillé's wont. Not less charming were the stopped ranks and the Swell Gamba and Celeste. Page told me that the organ was shortly to be dismantled and rebuilt by the Walker firm. On my registering some concern at such a possibility (for the style was so unlike their current work in every way), he assured me, "Nothing will be changed: I am going to sit by the voicing-machine with a cigarette on and see that nothing is altered." I felt reassured at this statement, for the moment. We shall see later how this materialised!

The next event was the purchase, by the Oratory, of a superb Mustel organ, on my recommendation, to replace a small accompanimental organ by the Positive Organ Company (Casson) used for certain services sung by the clergy alone around the Feast of Corpus Christi. The Positive was no longer satisfactory: the Mustel was put on castors so as to be mobile and could be wheeled into the Sanctuary as needed. It will be remembered from the Derby cinema-theatre days that the Mustel had quite remarkable power, and was thus adequate in such a large church; also that I was an expert performer on this complicated instrument. This was a fine vintage model, with two manuals, so that most foundation stops ran right through the compass: the broad-toned ones (Bourdon-Clarinette 16, Cor anglais-Flute 8, Voix celeste 8) on the front soundboard controlled by the lower manual; the 'fierce'-toned reeds (Baryton 32, Basson 16, Hautbois 8, Clairon-Fifre 4, Harpe Aeolienne 8) played by the upper manual; there was a coupler, two sets of swell-louvres for the 'back' reeds, and of course the all-important 'Expression' stop — whereby one blows with the feet *directly* into the reeds without using the reservoir, thus commanding a dynamic range from *ppp* to *fff* — in addition to the Mustel 'Double-expression' which enabled solo stops to be used without fear of being drowned by the accompaniment from the other reeds. This was all remarkable enough, but as heard in the Oratory acoustics, in such works as the 24 Pieces *'en style libre'* by Louis Vierne, the French aura was quite overwhelmingly beautiful to the ears of one accustomed to play these pieces on typical English stops: this again was a great breakthrough of 'the authentic voice'.

The third incident was far-reaching indeed. Through the agency of Mrs. A. C. D. de Brisay (wife of the one-time gramophone-recording critic), I was summoned to the Walker organ-factory to meet a Monsieur Louis Eugène-Rochesson, who was visiting London from Paris, and would like to be shown some interesting London organs. We went the rounds of various instruments to which I could get access (not forgetting Southwark Cathedral) but not before we had visited Walkers' head voicer in the factory voicing-shop — the celebrated W. C. Jones, generally regarded as something of a wizard with reed pipes amongst his colleagues in the trade. I told Rochesson of my visit to Leicester Square and my amazement at the speech of the reeds there, and my general dissatisfaction with English reeds, the basses of which were nearly always sluggish, and always thick and 'throttled'. Was it not an absurdity — would such poor emission ever be tolerated in an orchestra, if the trombones performed like this? It did not take long to find that we were in complete agreement about many other aspects of good organ tone and practice; and the final upshot was that he took me back to Paris at the week-end, taking advantage of the cheap fares granted for visiting the great Exposition of that year — I was too penurious to have gone otherwise. After dinner in his flat, Rochesson brought out a huge volume which he described as "The Law and the Prophets", viz, *L'Art du Facteur d'Orgues* of Dom Bédos de Celles. It was my introduction to this work; of course one could only glance at some pages of illustrations in the short time available, but it was a beginning.

On Sunday morning we set out early to see and hear all we could, even though many organists were *'en vacance'*, as it was the month of August. In spite of Dupré's absence, there was much to admire in the organ at St. Sulpice insofar as a mediocre performer was able to reveal its character: far more rewarding was the Mass at La Madeleine, whose organ was still in its pristine splendour as Cavaillé had left it in 1846. This large 4-manual organ of 48 speaking-stops had only one Mixture, a *Plein Jeu* on the Great, and one solitary mutation-stop, a Quinte 2⅔-feet in the same division. Yet, as I listened to this remarkable organ, and especially to the *tutti*, the *'Grand Choeur'*, trying to imagine what stops could be added to such an ensemble, I had to admit to myself that it was perfect: no addition could be conceived. The wonderful transparent brilliance of the reed-voicing was such as to compensate for any lack of mixture-work: the basses, of course, full and majestic — though not going below the 16-foot range — the trebles penetrating but essentially refined and in perfect balance. (In this Exposition year all the Paris organs had been put into good tune, which, I gather, was rather a rare occurrence!) the Bach Toccata and Fugue in D minor, played as the *Sortie*, was truly splendid, completely and musically satisfying!

But much more was still to come! We went to Vespers at Notre-Dame, and the first sounds I heard as we ascended to the tribune were those of the coupled *'Fonds'* 8-feet, mellow and broad, with rich, clear tenor and slightly fluty treble, albeit with an 'edge' to the tone, in every sense plastic, and thus *moving* as an experience undergone. "Super-Cavaillé" was how Rochesson described this instrument, designed by its builder on absolutely unique lines to project its tones throughout the length of that magnificent nave. All the music was improvised, by Vierne's successor — the former had been two months dead — and in true French style each piece was a Verset, alternating with the liturgical chants from the choir, far below; each verset was based on one characteristic registration, as in the works of Couperin, De Grigny, Guilain, etc, and in our times, Dupré. We heard the limpid Flûtes harmoniques, Bourdons, the heavily 'perfumed' Gambe and Céleste of the *Récit expressif*, paired with the Salicional and (flat-intoned) Unda Maris of the *Positif*, all homogeneous yet contrasting; and then the thrilling crescendo from the *tutti* of the *Récit*, opening gradually and successively amplified by the coupling of all the other four *tuttis*, with the final climax coming from the trenchant sound of the Pedal *Bombardes*, 32-feet and 16-feet. Each division was truly the complement of the others in a way quite unknown in English organs, though equally true (by a different method) of the finest of the baroque instruments. But in this organ (as I discovered later at Rouen and St. Sulpice) the genius of its creator had distilled a subtle alchemy — just as it happened in the finest works of Father Willis (when unaltered by later hands): the addition of one comparatively mild register to another produced a vehemence and complexity of sound in the General tutti which was truly astonishing and musically most exciting. How very flat the English Full Great with Tubas seemed in comparison — distinguished mainly by bulk or even sheer *din*, but lacking in any ability to rouse the musical sense! It was an unforgettable experience, this afternoon at Notre-Dame. Circumstances were at the time set against a possible closer scrutiny of the organ — such as I was able to make eleven years later, stop by stop — but a predominant impression which I carried away was the extraordinary clarity of the unison (and even sub-unison) pitch in the *Grand Choeur*, in spite of the enormously wide frequency-band of the sound: this was clearly due to the fact that Cavaillé had developed the harmonic series, 8, 12, 15, 17, 19, 21, 22, in Principal sonority for the 8-foot pitch (*Grand Choeur* manual), the 16-foot pitch (Solo, or Bombarde) and the 32-foot pitch (Pedal): the synthetic effect of this gave a reedy 'tang' to the fluework, making a perfect fusion with the reed chorus, and increasing the carrying power of both. (The late Albert Schweitzer remarked on the extraordinary clarity imparted to Bach's music, played at Notre-Dame.) The tonal pinnacle was, in no uncertain manner, the 1-foot stop of the *Grand Choeur* manual: the actual Mixtures were more foundational. The emission of all the reeds was instantaneous, rich and full-throated: the precision of a great orchestra was its only equivalent, yet it was true organ sonority.

The next morning, spent at St. Gervais, 'the organ of the Couperins', playing the first, 'parish' Mass of François 'Le Grand', gave a new insight into French classical registration even though (as I learnt much later) the pitch had been lowered one semitone in the late eighteenth century, and was thus a full tone below our normal. The reeds there were the ultimate in tonal output and grandeur — again the Bombardes, manual and Pedal, were the climactic registers. But the other reeds, Hautbois, Cromorne, Voix humaine, had an uninhibited directness of speech, brilliance without roughness, colour without over-refinement. The Voix-Humaine truly resembled a French operatic tenor, consonants and all! The other memorable effect was that of the creamy flavour of the Cornets, four in all if one included the *Cornet Décomposé* of the *Positif*. In this organ, as well as in a small late Cavaillé instrument, it was possible to inspect the reed pipes, noting the long, unweighted tongues with very pronounced curve at the free end, the long, parallel open shallots — everything calculated to give the full natural 'un-retouched' sound of each pipe according to the shape, scale and length of its resonator.

The actual specification of the organ in 1937 was as follows:

SAINT-GERVAIS-ET-SAINT-PROTAIS, PARIS

GRAND ORGUE		POSITIF	
Montre	16	Montre-Flûte	8
Bourdon	16	Bourdon	8
Montre	8	Prestant	4
Bourdon	8	Nazard	2⅔
Flûte	8	Doublette	2
Prestant	4	Tierce	1³/₅
Nazard	2⅔	Plein jeu	IV
Doublette	2	Trompette	8
Quarte de Nazard	2	Cromorne	8
Tierce	1³/₅	Basson-Clarinette	8
Grand Cornet	V	Clairon	4
Plein jeu	V		
I. Trompette	8	RECIT	
II. Trompette	8	Cornet	V
Voix humaine	8	Hautbois	8
Clairon	4		
		ECHO	
BOMBARDE		Flûte d'écho	8
Bombarde	16	Trompette d'écho	8
PEDALE			
Flûte	16		
Flûte	8		
Flûte	4		
Bombarde	16		
Trompette	8		
Clairon	4	Tremblant	

The Positif could be coupled to the Grand Orgue by pulling forward the keyframe of the latter: the Bombarde manual automatically activated the Grand Orgue, permanently coupled. There were no pedal couplers.

Returning to the Oratory — coming back to earth, as it were — one felt that *something* must be done to improve the balance and speech of flues and reeds.

The next 'event' was a curious one, which gave a clear lead forward. A bass note on the Great 8-foot Trumpet suddenly jumped to a higher note. I had the pipe out, and discovered that the weight on the end of the tongue had come off — it consisted of a small piece of thick leather lined with a small strip of brass. Experimentally, I knocked the spring up, and was surprised to find that I could tune it right down to its proper note; also, that the pipe gave an excellent Trumpet note (as compared with the rather stifled Bassoon quality of its neighbours): and it also spoke *quickly*, where they were all slow in speech! The next step required some courage (for I was not the sole organist: my colleague, Henry Washington, played for many services too): however, I removed the other weights, one by one — they were only put on the tenor and bass register. The final result was a little 'rough' in quality, but the Cs now balanced admirably, and the effect of the whole stop in the church was vastly improved; the size and ambience of the building could 'take it' and the musical gain was considerable: one could play the bass ornaments in Couperin!

I soon removed most of the weights from the Clarion. Of course, I had to notify Walkers': they replied, "The reeds must have been well-voiced[18] to speak at all." It looked as though the revoicing since Bishops' lost care of the organ had only consisted of Walkers' loading the tongues and raising the wind-pressure — the curve of the tongues had remained intact, unaffected by their now shorter length. A visit to an old intact Bishop 3-manual organ in the East End of London[19] shortly afterwards, confirmed this and also provided an invaluable source of information on the treatment and sonority of Bishops' flue-work of the Oratory period: the little wooden flutes of the Choir Organ, identical in design but speaking with peculiar charm and piquancy on their original wind-pressure[20]; the 'old-fashioned' mild but clear Mixture chorus and separate stops of the Great, all fitting in with a fierce Swell Trumpet, and conveying an intriguing musical impression of real character. Could not the Oratory stops be restored to this? It was a tempting, tantalising thought: one to be stored in the department of ideal fantasy.

In that realm of fantasy also, as hinted earlier, 'change was in the air': for though the move to Brompton was the product of much wider and deeper issues than this or that style of organ-building, or indeed, organs at all (and in any case the Oratory organ in the circumstances was tolerably acceptable in its general effect combined with the sympathetically reverberant acoustics of the building), yet the foretaste of the Classical Revival in the USA, and the continuation of my correspondence with Donald Harrison were influences too powerful to lie dormant for very long. Donald, after visiting some celebrated old organs in Germany in 1936, had evolved his own improved classical design with an *unenclosed* Positive section on light wind-pressure (about 2½ inches), tonally related to the Great in the same way as the older traditional *Rück-positiv*: the new Swell divisions retained the Romantic voices with French-style chorus reeds on fairly light wind (perhaps 3½ inches) and a large completely independent Pedal division. If a second Romantic division was called for, this took the form of an *enclosed* Choir (played from the lowest manual) which was also given a chorus structure with perhaps a 3-rank Carillon (12, 17, 22), again in Cavaillé-Coll fashion, as the tonal pinnacle.

Still technically British (resident in the United States), Don would have been willing to co-operate with an English firm in building a new classical organ for me, if such a firm could be found: he would make the main choruses, the design and voicing of which would represent a complete about-face from current English practice, using light wind-pressure, 'full wind' at the pipe-foot with more control of the tone at the embouchure, and a larger proportion of tin in the pipe-metal: any old material re-used would be put inside the swell-boxes.

But there were considerable local obstacles to any such fundamental scheme of change: enumerated briefly, these were:

(1) A strong mental resistance (and hence, lack of confidence) on the part of my Musical Director, who also had a natural aversion to any immediate artistic project emanating from abroad, and especially from America — it was bad enough to have put up with a quasi-American organist!

(2) The non-existence of any church funds for such a project, and a fundamental disinclination on the part of the authorities to make any change in the *status quo*, even had money been available, and a strong case made.

(3) The unlikely chance that any English firm could be induced to 'step out of line' to the extent of collaborating with Don Harrison and his American company and taking direction from him in the technical sphere. The wide divergence of views and styles could be seen even in a comparison of lists of stops, but far more apparent was it in the spheres of pipe-material and construction, voicing, layout, wind-pressure, and above all, the finished 'sound-picture' in the mind of the organ-voicer: in the contemporary English style, I found this harsh, unmusically top-heavy in the manuals and bottom-heavy in the half-starved Pedal section.

At this point we must return to Cavaillé-Coll and Notre-Dame de France, Leicester Square. On one of my visits to the Walker factory I was again ushered into Mr. Jones' voicing room: he produced the bottom G pipe of the Pedal Bombarde, and put it on its wind. It gave a superb note, with splendid 'round' attack and full harmonic development, which delighted my ear. Said Mr. Jones, "Everything possible is wrong with that note," obviously failing completely to appreciate the style and its merits, and most probably horrified to hear what is vulgarly called the "death-rattle" — a slight after-vibration of the tongue, which can be perceived at close quarters and which results from the particularly sensitive curve of the long unweighted tongue, lying very close to the shallot at the wedged end. Of course all this was changed — 'revoiced' — as was much of the fluework. Happening to drop into the church itself some time later, I heard someone struggling unsuccessfully to get decent speech from those front pipes whose promptness I had so admired a few months previously. Adieu, Monsieur Cavaillé! Yet this revoiced organ was regarded by many as an unqualified success, and one boast of the time was that it was easier to keep in tune. Happily, perhaps, the issue was finally settled by 'enemy action' during World War II: it had been a complete misunderstanding on the part of the restorers, and it destroyed for me any hope of musical betterment in the officially established tradition of British organ building of the time. Improvements at the Oratory — on which I was certainly resolved — could only be brought about unofficially, as it were, by continued discreet re-regulation of the fluework, carried out by sympathetically inclined tuners: the Swell and especially the Pedal reeds and Tuba were for the moment incapable of improvement.

Yet there had been renewed grounds for hope in an unforeseen happening: Reginald Walker made a trip to the United States! While there, he visited Donald Harrison at the Aeolian-Skinner works, and they became quite friendly. Bearing in mind the already mooted possibility of some collaboration, Don went to some trouble to show him their latest work and methods (some of which, as Don observed to me, must have come as quite a shock to Mr Reginald): at all events, an impression was made in a favourable sense, as I was to learn later. All this was splendid for the cause, though it would still be a very long journey to get through the natural resistance to change among the Walker staff; and still, alas, the Oratory situation was utterly unfavourable. But then another avenue opened, suddenly and significantly.

One of the monks of Buckfast Abbey was living with the Oratory Fathers while working at the adjoining Royal College of Art, and having observed what I was trying to do, he passed on to me an invitation from the Abbey organist to go and make a survey of that organ. My considerable recommendations had to be shelved, but after the then Abbot's untimely death, the matter was re-opened. The organist being very much of the same mind as myself — he had studied in Germany — he was easily persuaded to accept my advice that

Donald Harrison be engaged to design and supervise the building of a new organ which would incorporate all that was of value in the old, but would follow the principles of classic design. Thanks to Reginald Walker's visit, which had prepared the ground, the Walker firm agreed to collaborate, and as the first stage, a new 4-manual console was ordered from them: on the stop-keys was engraved the new specification which I drew up in consultation with Harrison! But in mid-1939 the clouds of impending world war were gathering, and by the time the console was ready, the American project had been posponed *sine die*. What to do?

As the existing console and action had been largely condemned in my report, the obviously best course now was to connect up the existing organ to the new console — which incidentally facilitated a much better co-ordination of a rather haphazard collection of organ material, partly built piecemeal as the Abbey had grown — built by the monks themselves — and partly second-hand from at least two sources[21]. Even as a temporary measure, the best musical effect was desirable, and I decided at once to omit the existing chorus reeds, which were all on heavy wind, of an undesirable tonality. By dint of finding some of the better second-hand pipes amongst material which one of the monks had amassed up in the tower for a well-intentioned 'Echo Organ', it was possible to improvise two acceptable mutations, Nazard and Tierce, on the newly constituted (enclosed) Choir division.

When all was ready for the necessary tonal regulation, we were already into 1940, and Britain was at war. Organ-building was almost at a standstill already, and thus it was possible for two of Walkers' top technical staff to do this work — Mr. Earlam and, of course, the voicer, Mr. W. C. Jones: both of them applied themselves most generously to carrying out my wishes in spite of the odd appearance of things. We started the regulation of the pipes of the Great division, the first stop being the important 'tuning rank', Principal 4-feet. Mr. Jones began with middle c, and up the scale therefrom, note by note, in a perfectly graded crescendo for an octave-and-a-half or so, and down into the tenor octave in an equally graded diminuendo, according to the rule-book, so to speak. He was obviously pleased with the result. "But Mr. Jones," said the organist and I, "let us weigh the C's against one another, like this." and I applied the 'Gottfried' balancing test: of course, treble C spoke out thinly, while the tenor C mumbled politely in the accepted manner of the style and time. A short musical example played, sounded rather thin and miserable, like a third-rate village organ. "Let's get these C's in balance with one another", and reluctantly, though not without interest, this was done; treble C sounded better for not being so forced; tenor C, a substantial-note, not without some sort of slight 'cough' or initial transient tone. The other intervening notes were re-regulated accordingly right through the compass, and the 8-foot Diapason treated likewise. "See now, Mr.

Jones, how much clearer the music sounds," we said, as indeed it did, and the general sonority had gained in breadth and even a certain 'nobility' of timbre. This method was continued throughout the fluework: there was only one tiny Mixture ('Echo') in the Swell — but that was immaterial: a Bach fugue as now played was completely clear for the first time, and everyone present noticed it! I felt that an effectual death-blow had been struck against the prevailing 'melodic' practice of 'keeping up the trebles' which had bedevilled English organ-voicing for thirty years.

Another interesting object-lesson was brought home to me: during my brief absence from the scene, the pipes for the Nazard and Tierce were fitted into two vacant places in the Choir section; but when I came to try them, they were too prominent: when softened, they sounded like the so-called 'synthetics' which were being incorporated as a matter of course by most builders by now, in enclosed and rather anaemic Choir divisions — equally unsatisfactory. Suddenly I realised that there was only one solution — a large increase in scale (diameter) for these pipes. This would make the sound more foundational, more fluty, more *blending*, which after all is the one quality a mutation 'off-pitch' stop *must* have. Rather reluctantly, the pipes were cut down several semitones, perhaps four or five, and moved along to their new places. This proved to be successful, and they combined excellently with a fine Flute 4-foot and wide-scaled Flageolet 2-foot to make a full-bodied *Cornet Décomposé*. It was a lucky fluke, and the voicers' reluctance was founded on a legitimate artistic scruple: when a pipe is shortened, the relative cut-up of the mouth, *vis-à-vis* the length scale, is increased; and when that cut-up passes a certain point, stability of tuning becomes a crucial issue: Earlam and W. C. Jones were already rather concerned that the limit had been passed when the main Diapason was softened in the treble range — "Those pipes are under their speech," they exclaimed. Short of wind or not, I found them better musically than when they had been so forced, and when it came to a choice of evils, I was all for the musical effect as the priority; again, it was a lucky fluke that the acoustics of the Abbey church were on our side — the offending pipes sounded better than they should have done! Considering that some reduction of wind-pressure had also been made, we were doubly lucky, for that also was working against the cause of firm speech and tuning — the pipes could reach the point of 'gasping for breath'. Considering also the rather odd stop-list now produced, it was remarkable that the organ sounded so well: and so it had to remain for nearly seven years. Mr. Jones' final gesture was the improvement of the Pedal Trombone-Trumpet extension, lowering the pressure slightly, and letting the pipes speak out more freely.

A mooted plan to give the Great a Mixture and Sesquialtera at this juncture was abandoned on the grounds of expense, and the specification was now as follows:

GREAT			SWELL			ECHO (unenclosed)	
Subprincipal		16	Gedeckt		16	Lieblich gedeckt	8
Diapason major		8	Open Diapason		8	Dulciana	8
Principal (ext)		8	Violin Diapason		8	Lieblich flöte	4
Claribel Flute		8	Gedeckt (ext)		8		
Rohrflöte [sic]		8	Flauto		8	CHOIR (enclosed)	
Octave		4	Rohrflöte [sic]		8	Diapason	8
Harmonic Flute		4	Salicional		8	Hohlflöte	8
Twelfth		2⅔	Aeoline		8	Gedeckt	8
Fifteenth		2	Voix celeste		8	Quintatön	8
Clarinette (open tone)		8	Geigenprincipal		4	Viole	8
			Gedeckt (ext)		4	Viole celeste	8
PEDAL			Salicetina		1	Cone gamba	8
Acoustic Bass		32	Sesquialtera		III	Vox angelica	8
Contrabass (Great)		16	Musette		16	Principal	4
Bourdon (ext 32-feet)		16	(improvised bass)			Concert Flute	4
Sub-bass		16	Musette (ext)		8	Octave viole	4
Dulciana		16	Musette (ext)		4	Nazard	2⅔
Gedeckt (Swell)		16	Tremulant			Flageolet	2
Octave wood		8	Octave			Tierce	1³/₅
Principal (Great)		8	Suboctave			Trumpet	8
Gedeckt (Swell)		8	Unison off			Corno di bassetto	8
Gedeckt (Swell)		4				Tremulant	
Trombone		16	Unison couplers.				
Trumpet (ext)		8	Wind pressures:				
Musette (Swell)		8	Great: flue 4½" reed 5"				
Musette (Swell)		4	Swell: flue 5" reed 5¼"				
			Choir: 4¼"				
			Echo: 3¼"				
			Pedal: flue 4½" reed 6"				

Odd though it appears on paper, the musical effect of this instrument was quite presentable: it certainly proved that clarity is by no means wholly dependent on the presence of Mixtures and highly developed mutation stops. This we knew; for a number of organist-musicians unable to tolerate (or even analyse aurally) the sound of a Bach fugue played on the heavy-pressured hard-toned choruses of contemporary English organs, had discovered with joy and satisfaction that such Bach works sounded best when played throughout on a single small diapason — usually 'Great No. 2'. But clarity, vital though it is, is not the *sole* issue: *character* (in which is included the quality of timbre, dynamic intensity, etc) must also be right; and the character of this organ was really too neutral and monotonous for certain works ever to sound their best. This phenomenon was confirmed in one of my exchanges of views with Donald Harrison, relative to the desirable loudness of mutation and mixture ranks, and his reply that the sound of an organ chorus is a *special* sonority, and thus the artificially produced harmonics must *not* be completely subordinated to the unison pitch: and that there could be considerable variation in the conception of a good organ ensemble, the tonal centre of gravity of which could be of high, low or middle pitch. This was a most important pronouncement, expressing an architectural basis for making a two-, three- or four-tiered tonal scheme, each division of which, while complete in itself would interlock effectively with the others, to produce a grand and rich tonal synthesis. The full realisation of this principle and its practical application was still to take some years for me to grasp fully — largely as a consequence of later study of Dutch and German baroque organs — even though a like synthesis had already been noted in the best Cavaillé organs, where it was produced rather by skilfully conceived *duplication* of stops, scales and sonorities from one division to another.

Returning to the Oratory, mention must be made of an unexpectedly generous move on the part of Reginald H. Walker and W. C. Jones, who came one day with two or three reed pipes made on the French principle, and sounding 2-foot, 4-foot and possibly 8-foot C: these had been voiced on 3¼ inches pressure, and they were put into position on the back soundboard (reeds) of the Great division. Alas for good intentions! We had all been misled (probably by Gilbert Benham's article in *The Organ*[22]) into thinking that the whole Great was on this pressure — whereas, as mentioned earlier, I discovered later that it was one inch higher. Of course the trial pipes would not tune, and when slots had been opened in the resonators, and the tongues had been flattened at the tuning-springs to bring them to correct pitch, the tone was certainly powerful but unpleasantly rough and rasping! It was, however, admitted all round that this gave some indication of what might be attempted if the necessary money were made available — but there was still no hope of that.

When the 4¼ inch pressure was discovered, and was found to apply also to the Choir department, both were dropped to 3¼ inches, and all the relevant pipework on Great and Choir was restored to something like its original speech by opening up the foot-holes. Meantime the Blockflute on the Great was moved up four pipes to make a Tierce; one of the two 4-foot flutes on the Choir was moved up as a Quintflute 2⅔ feet; and the tierce-rank was extracted from the Choir Mixture-stop and cut down a few semitones to increase its scale; and the Swell and Choir Mixtures were both 'cannibalised' a little so as to give a higher pitch for the bass and tenor ranges, with breaks on all C's (concealed, of course, by the method employed earlier at Princeton) instead of a great jump back at middle C sharp.

But that is not to say that all this tonal regulation was not constantly hampered by acoustical difficulties: it was one thing to balance C's (or other notes) at the console in the gallery, but as heard down in the church they could sound quite otherwise; the upper notes came out louder, the lower softer, indistinct or characterless. Nor was this imbalance constant — it changed as one moved about the building. We struggled for hours with this phenomenon, and the tuner-voicer, although conscientiously working for the attainment of my purpose, said, "I don't think you will ever achieve a true balance in this building." Undoubtedly, with hindsight, we were up against 'standing waves', which can make a pipe *inaudible* from one position and almost twice its strength from another! We did our best! I only discovered the complete solution of this problem ten years later by dint of practical research and experiment. So much for the fluework.

The next task was to tackle the Swell, Pedal and Solo reeds. The 8- and 4-foot trumpets in the Swell responded to the removal of the loads on the tongues and the lowering of the wind-pressure to 3¼ inches — like those on the Great. But whereas the Walker Double Trumpet on the Great — a reed with 'capped' (pepper-pot) resonators — had accepted the lower pressure without much trouble, the Swell Contra Fagotto became sluggish and unusable. Mr. Jones came, and I of course wanted unweighted tongues, thinking of the French sound and attack. He did remove one or two weights, to my delight; but habit was too powerful, and my heart sank as he produced his own 'armoury' of felt pellets and small metal discs, to replace the original hard leather and brass loads. A rather muffled tone resulted, and my only remaining concern was that the pipes be made to speak quickly enough: this could only be achieved by reducing the curve of the tongues to a minimum, (the only permanent cure would have entailed the substitution of thinner, softer tongues): the tone was then so devitalised that I realised that we must say "Goodbye"; I felt that Mr. Jones and I could never agree — indeed I tried to get the tuner to try his hand at voicing, if only we could get some new brass of the right specification from the firm. This only embarrassed all concerned, and was a 'non-starter'.

We did, however, try to improve a note — low B — on the 32-foot reed. I discovered then that this stop had enormous wooden shallots — the block and shallot all of a piece, beautifully made! The tongues were very thick, with a heavy weight screwed on. The tuner removed the latter, substituting a much lighter one, stuck on with 'Chatterton compound'. When the note was tried, the weight was blown off immediately, just as my Reverend Prefect of Music walked through the church. Describing the sound as "like an elephant in travail", he gently admonished me not to repeat this performance while people were trying to pray — and there our operations ceased.

Soon, well into World War II, the air-raid sirens took over. The Oratory lost nearly all its windows, but sustained no further damage.

The Sunday services continued normally, and the organ sounded more musical on account of the work already done. It was not long before I myself was called to Other Duties for week-days, and apart from necessary patching of leather on the feeders of the powerful hydraulic blowing-plant which was still giving yeoman service, all work was postponed.

By the autumn of 1942 the war situation had quietened considerably, and as my activities were now transferred to the London area, I was soon trying again to tackle the Pedal reeds and the Tuba. But by now Walkers' were under severe war restrictions, although disinclined to let any other smaller firm 'have a go'. They did, however, send their old and trusted senior voicer, Mr. Eagle, to try and effect some improvement in the speech of these heavy Pedal stops, but alas, to no purpose — they remained completely intractable. (An amused spectator of this operation was his 'boy', one Dennis Thurlow.)

Owing to the same restrictions, the firm was unable even to undertake the re-engraving of the changed stops, the paper labels of which were always coming off. Discovering that R. W. Davidson ('Kingsgate Davidson') was at this time actually rebuilding the organ at the church next door (Holy Trinity, Brompton) under the moral guidance of the late Colonel George Dixon, I asked Mr. Davidson whether *he* could not perform this small service for me, which he did, by arrangement with Walkers'.

It soon became obvious that he was able, and prepared, to help me further to attain my ideals, and I arranged for him to take over the maintenance of the Oratory organ from 1944. His first good service was the revoicing of the Tuba, using thinner tongues and only a few small weights for bottom notes — wind-pressure 5½ inches. Whatever the scoffers might say about such a pressure, this became a very effective stop, a trifle more fiery than before, and still profiting from its forward position, but much more in harmony with the rest of the organ, though far from feeble!

All my operations up to now had been performed on existing pipework, occasionally transposing the pitch of a stop, sometimes enlarging its scale (by shortening existing pipes) to the point where (in the case of quints and tierces) a good blend was reached empirically, subject to the restrictions imposed by the cut-up of mouths in the trebles; if this were too high, good steady speech would be inhibited, or indeed the pipe might refuse to speak at all. I was lucky! Nothing had to be thrown out or replaced.

And now in the spring of 1945 another new avenue opened up: Michael Howard, for whose Renaissance Society concerts I often played, told me that the Dolmetsch family actually possessed a copy of Dom Bédos, and he obtained permission for me to go a number of times to consult it at Haslemere — a facility not otherwise open to me at that time. It was my real initiation into the traditions of French classical organ-building, and of special interest were the list of the stops, the pipe-construction, both flue and reed, and, of course, the width-scales of all pipes including the mutations, cornets and pleins-jeux, and the composition of the latter — consisting of fournitures plus cymbales. Particularly intriguing was the simplicity of the system of scaling the flue-pipes — as an organ-builder he naturally worked in terms of circumferences, to be inscribed on the flat metal sheet. All that was necessary was the erection of ordinates on a horizontal line marked out with the length-scales (in the octave-ratio 2 : 1) from C to c''', then to mark the scale of the largest pipe (C) and the smallest (c''') on their respective ordinates: a straight line joining these two points and intersecting the other uprights would then give the scales of all the intervening notes. This was an ingeniously simple method of relating the width-scale to the octave-ratio of 2 : 1, but only made possible by the addition of an empirically determined constant to counteract the too rapid diminution of widths from octave to octave, in the direct 2 : 1 ratio.

The scale-widths of the mutation-stops, Nazard, Tierce, Quarte, Larigot and the Cornets, were quite a revelation — for all such stops in English organs up to now were made up of meagre little flutes or gemshorns or dulcianas, producing at best only feeble 'synthetic' effects. A 2⅔ foot Twelfth was always made narrower than either the 4-foot or 2-foot, and when loud enough to be heard was then too 'stringy' to be usable with the flute-stops — or indeed with any stop without the presence of its neighbouring 2-feet. Against this poor background of contemporary practice, the Oratory mutation-changes did not come out badly at all. What could now be more natural than to attempt some classical mixtures — and first, the Fourniture?

The composition and scale particulars were duly noted: Mr. Davidson reckoned that we could convert the Great 3-rank Mixture into a 5-rank Fourniture if the pipes could be planted on a "cheek", screwed on to the back of the Great "front" soundboard to give additional area for planting the two extra rows; and I worked out the scheme of the breaks, à la Bédos, fitting round the existing three ranks, which are underlined:

	C	15	19	22	26	29	(17 notes)
	f	8	12	15	19	22	(12 notes)
c' sharp		8	12	15	19	22	
	f'	1	5	8	12	15	(to top)

(The necessary correlated Cymbale, of three ranks (29, 33, 36) was left in abeyance for the moment.) The new pipes were ordered, and arrived as soon as post-war conditions allowed, probably in 1946 or early 1947.

Meantime we began work on the Pedal reeds. Davidson took a great interest in trying to improve them: he, like myself, was conversant with Lewis's work in the same direction.

The specification of the pipes has been mentioned already. The lowest 27 notes (from 32-foot C) had wooden blocks and shallots, the latter being parallel, not tapered, with a fairly long but certainly not *full* opening down the side, and in addition to being wood, this was faced with hard cardboard. The 16-foot part was older, dating from 1914; the 32-foot extension was put in in 1924: the scale of the older part was reasonably moderate, that of the big pipes much larger: in the whole stop the recipe was perfect for encouragement of a dead heavy sonority with no harmonic development beyond what might be termed a 'massive toothache'! The shallots of the bottom octave were so enormous, and the tongues were so thick and weighted, that it ceased to be a reed at all — it was potentially a diaphone, and even on the heavy wind was painfully slow in speech. Our first step was to open up the shallots and drop the pressure to about 4½ inches, and Mr. Davidson cut out and curved some new tongues, on the spot. No weights were used, and there was some likelihood that the tongues would not be long enough to tune down to the fundamental pitch, and this necessitated still thinner scale. One problem which arose came from the fact that the sheet brass came from the rolling-mill with a slight curvature already imprinted. If one cut the tongue with the length following the direction of the curve, then the original curvature would tend to return and falsify the implanted curve, causing slowness or rattle or some other defect of speech. Thus, most voicers put the new curve on at right angles to the initial curve: but if one was working with thin brass, this could cause a kind of extra inertia against which the wind-stream would have to work, and this brittle effect would also cause slowness or a harsh tonality. Truly, the 'added-weight' technique was a god-send to a commercial voicer who aspired to finish voicing a manual reed stop between breakfast and luncheon!

Many of our essays — and I count myself as part of the operation — failed in some way or other at first; but Davidson persevered, and eventually we got some good round notes, not really French, but not wholly English either — somewhere between the two. Davidson observed to me that the best result seemed to come when the tongue never *completely* closed the opening in the shallot: if it did, then there was a most objectionable grating or rattling sonority — and of course the same thing happened if there were a flat place in the curve. Again, one could obtain a splendid note with a fine curve, only to discover that after a moment's repose the note was *slow*, or wouldn't speak at all! Then it would be necessary to reduce the curve and run back into all the ancillary risks, 'flats', 'tip-clatter', etc, as at 'Square One'! (As a consolation, I remembered Rochesson's saying that once you had the "right curve", the acoustical "pull" of the resonator-pitch would help to preserve it permanently.) *Ars longa* ...!

A similar plan of revoicing was successful in getting more 'drive' from the Swell 16-foot Fagotto, which was then renamed Bombarde in spite of its modest scale. But the overall effect of the Pedal reeds remained, on reflection, dull and lifeless, even though they spoke more *promptly* than ever before. C. H. Trevor could still find little to admire in their tone, though he had regarded very favourably the improvements in the flue-choruses.

In despair, I wrote to Rochesson in Paris, and to my surprise received in reply a most generous *exposé*. (It will be recalled that he had worked initially under Monsieur Prince, Cavaillé's head voicer, and was expertly conversant with the style and techniques involved.) According to him, the brass used for reed tongues by English organ-builders was much harder and less flexible than that used by the French, which, incidentally was cut and supplied *in the flat*, not rolled: (see above, where our experience had confirmed this). The full beauty of French reed-voicing was also dependent on the use, for all except certain romantic stops, such as the Clarinette or Bassoon, of the French open shallot, a long cylindrical brass tube with a domed end and a parallel opening (and flat face) down its whole length. More particularly was it dependent on the correct curvature (*'tournure'*) of the long, unweighted tongue through three distinct zones: around the contact-point of the tuning spring it should lie *flat*; a little way further towards the free end the curve should begin very gradually; but in the third zone, nearer the tip, it should be accentuated 'energetically' — this final tip-curve secured a fine round-toned attack, thus fulfilling the function usurped by the commercial practice of loading the tongues — the latter 'technique' robbing the sound of its full natural vitality, as well as producing eventual slowness due to the inertia and also the thrashing action of the weight. Of course, as Rochesson admitted, only an actual demonstration could illustrate the matter clearly: untoward circumstances debarred such a thing so soon after World War II while all kinds of controls were still in force; but in the following year it was arranged and took place in May 1948.

In the meanwhile, the complete revision of the fluework structure and a plan for further, final enlargement were worked out with Mr. Davidson, to include a new stop-key console similar to the interesting pneumatic one made by the old firm of Nicholson at the Birmingham Oratory, but electrically powered. The stop-keys, of an unusually substantial pattern, were made of wood with circular ivory name-plates. They were comfortable to operate, and were ranged in a long horizontal row over the top manual, overlapping at the ends, with a second and third row at the bass end for Pedal stops and Pedal couplers. By this means the console height was kept down; and the site planned for it at the front of the choir gallery ensured easy communication with the Choir-Director, and a hitherto denied full view of the church below.[23]

An important acoustic improvement was the planned addition of five unenclosed stops to the Solo division, to stand on a new soundboard high in the arch communicating with the 'south' transept, where they would be joined by the existing Tuba — the whole to project a substantial body of sound primarily into the transept and dome area, but also backward through the other gallery-arches into the nave. I had by then obtained the necessary support of the authorities, the order was given to go ahead, and the complete specification was to be:

GREAT			SWELL			POSITIVE (open)	
Subprincipal	16		Bourdon	16		Bourdon	16
Principal	8		Diapason	8		Stopped Diapason	8
Diapason	8		Stopped Diapason	8		Flauto (grooved)	8
Claribel	8		Viole de Gambe (new)	8		Bell Gamba (grooved)	8
Harmonic Flute (g)	8		Violes Celestes (new)	8		Principal	4
Stopped Diapason	8		Octave	4		Flute	4
Octave	4		Superoctave	2		Quint Flute	2⅔
Wald Flute	4		Sesquialtera	III		Octave	2
Quint	2⅔		Bombarde	16		Blockflute	2
Superoctave	2		Cornopean	8		Tierce	1³/₅
Tierce	1³/₅		Oboe	8		Larigot	1⅓
Grande Fourniture V	2		Clarion	4		Petite Fourniture	III
Cymbale III	½		Tremulant			Petite Cymbale	III
Posaune	8					Tuba Magna (Solo)	8
Clarion	4		SOLO (open)			POSITIVE (enclosed)	
			Sub Bass (part Pedal)	16		Principal-à-Echo	8
PEDAL			Major Principal	8		Unda Maris (c)	8
Sub Diapason	32		Rohrquint	5⅓		Cromorne	8
Major Bass (wood)	16		Grosse Octave	4		Tremulant	
Principal (front)	16		Grand Cornet	III-V			
Violone (wood)	16		Trombone	16		WIND-PRESSURES	
Bourdon	16		Tuba Magna	8		Great:	
Echo Lieblich (Sw)	16		SOLO (enclosed)			3¾ and 3¼ inches	
Principal (extension)	8		Orchestral Flute	8		Positive:	
Bourdon (extension)	8		Harmonic Flute	4		3¼ and 3½ inches	
Flute or Octave (new)	4		Fagotto	8		Swell:	
Contre Bombarde	32		Vox Humana	8		3 and 3¼ inches	
(extension)			Tremulant			Solo:	
Bombarde	16		Enclosed Positive on Solo alone			3½ and 5½ inches	
Trumpet (extension)	8					Pedal:	
						3¼ and 4½ inches	
						Action:	
						7½ and 10½ inches	

Comparison with the original Bishop specification will account for much of the above, though not all. The Tierce on the Great was the old Blockflute, cut down, still with its wood bass; the scale of the Octave 4-feet was to be increased by two pipes, those of the Quint and Superoctave by three and four pipes respectively. The Bell Gamba on the Positive was new (old Bevington), while the old stop was to be cut down to make the new (conical) Blockflute, shorn of its dilapidated, torn bell-tops. On the same division the old wooden Piccolo became the Larigot, and the Fifteenth was absorbed into the Mixtures — the old (tenor c) Diapason and the 4-foot Principal becoming the new 4-foot and 2-foot stops.

The three enclosed stops of the Positive section would occupy the former 'Echo' box behind the Swell at the very back of the organ, and consist of the two old ineffective Dulcianas, scaled up to make a Principal à Echo and an Unda Maris 8-feet (tenor c) standing in place of the former Viole d'orchestre and Clarinet (tenor c); a new (second-hand) Corno di Bassetto 8-feet, of 58 notes, to stand in place of the old Orchestral Oboe; and all on a wind-pressure reduced to the reasonable level of 3½ inches. This whole operation was completed quite soon, and the effect of the undulants with swell-box closed was ethereally beautiful — these quiet sounds penetrated into every corner of the large building. The soft metal pipes of both stops were newly slotted at the tops: this imparted to them a slight stringiness of unusual character, mostly suppressed when the shutters were closed, but emerging gradually as the box was opened, and in charming contrast with the keener (old Lewis) strings made of good spotted metal, now in the Swell division.

On the new (unenclosed) Solo division the Rohrquint was the old Gedeckt — the pipes had been transposed up since 1941, *inside* the box; the new Major Principal and Grosse Octave were, by Mr. Davidson's recommendation, to be made to the scale of Schulze's largest Diapason scale, that at St. Mary's, Tyne Dock, the 8-foot stop to have the wide $2/7$ mouth; and the Cornet was, by my advice, to be made to the Dom Bédos 'Grand Cornet' scale — the maximum. The 16-foot Trombone was to be an old Hill stop in Davidson's possession, with half-length pipes for the bottom octave. Mr. Davidson was very enthusiastic about Schulze's work, and had recently installed a new Schulze-style [sic] diapason chorus at the church next to the Oratory (Holy Trinity), under the advice and supervision of Colonel George Dixon, the well-known organ-connoisseur already mentioned, who had had a finger in the pie in many British organs from Ely to Norwich! After reading a most interesting and fully documented report on the Tyne Dock organ, written in *The Organ* by D. Batigan Verne[24], I was frankly somewhat sceptical about the authenticity of the voicing of Davidson's copies: their tone seemed too opaque and the mouths looked rather high-cut — certainly higher than the $2/9$ proportion of their width, which was cited by Verne. Obviously here was a matter for further investigation, and one day I got on a train to South Shields, and arrived at St. Mary's. Sadly the Vicar informed me that the organ was all to pieces for cleaning, by Norman & Beard! However, the Great pipes were back in place, and almost perfectly in tune: alas, the sound of the Diapason did not attract me: I felt that a change had taken place since Schulze had left it: it did not correspond to Verne's account at all; and the effect of the Mixture V ranks was equally dull and unattractive. In despair, I decided to visit Armley[25] on the way home. (This was in 1947, and nothing had been done to it since about 1906.) There I found what I had sought; the Major Principal had a breadth and nobility combined with a warm string-like bloom — this was completely convincing and quite unlike the counterfeits. Of course I disliked the Choir Mixture with its growling sub-tierce; and the famous Great Mixture (now somewhat tamed?) made one's hair stand on end. But the memory of the big Diapason remained as a musical experience. *That* was what we must have at the Oratory! I told Mr. Davidson of my conclusions: his pipes were cut-up too high.

Meantime there were stirrings at Buckfast Abbey in favour of completion of the planned rebuilding, but now without Donald Harrison's supervision (owing to the international currency situation) and on simpler lines, utilising most of the existing pipes and two of the soundboards, which belonged to the Aeolian section, and were constructed on the Roosevelt, sliderless, principle. One of these was to remain within the Choir chamber, the other was to go into the Swell. The former posed problems of allocation of stops which would fit the available spaces and still make a good chorus-structure. Indeed the basis of the whole project was the provision of adequate new 'chorus' material, and in this context nothing seemed simpler than to adopt the scheme and scaling given by Dom Bédos for both the mixtures and some separate mutations. In the limited spaces of the enclosed Choir division I decided to 'double up' two wide-scale mutations (a conical Nazard 2⅔ feet, *'grosse taille'*, and a cylindrical Quarte de Nazard 2-feet, *'menue taille'*) as a Rauschquint, and as the sole 4-foot I specified a 'cooked up' Spitzprincipal of heroic width-scale derived from that of the conical Nazards. Other wide scales were proposed for the unenclosed Positive. The whole scheme shows some resemblance to the new Oratory stop-list:

GREAT		PEDAL	
(in Choir-aisle, east and centre)		(Choir-aisle, west and centre)	
Subprincipal	16	Sub Bass (real to E)	32
Major Diapason	8	Contrabass (old Violone)	16
Gross Flute (old Choir)	8	Principal (Great)	16

DEVELOPMENT

Principal (extension)	8
Rohrflute (existing)	8
Octave	4
Flute Couverte (wide)	4
Grosse Tierce (old Echo, stopped)	$3^{1}/_{5}$
Nazard (new, open, wide)	$2^{2}/_{3}$
Doublette (old 12th cut down)	2
Tierce (old 15th cut down)	$1^{3}/_{5}$
Fourniture V	2
Cymbale III	½
Posaune (old Swell)	8
Clarion (old Great)	4

SWELL (triforium, east)

Gedeckt	16
Geigen	8
Gedeckt (old Choir)	8
Harmonic Flute (old Great grooved)	8
Viole de Gambe (old Choir)	8
Viole Céleste (old Choir)	8
Octave (old Diapason)	4
Concert Flute (old Choir)	4
Viole (old Choir)	4
Nazard (old Choir)	$2^{2}/_{3}$
Flageolet (old Choir)	2
Tierce (old Choir)	$1^{3}/_{5}$
Petit Pleinjeu VI	1
Contra Clarinet (old Great, new bass)	16
Trumpet (old Choir)	8
Clarinet (extension)	8
Clarion (new)	4

ECHO (encl, triforium west)

Rohrflute (old Swell)	8
Salicional (old Swell)	8
Unda Maris (old Swell, flat)	8
Dulciana (old Echo)	8
Flauto traverso (old Swell 8')	4
Lieblich Flute (old Echo)	4
Salicetina (old Swell)	1
Echo Sesquialtera (old Swell)	III

Bourdon (extension)	16
Dulciana Bass (old)	16
Gedeckt (Swell)	16
Flute Ouverte (old)	8
Viola (extension)	8
Gedeckt (Swell, extension)	8
Octave Bass (part new)	4
Flute (extension)	4
Gedeckt (Swell, extension)	4
Bombarde (old, new tongues)	16
Clarinet (Swell)	16
Trumpet (extension)	8
Clarinet (extension)	8
Clarion (extension)	4
Clarinet (extension)	4

CHOIR (triforium, centre)

Bourdon (part old Pedal)	16
Hornprincipal (old)	8
Claribel (old Great)	8
Spitzgamba	8
Vox Angelica (flat)	8
Spitzprincipal (wide)	4
Rauschquint II	$2^{2}/_{3}$, 2
Scharff IV	1
Corno di Bassetto	8
Musette (ex Swell)	8

POSITIVE
(open, in Choir-aisle, centre)

Quintatön (old Choir)	8
Rohrflute (new)	4
Nazard (stopped) (new)	$2^{2}/_{3}$
Spitzprincipal (new, v. wide)	2
Tierce (new, wide)	$1^{3}/_{5}$
Larigot (new, wide)	$1^{1}/_{3}$
Petite Cymbale (new) III	¼

Enclosed Choir on Swell

The large number of wide scales quoted to Walkers', as well as the risks attendant on cutting down old pipes (thus effectually increasing their cut-up of mouths) occasioned them considerable consternation. Reginald Walker could find no rational connection with the dimensions of the existing pipe-diameters — indeed, by normal contemporary British standards there *was* virtually none! That the procedures cited were a radical departure from the firm's normal practice (which I did not admire) did not seem to me anything but advantageous: therefore I stuck to my figures as well as to the idea of increasing some flue-scales by cutting down the pipes. I also required the removal of all weights from the reed-tongues; while to juggle with resonator-lengths and moving shallots along to gain tuning-length seemed to me quite sensible, though this idea also aroused much apprehension, probably on grounds of unpredictable labour and cost. Walkers' felt that they should not be expected to achieve the impossible with existing (and sometimes inferior) material, and that some measure of prior experience was desirable. To my surprise, perhaps, Reginald Walker was very keen on this, and he spoke wise words about the right methods of achieving my musical aims and objects — obviously he had appreciated what he had seen and heard during his visit to Aeolian-Skinner in the US.

To obtain good stable speech, on lower wind-pressures, and especially in conjunction with large scales, wind-chest design would be all-important, to ensure a copious supply; while at the same time, mouths must be kept low, with very sparse nicking of languids, and the use of thin hard metal (such as tin or 'spotted') and possibly conical construction could be vital to success. All this was a little alarming in view of the probable expense involved, but I agreed that experiment was worthwhile: in my heart of hearts I was by no means secure — a point brought home to me by Walkers' final request that I might take them to look at an organ where my ideas had been carried out, especially those derived from 'old French practice' which I had cited. *I could not*, yet! However, that was not the end of the matter: it was only the beginning.

CHAPTER THREE

Crises of Trial and Error

The new Fourniture pipes (made ostensibly to the Dom Bédos scale) arrived at the Oratory, and Mr. Davidson fitted the new cheek on the rear of the Great 'front' soundboard. I had briefed him with words culled from Arnaut de Zwolle's Treatise, the modern reprint of which had been lent me by Cecil Clutton, to the effect that the purpose of the stop was to add richness not shrillness to the chorus; and I then left him to get on with the voicing and regulation. I had to admit to myself that, there being no actual examples to hand — and English mixtures were mostly of 3-ranks at the time, and very hard-toned and unblending — I could not really imagine *how* it was going to sound. Returning to the console in the evening, I was delighted with the discreet sparkle of the 26th and 29th in the tenor and bass ranges — quite charming as heard at close quarters! But when I listened in the church the next day, with Davidson at the keys, I could not hear it at all! The blend was complete — total absorption! Alarums and recriminations! (Here was born my sometime reputation of always blaming the organ-builder for anything which did not succeed.)

As it turned out, on further close investigation, the cheek had not been securely bolted to the soundboard (and possibly the borings through had not been sufficiently generous), thus occasioning a significant loss of air-pressure, so that the Fourniture pipes barely spoke! After some labour, this fault was rectified, but then the Fourniture was too loud, and despite my own efforts (*à la* Gottfried) and a very discouraged Mr. Davidson's further revision, the effect was muddy and unbalanced, particularly in the middle octave where the 8-foot and $5\frac{1}{3}$ foot pitches arrived. (Though I had not realised it, I had in fact reproduced Schulze's misconceived mixture-recipe at Tyne Dock and Armley — though with a difference, a *great* difference, and not for the better!)

With hindsight, I could put my finger on more than one contributing factor to this failure: item, the scaling of the added pipes was too wide. To understand how this happened, it is necessary to compare the scaling methods of Dom Bédos with other, later methods which became fashionable in the nineteenth century, especially those of Professor Johann G. Töpfer, which were based on a mathematical progression; and this comparison can be most conveniently made in graphic form.

In his justly celebrated work on the theory and practice of organ-building, Professor Töpfer singled out as ideal an octave progression for the cross-section areas of his pipes in the proportion of $1 : \sqrt{8}$, and in this progression the diameters were halved on the 17th pipe, the major 10th. At the first important conference of the Organ Reform, held at Freiburg in 1927, this progression was unanimously adopted as the Normal Scale for Principal registers, the diameter for 8-foot C being fixed at 155.5 millimetres. (4-foot c then came out as 92.2 mm, 2-foot c as 54.9 mm, 1-foot c as 32.6 mm, and so on.)

If the Normal Scale is then represented graphically as a horizontal straight line, it is easy to compare deviations from it in terms of Half-Tones greater or less. Töpfer's two other workable progressions, halving on the 18th or 19th pipe respectively, would then appear as oblique straight lines on this graph, with a clear increase of one HT at each halving-point. Dom Bédos adopted, ostensibly, the length-scale octave-ratio of 1 : 2, which if transferred to this graph will appear as a steeply sloping straight line, since four Half-Tones are lost in each octave — the diameters are halved on the 13th note: but the addition of the (empirically determined) constant, referred to earlier, produces a curve which begins in a downward direction to a certain point whence it turns upward. This simply expresses the greater effect of the added constant in proportion as the absolute measurements decrease: as explained earlier, it should be noted that without such an addition to the simple 2 : 1 ratio from octave to octave, diameters for the treble pipes would become impracticably small, and for the basses impossibly large. The Dom Bédos scale for a Fourniture 2-feet is about 1.80 inches for C, and .266 inches for c 49 (½-foot): (the 2-foot pipe of the existing Mixture had a diameter of 1.75 inches — so this was a fairly good fit).

Figure 1

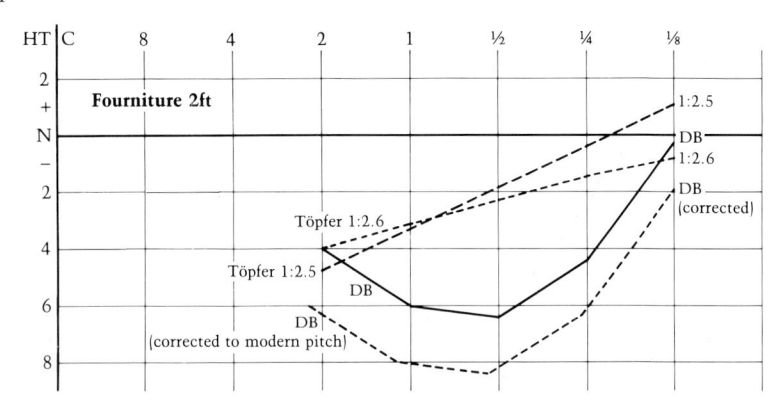

The added-constant being ascertainable as .164 inches (added to 1.636 inches proceeding on the 2 : 1 octave ratio), the diameters of the other Cs are obtained as follows (see Figure 1, firm black curve):

C	1.636 + AC .164 =	1.80 inches	(N − 4 HT)
c	.818 + AC .164 =	.982	(N − 6 HT)
c'	.409 + AC .164 =	.573	(N − 6⅓ HT)
c''	.205 + AC .164 =	.369	(N − 4½ HT)
c'''	.102 + AC .164 =	.266	(N − ²/₅ HT)

However, it is possible to connect these two extreme points, C and c 49, by means of Töpfer's ratios − 2.6, halving on the 18th note:

C	=	1.81 inches	(N − 4 HT)
c	=	1.11	(N − 3½ HT)
c'	=	.64	(N − 4 HT)
c''	=	.42	(N − 1½ HT)
c'''	=	.26	(N − 1 HT)

or 2.5, halving on the 19th:

C	=	1.75 inches	(N − 4½ HT)	— (the existing scale of
c	=	1.10	(N − 3½ HT)	the Mixture)
c'	=	.70	(N − 1⅔ HT)	
c''	=	.44	(N − ½ HT)	
c'''	=	.28	(N + 1 HT)	

Both these scales show a marked increase in width over that of Dom Bédos, especially between c' and c''.

What is the connection with the Oratory Fourniture? Simply this — and I have to speak now in the absence of any confirming evidence, for all the flue-pipes were lost in the fire which wrecked the organ in 1950; Mr. Davidson is no longer alive, and all records must be presumed lost — Mr. Davidson certainly used the Töpfer scales himself: indeed it was he who first made me aware of their use as listed in G. A. Audsley's great book on *The Art of Organ Building*, and the smaller work by F. E. Robertson, both of which he lent me. So part of the reason for the lack of 'sparkle' in the Fourniture was undoubtedly due to the excessive width of the new pipes, possibly cut a little too high in the mouth also. Part was also due to the metal used, with a low percentage of tin (matching the existing pipes), while the French *Plein jeu* was invariably made of nearly pure tin. Another significant addition to the scale-width was due to my failure to advert to the Normal Pitch of Dom Bédos' time — approximately one whole tone below ours: this pushed up the Fourniture scale we used by an additional 2 HT. In conjunction with my general tendency to keep mixtures on the quiet side (*à la* Gottfried), it was small wonder that the total effect was rather dull and fluty. C. H. Trevor used to cite the *alla breve* section of Bach's Fantasia in G as *the* test piece for contrapuntal clarity, and when I showed him the Fourniture, we had to agree that it did not pass with distinction. Here again, however, there was a faulty judgement: for in the French classical organ the *Fourniture* was never meant to be used alone, but always combined with the *Cymbale*, the highest rank of which was pitched an octave above, and which broke back, one rank at a time, twice in each octave. It was natural, therefore, that when the Oratory Cymbale of 3 ranks arrived on the Great Organ (deposing the Walker Double Trumpet), the effect improved.

Nevertheless, a comparison of the complete scale-plan of a Dom Bédos *Plein jeu* (8, 4, 2-feet and mixtures) with that of the Oratory at this point is interesting. (In order to read this clearly it should be noted that the separate stops are shown at their actual musical pitch: to obtain tenor c, for instance, one must read the 4-foot scale of the Montre 8-feet, the 2-foot scale of the Prestant 4-feet, the 1-foot scale of the Doublette 2-feet, and the Mixtures will begin from the 1-foot scale of the 2-foot rank, and so forth.) The varying interrelations for all the registers can be clearly grasped: the streamlined appearance of the Dom Bédos plan is in marked contrast with the untidiness of ours, with its over-wide typically English 8-foot basses, the 'bumps' in our treble progressions of the 2⅔ and 2-foot stops (due to old pipes inherited), and the confusion created by the interpolation of Töpfer scales (Figures 2 and 3). In Figure 4, the increases in scale of the 4-foot, 2⅔ foot and 2-foot are shown, and are possibly slightly more coherent, though the 2-foot is undesirably wide in the whole of the middle octave — a fluty sonority here would be inescapable in this case.

Figure 5 is the scale-plan of the Swell division, and will partly explain the rather insignificant contribution of this department to the flue-ensemble of the organ, a defect further aggravated by its position partly behind the enclosed Solo and the fact that its wind-pressure was still 3 inches, whereas the main Great had been raised to 3¾ inches, to compensate for the excessive cut-up of the mouths of the treble pipes

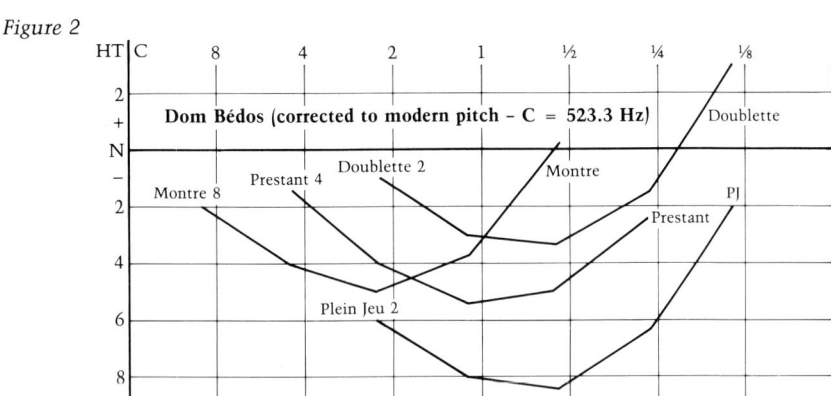

Figure 2

CRISES OF TRIAL AND ERROR

Figure 3

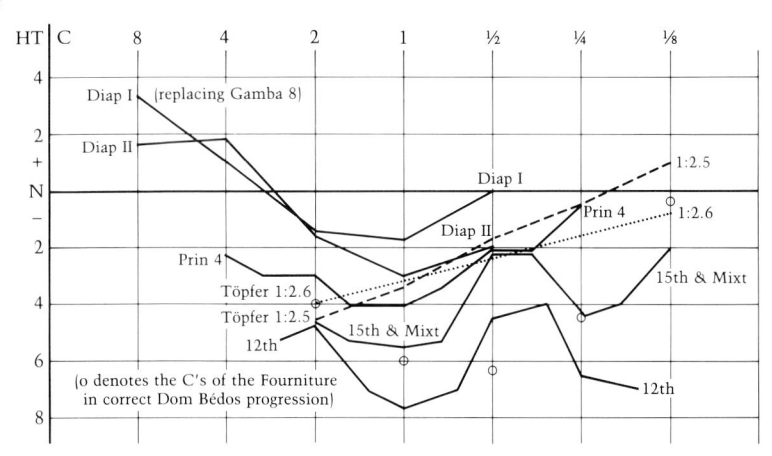

Figure 4

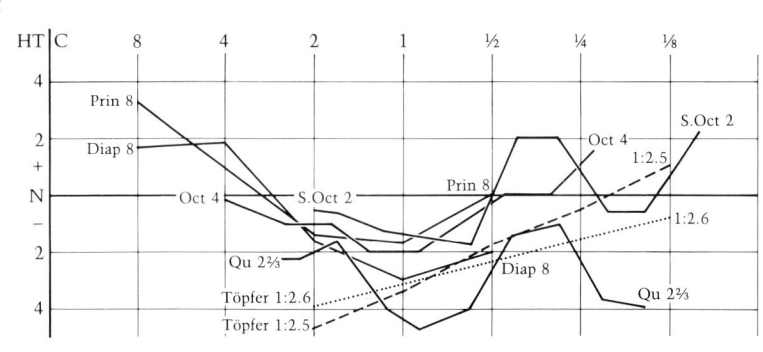

Figure 5

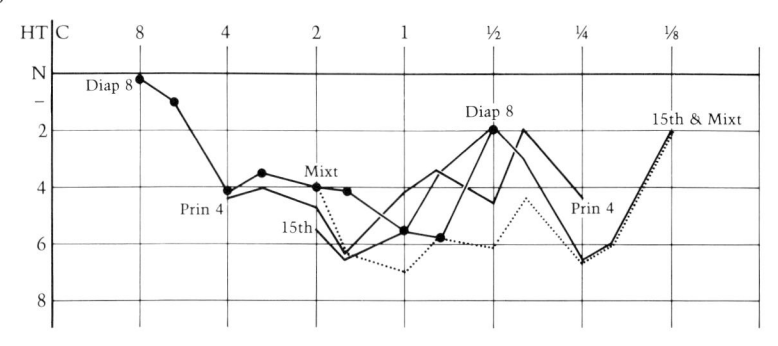

transposed to higher pitch. In the performance of French music this disadvantage was minimised by the telling character of the Swell reeds, and the presence in the Choir (Positive) of fairly wide-scaled mutations, Nazard, Tierce and Larigot, and the Quint and Tierce on the Great, as well as the generally fluty sonority of the trebles and the strong tenor range: in German music, matters were less satisfactory, as will be shown later.

This is a suitable place to digress into the sphere of my considerable musical activity in the immediate post-World-War-II period, both as a frequent solo recitalist and broadcaster in a repertoire ranging from French, German, Italian and English music of the seventeenth and eighteenth centuries to Schumann, Liszt, Brahms, Franck and Reger and a fair sprinkling of contemporary works: and also as a *continuo* player and orchestral and choral organist in a variety of works, playing under conductors of widely different tastes and attitudes to the organ. Always the problem was the same — to make *music* by the means available, always keeping in mind the art-historical background of the works performed; which usually entailed rejection of the conventional use of the organ stops. For this one naturally had to develop a sense of an ideal organ-character in each case, and this tied up with practical considerations of organ-design or re-design in possible future operations in that field. Donald Harrison in the USA had successfully evolved a *classical* instrument which could match up when required to full orchestral dimensions without loss of clarity or good musical sonority, and I could only deplore the complete absence in this country of any such development.

A fair amount of continuo accompaniment at this time was necessarily done on 'chamber-' or positive-organs of various kinds, old and new, good, bad and mostly indifferent in quality, loud and feeble. Conductors, especially in the last case, usually expected the constant use of 'high squeaks' in order to achieve *audibility* in this ensemble and vitalise the tone somewhat. With some hindsight I can say that some of them (even when larger organs were in use), and broadcasting engineers and producers (who often followed this procedure to avoid the organ's merely duplicating orchestral or choral sonority and pitch) fell into the mistaken idea that this was 'Baroque style' — thus confusing the solo and accompanimental functions of the instrument. All the Baroque authorities in fact unanimously prescribe 8-foot stops with a very sparing use of mild 4-foot — nothing higher — in any combination of organ and other instruments, with the sole exception of organ *concertante* movements with organ solo obbligato, which are rare enough indeed.

But I could not be unaffected by these notions: the late Arnold Goldsborough, a distinguished and sincere musician, whom I had known personally and admired for years as a first-rank organist — and a most painstaking conductor-interpreter of Baroque music — opted for 'soft mixtures': this seemed musically viable, to my mind. He came with a BBC producer to see my new Cymbale on the Oratory organ, which I had described to him: but it was soon clear that he did not find it musically acceptable, even though it *was* soft. Again, with hindsight, I expect he was hankering after Handel's reputed prescription of 8, 8, 4, 4, 2⅔, 2, 1³/₅ (all drawing as separate stops): my Cymbale broke back too much and was too high-pitched in the bass for his taste.

But in many concerts with larger ensembles, chiefly at the Royal Albert Hall with the London Philharmonic, I *was* excited at the possibility of using the phenomenal Great flue-chorus there — never heard without the reeds at the hands of the incumbents of the time: this was suggested first to me by my friend and colleague, Osborne Peasgood, who for many years was organist of the London Bach Choir, and also acting-Organist and Master of Music at Westminster Abbey during 1941-46: he had been instrumental at that time in effecting a great improvement in the sound of the Abbey Great flue-chorus, which had to undergo repairs after some trifling war-damage to the central lantern. Walking in, one Sunday afternoon, I was much taken with the fine Mixture-ensemble on which he was playing Bach's B minor fugue. Concerning the use of the Royal Albert Hall organ, he took the view that the larger 8-foot stops should be suppressed so that the upperwork (and the 16-foot) plus the Pedals would make an effective 'frame' for the choir and/or orchestra. (Apparently he said this quite outspokenly to the *Times* critic who, surprisingly enough in a later context, made no demur! But then one recollects that most of OHP's pronouncements were made with such self-assurance as to be unanswerable — that was one of the most attractive traits of his personality.) Whether right or wrong historically, this effect was in many ways preferable to the more or less complete *obliteration* of an orchestra in many parts of the building by the use of the opaque, monstrously overblown Trombas and Tubas and Pedal 'Open Woods': incidentally, such blatant sounds were never heard in the Father Willis days of this organ, as I myself can testify.

My idea received a signal confirmation at my very first performance there, playing the Bruckner *Te Deum* in 1947 with the London Philharmonic under Dr. Bruno Walter, who after hearing my first 'trial' chord for the beginning, exclaimed, "That is a sound after my own heart!" Of course I had the Great flue-chorus, entire, plus all the *metal* stops and most of the reeds of the Pedal division, 32-, 16- and 8-feet. It was still possible to use the small 16-foot Open Wood without overbalancing the effect — this made for greater warmth, and also rendered the bass line more audible to the player. Avoiding the Great and Solo reeds altogether, I found this made a convincing tone-picture, which stayed in my mind as a potential future inspiration. All the other manual sections, apart from the Swell reeds, were very subsidiary and had little significance in the general ensemble. (Various modifications of a trifling nature have been made in recent years, but that is a story in itself: a sad one, in which I have no concern.)

But to return to the Oratory scene, I was due for more disappointments: Lady Susi Jeans (who was a close friend of mine at this time, giving me much help and encouragement, acquainting me with the masterly reference work of Christhard Mahrenholz, *Die Orgelregister*, and even allowing Mr. Davidson and me to study in detail the scales and voicing of the pipes in her German 'Neo-barock' organ) — Susi came to look at our achievements. I myself was convinced of their adaptability for much French music: but as she tried one stop-combination after another in her habitual German style, *nothing* succeeded! Not a word was spoken: I merely noted the failures and frustrations, whether in trio-formation or inter-chorus relation!

My acquaintance with Reger, both in playing and through fine German pre-war recordings, had already made me aware of the importance of their flue-choruses (even in the Romantic organs), and the need for at least three such choruses well balanced against each other. At the Oratory, as was noted earlier, the Swell division was too insignificantly scaled and voiced to match the Great (a very common English failing), while both it and the Choir (positive) lacked impact on account of buried positions. There was no Solo to Choir coupler, which might have helped: thus Reger was 'out' for all his larger works, though there might be greater hope when the new unenclosed Solo arrived.

In July 1948, M. Rochesson came: his object was to demonstrate the French reed-voicing technique, and he brought with him a convenient number of 'samples'. Mr. Davidson had looked dubiously at the rather moderate scale (diameter) of the existing 16-foot Trombone, and decided to replace it with a second-hand set of stout zinc tubes of larger scale by the old firm of Brindley and Foster. When Rochesson saw the largest (C, 16 feet), a momentary expression of astonished awe flitted over his face — the scale could have been all of 10 inches! The wind-pressure was to be 4¼ inches, reduced from 10½ inches (with no separate bellows), on which the 16-foot portion of the stop had only fairly made its presence felt, unlike its 32-foot extension of which we have spoken earlier).

Armed with a Labour Permit, a curved, hollowed out burnishing-block, a burnishing-tool shaped like a very slender fish stuck into a handle, a set of French shallots (open, parallel), and a quantity of soft brass tongues, he set to work from somewhere in the 8-foot range, going downwards.

The burnishing of the tongue (already cut to the exact length and width required, and fastened securely at one end to the flat surface of the hard-wood block) begins with a number of strokes straight along towards the free end: the burnishing tool must be kept accurately at right-angles to the tongue, or the latter will be given an inconvenient twist. The amount of manual pressure applied is a matter of experience; I noticed that Rochesson always ran the tool through his hair first, obviously using this natural fine oil as a lubricant! As the brass was quite soft, the free end of the tongue soon began to lift away from the block, and was then capable of vibrating against the shallot when mounted thereon, and thus of sounding a definite note. After getting this result, roughly at the right pitch, Rochesson said, "Ça vient," and began to accentuate the curve at the free end, using the hollowed out block. An important implement for securing this result with the larger tongues consisted of two steel pins driven parallel into a chisel-handle (Figure 6). By its use the curve could be varied more smoothly and accurately than with the burnisher for the last stages: a 'flat' or a 'kink' or any other irregularity would produce a horrible grating rattle when the tongue was mounted in the pipe and put on its wind-supply; everything depended on the right *kind* of curve, too: if too straight, it would give a bassoon-like character to the sound: the true trumpet sonority needs a bold curve at the tip of the tongue.

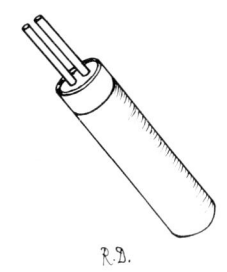

Figure 6

Every pipe was then subjected to the 'doubling' test: the spring was knocked down the tongue while the note was sounded, until it could no longer hold its fundamental pitch, and 'flew up' to a higher note, about a third or fourth higher. The spring was then lightly tapped upwards again until the tongue returned to pitch — hopefully quite suddenly — demonstrably the product then of the respective lengths of the tongue and the resonator. Another tap upwards to free the tone from any constraint and give some margin for tuning: and any further tuning required would have to be done by adjusting the resonator-length, usually by cutting a little off the top (if the correct amount of over-length had been allowed when the pipe was made). In order to safeguard the tuning in very hot weather, a slot could be cut — a full diameter from the top of the pipe — for further sharpening of pitch without materially changing the sonority: but this slot would normally be kept *closed* (Figure 7). This was in contra-distinction to normal English practice which first adds weights to the tongues (thus stifling free speech, generally on heavy wind-pressure) and then opens a slot near the top of the pipe in order to make the sound more nasal — they would say "brilliant"! The true French character is based on long resonators (for volume and roundness of tone) and long, well-curved unweighted tongues (for brilliance and attack): at its best it strongly resembles the sound made by a good brass-player playing *fortissimo*: in a snugly-fitting swell-box, the shutters can reduce the brilliance but leave the roundness as the box is closed — a valid and 'natural' musical effect.

Figure 7

Some excellent Bombarde notes began to emerge. Mr. Davidson was fascinated, and it was entertaining to see M. Rochesson, tall and thin, normally a voluble talker with a great sense of humour (but who spoke no English) silently looking very solemn over the operation; while Mr. Davidson, equally tall and thin, a thoroughly good-hearted, frugal, sincere Englishman (but who spoke not a word of French) looked on ingratiatingly, obviously enjoying a slightly 'naughty' new range of organ-tone in the French manner! Everything went swimmingly, and the pipes were pronounced finished, and laid by for the time of insertion into the organ, where we shall join them later in this account.

CHAPTER FOUR

Portentous Interlude

Early in 1948 I had had to accept the decision of my Director of Music at the Oratory that the console should not be moved: and indeed no other work was done on it due to the non-arrival of the electrical components for the new stop-keys, after a year of waiting. A similar period of inaction set in at Buckfast owing to a back-log of work, and various other shortages experienced by the Walker firm.

During this lull, a new star burst upon the firmament for me: an 'early warning' came in the form of a telephone call from my old friend and associate, Felix Aprahamian, till lately Orchestral Secretary and Concert Director of the London Philharmonic, Secretary of the Organ Music Society, Critic and Concert Promoter, etc. Did I know about the new concert hall to be built on the South Bank of the Thames? Well, no! I did not — was it the Henry Wood Hall to which the public had subscribed? No: it was to be built by the London County Council: the London Philharmonic would probably become the resident orchestra, and I was going to be invited to be Consultant for the designing of an organ for it; and *on no account* was I to refuse on grounds of diffidence: if I were in difficulties I could call in M. André Marchal, for instance, to give a second opinion.

Sure enough, the invitation came the next day, also on the telephone, and practically word for word, and upon expressing my willingness to accept this impressive commission I was immediately put into touch with the Executive Architect, Edwin Williams, at County Hall, in whose office I was shown the blue-print for the new Auditorium, where the organ was obviously banished into the roof-space over the orchestra by the Acoustics team, headed by the late H. Bagenal — a position I (this time) categorically refused to countenance! Happily, Edwin Williams responded with a counter-suggestion that the organ be totally visible and accepted as a decorative feature of the hall, the designs for which were still in the early stages, but which was planned to seat an audience of about 3,000.

It was pointed out to me that there would have to be tenders from several organ-building firms: one firm, with a strong 'nose' for business, was already intent on staking a claim, and a Director (now dead) became a constant source of irritation — perhaps this was good for me! Of course the pre-tender situation meant that I myself must shortly provide the Architect with all necessary specifications of requirements, material and spatial, inasmuch as the building

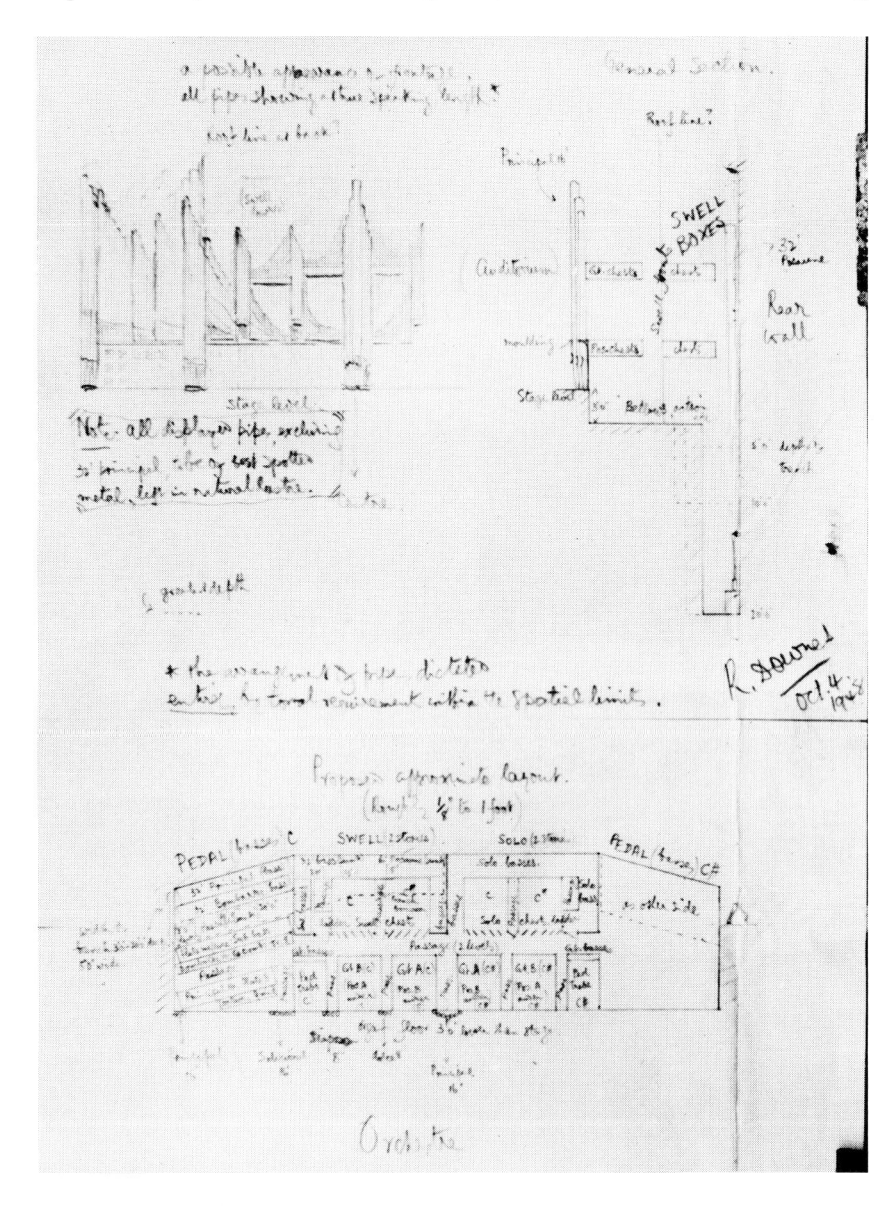

PLATE VII *Festival Hall organ, outline sketch showing possible front elevation, section and plan, October 4th. 1948.*

programme was advancing very quickly, and the target-date for completion of the hall was the 1951 Festival of Britain.

At this point I sketched out a list of stops accompanied by a possible front elevation, a plan and a section (Plate VII), for a sizeable 4-manual organ of an eclectic classical design, suitably ensconced at the rear of the stage. It will be seen to be clearly related to my other current projects:

Proposed specification

Four manuals, C to c''''', 61 notes; Pedals, C to g', 32 notes

GREAT ORGAN

1	Principal	16	metal
2	Bourdon	16	wood and metal
3	Diapason	8	metal
4	Gemshorn	8	metal
5	Harmonic flute	8	metal, open throughout
6	Bourdon	8	metal
7	Octave	4	metal
8	Rohrflöte	4	metal, large scale
9	Nazard	$2^{2}/_{3}$	metal, conical
10	Superoctave	2	metal
11	Quarte de Nazard	2	metal, large scale
12	Tierce	$1^{3}/_{5}$	metal
13	Grande fourniture	V	
14	Cymbale	V	
15	Bombarde	16	
16	Trumpet	8	
17	Clarion	4	

SOLO ORGAN (enclosed in a swell)

18	Flûte conique	16	metal
19	Major principal	8	metal
20	Flûte majeure	8	wood
21	Viole de Gambe	8	metal, conical
22	Violes célestes	8	metal, conical
23	Quint	$5^{1}/_{3}$	metal
24	Grosse octave	4	metal
25	Harmonic flute	4	metal, large scale
26	Grosse tierce	$3^{1}/_{5}$	metal, conical
27	Septième	$2^{2}/_{7}$	large scale
28	Blockflute	2	large scale, conical
29	Grand cornet	III-V	
30	Orchestral bassoon	16	
31	Orchestral Hautboy	8	

32	Clarinet	8	
33	Tuba major	8	(higher pressure)
34	Tuba clarion	4	(higher pressure)

Tremulant to light pressure stops

POSITIVE ORGAN

35	Salicional	16	metal
36	Claribel flute	8	wood and metal
37	Bourdon	8	wood and metal
38	Dolce	8	metal
39	Unda maris	8	metal
40	Spitzflöte	4	metal
41	Cor de nuit	4	stopped metal
42	Nazard	$2^{2}/_{3}$	stopped metal, large scale
43	Octave	2	metal
44	Quarte de nazard	2	metal, large scale
45	Tierce	$1^{3}/_{5}$	metal, large scale
46	Larigot	$1^{1}/_{3}$	metal, large scale
47	Septième	$1^{1}/_{7}$	metal, large scale
48	Blockflute	1	conical, large scale
49	Petite fourniture	III	
50	Petite cymbale	III	
51	Trumpet	8	
52	Cromorne	8	
53	Clarion	4	

Tremulant

SWELL ORGAN

54	Quintatön	16	wood and metal
55	Harmonic flute	8	metal, open throughout
56	Rohrflöte	8	wood and metal
57	Violoncelle	8	metal
58	Voix célestes	8	metal
59	Gemshorn	4	metal
60	Harmonic flute	4	metal
61	Harmonic piccolo	2	metal
62	Cornet de récit	III-V	
63	Plein jeu	VI	
64	Bombarde	16	
65	Harmonic trumpet	8	
66	Harmonic horn	8	
67	Oboe	8	
68	Vox humana	8	
69	Harmonic clarion	4	
70	Octave oboe	4	

Tremulant

PEDAL ORGAN

71	Principal	32	metal
72	Flûte majeure	16	wood
73	Principal	16	metal
74	Sub Bass	16	wood
75	Flûte conique	16	(No. 18)
76	Salicional	16	(No. 35)
77	Quintatön	16	(No. 54)
78	Quint	$10^{2}/_{3}$	metal, conical
79	Octave	8	metal
80	Flute	8	wood
81	Tierce	$6^{2}/_{5}$	metal, conical
82	Septième	$4^{4}/_{7}$	metal, large scale
83	Spitzflöte	4	metal, large scale
84	Nazard	$2^{2}/_{3}$	stopped metal
85	Blockflute	2	metal, large scale, conical
86	Sesquialtera	II	
87	Bombarde	32	metal
88	Posaune	32	metal in Swell box
89	Bombarde	16	metal
90	Trombone	16	(No. 88)
91	Trumpet	8	metal
92	Clarion	4	metal

COUPLERS, etc

Swell to Great
Positive to Great
Solo to Great
Swell to Positive
Solo to Positive
Solo to Swell
Swell Octave
Swell Suboctave
Swell unison off
Swell to Pedal
Positive to Pedal
Great to Pedal
Solo to Pedal
Swell Octave to Pedal

8 pistons to each manual (adjustable)
8 combination pedals (or foot-pistons) to pedal (adjustable)
8 general pistons (adjustable)
6 hitch-down pedals to intercept reeds, one giving General Tutti
General Cancel piston

Reversible pistons to all couplers
Reversible pedals to all pedal couplers

2 balanced swell-pedals (remote control)
All-electric moveable console (stop-key type?)

WIND-PRESSURES

Great: not to exceed 3¾ inches
Swell: not more than 4 inches, flue and reed
Positive: not more than 3 inches
Solo: flues not more than 3¾ inches, Tubas 5 inches
Pedal: flues 3½ inches, reeds 4½ inches

With hindsight, I could now regard this as a sound, conservative scheme with a perfectly practical layout, given the space allotted by Mr. Williams in our first conversations. I think it could have been effective and easy to control, even though it is strongly biased in the direction of Cavaillé-Coll-Mutin, and might have been much less suitable for German, Dutch or Italian Renaissance or Barock music. Yet it was received with indignation by a strong member of the Royal College of Organists' establishment, to whom I divulged details in return for a like confidence afforded me about the rebuilding of his famous church-organ! I suppose its greatest weakness lies in its lack of any great point of interest — it is rather prosaic, and certainly not in any sense baroque! The use of French-type reeds was, after all, only a resurrection of what had been done for generations by Hill and Lewis; even some of Father Willis's work bore a strong resemblance to the French school: for instance, *in its original voicing*, the Grand Bombarde 16 feet in the dome section at St. Paul's Cathedral — a sound which was conspicuously absent when the organ was rebuilt

PLATE VIII *Danish State Radio Concert Hall, Copenhagen, organ by Marcussen, 1946.*

and reinstated in the 1930s: I remember it very well indeed, having heard it two or three times weekly during much of 1922-23. But all English voicing had been moving more into the suppression of natural harmonic overtones, with constantly increased wind-pressures such as would have killed poor T. C. Lewis to listen to! Thus, one only had to mention French reeds to obtain a ribald rejoinder about 'bacon-frying' or some such ignorant, bigoted riposte, usually from people who, for all their vociferous condemnation, had never been outside the British Isles, and certainly not to France.

From the start, I had decided that Rochesson *must* voice the reeds, and even possibly the French mutations, Cornets and Harmonic flutes; and in December 1948 I slipped over to Paris to discuss the whole project with him. Before this, however, there were further developments here: for although Edwin Williams and his immediate associates had received my plan, elevation and section with enthusiasm, the Chief Architect's 'backroom boys', the designers of the hall's interior decor, liked it not at all. "Too gothic, too many conspicuous long pipes, breaking into the podium at the rear of the stage."

As a possible 'inspiration' for me, the new Marcussen organ in the Danish State Radio Concert Hall was cited (Plate VIII), and, of course, the organ in the Palais de Chaillot in Paris. Edwin Williams liked the idea of displaying wooden pipes and also metal pipes of conical construction — why not? It could be fun! After much soul-searching, I produced the next (rather too derivative) sketch, with sections and plan of layout, to serve as a preliminary guide for the organ-builders who were about to tender. With this design I felt less secure in my inmost mind, but I followed it through in detail (Plate IX).

Some tonal alterations were needed or seemed desirable at this point, and were as follows:

Great Organ No. 1 became Spitzprincipal 16-feet, tin pipes on front for the lowest octave; and the same treatment was given to the bass of the Diapason 8-feet. The Fourniture was specified as to ranks, 15, 19, 22, 26, 29, and the Cymbale 22, 26, 29, 33, 36.

Solo Organ gained an independent Plein jeu, VIII ranks, 12, 15, 19, 22, 26, 29, 33, 36.

Swell Organ The mixture renamed Pleinjeu doux, with ranks 19, 22, 26, 29, 33, 36, the 16-foot flue-stop became Salicional, the Harmonic Flute 8-feet a Spitzflute, and the Octave Oboe was dropped out.

Pedal Organ Nos. 73 and 79 were put in sight for most or all of their compass, with tin pipes, and the two open flutes 16-feet and 8-feet were displayed in full. The Sesquialtera II ranks (No. 86) was dropped out, and the two Trombones, 32-feet and 16-feet, were now borrowed from the Swell stop.

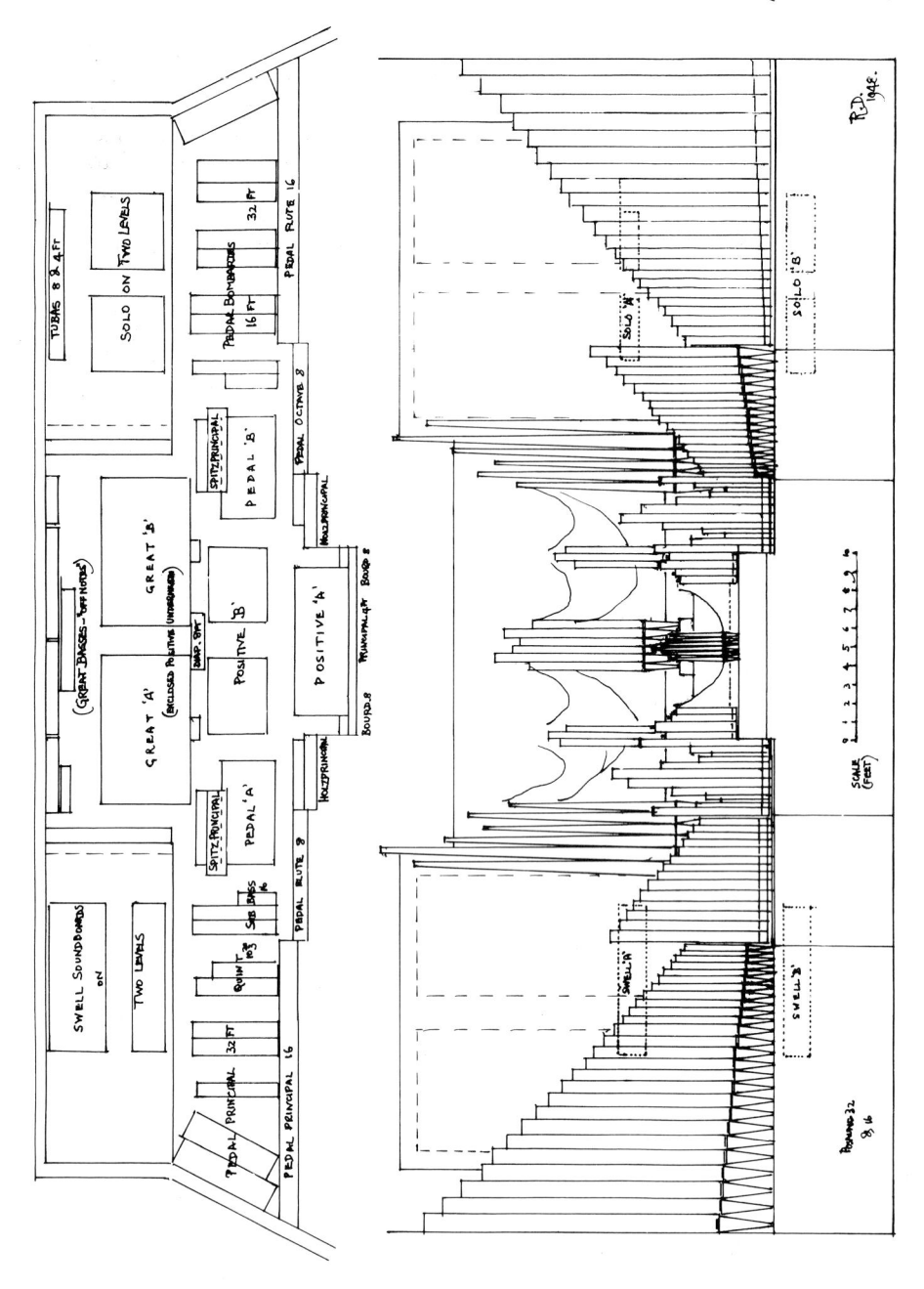

PLATE IX *Royal Festival Hall, proposed plan and front elevation drawing, 1948. A preliminary guide for the organ-builders who were asked to tender.*

The biggest changes occurred in the Positive:

Unenclosed section (projecting)			
Holzprincipal	8	\multicolumn{2}{l}{24 on front: 36 open wood (oak), rest metal}
Bourdon à cheminée	8	\multicolumn{2}{l}{12 wood, on front, rest metal with chimneys}
Spitzprincipal	4	\multicolumn{2}{l}{tin, on front}
Cor de nuit	4		
Nazard	2⅔	\multicolumn{2}{l}{metal with chimneys}
Octave	2		
Quarte	2		
Tierce	1³/₅		
Larigot	1⅓		
Septième	1¹/₇		
Blockflute	1		
Petite Fourniture	III	*Enclosed section (under Great)*	
22, 26, 29		Quintatön	16 wood and metal
Petite cymbale	IV	Dolce principal	8 metal
33, 36, 40, 43		Unda maris	8 from A sharp
Trumpet	8	Concert flute	4
Cromorne	8	Contra clarinet	16
Clarion	4	Corno di bassetto	8
Tremulant		Tremulant	
wind-pressure 3 inches		wind-pressure 3½ inches	

Figure 8 shows the foundation point of the flue-scales: the reeds began as follows:

Great:	16, 8, 4: 9 inches, 6 inches, 4⁵/₁₆ inches
Positive:	4⁷/₁₆, 2³/₁₆, 3⁵/₁₆ inches
Swell:	trumpets: 8, 5, 3½ inches
Pedal:	16 inches, 11 inches (from Swell), 10 inches, 6 inches, 4⅜ inches. Most of these were derived from Dom Bédos, and even Rochesson was a little alarmed at their amplitude, which would have been fine for a French cathedral!

As before, all unspecified metal pipes were to be of spotted metal, down to 16-foot C.

When I arrived in Paris, Rochesson was unable to obtain access to the Chaillot organ, owing to some public exhibition; but we went to see André Marchal at his own St. Eustache (Merklin, rebuilt recently by Gonzalès), and then on to Notre-Dame where I was at last able to try out and admire all the stops in detail, by courtesy of M. Léonce de St. Martin, Vierne's immediate successor. The three which stayed

86 BAROQUE TRICKS

Figure 8

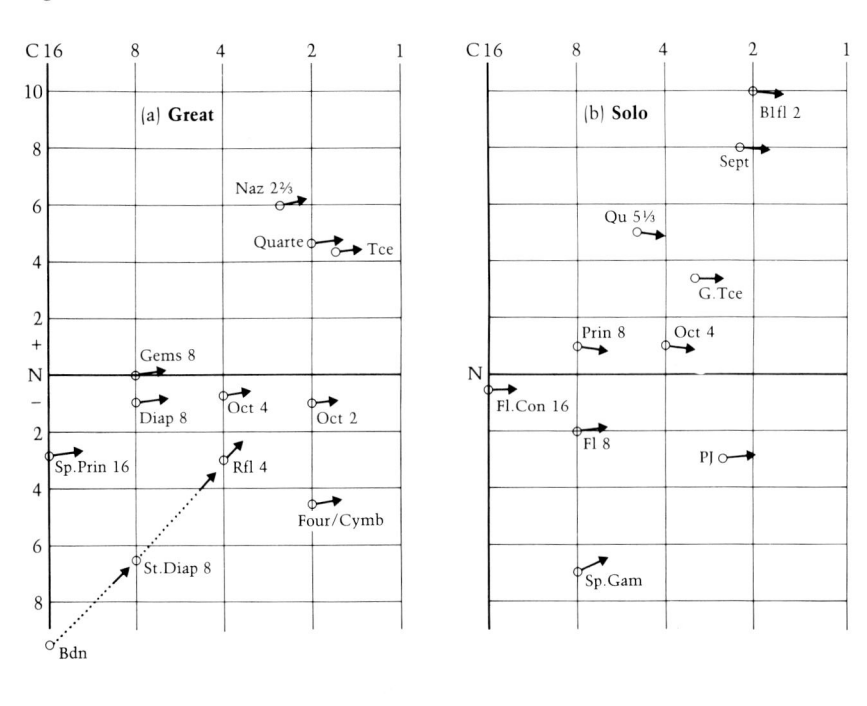

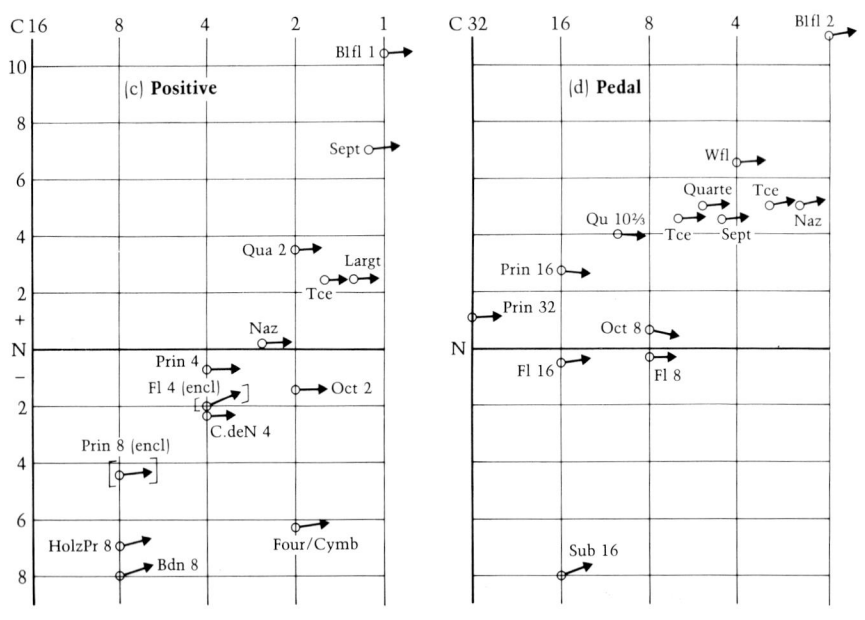

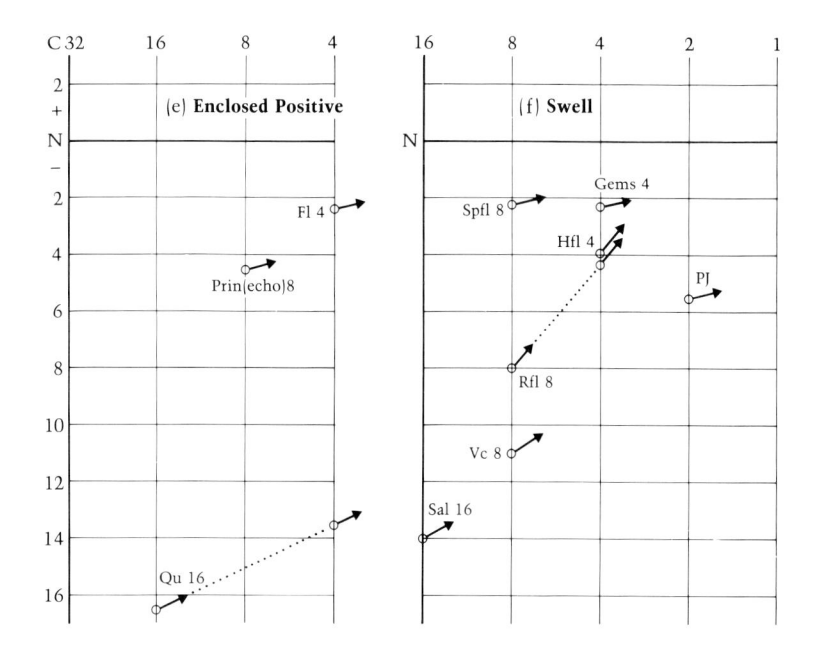

```
C 32      16       8       4        16       8       4        2       1
   2
   +            (e) Enclosed Positive         (f) Swell
   N                                    N
   -
                                                             Gems 4
   2                                        Spfl 8
                              Fl 4
   4                                               Hfl 4
                                                                         PJ
                         Prin(echo)8
   6
   8                                             Rfl 8
  10
                                            Vc 8
  12
                                       Sal 16
  14
              Qu 16
  16
```

most vividly in my memory were the (Clicquot) Cornet V ranks of the *Récit*, the superb Cromorne 8-feet (vastly superior to the stop of the same name at St. Eustache, which had a hard, thin 'grating' quality which Marchal (to my surprise) praised as *'pittoresque'*), and especially the magnificent richness of the Tuba Magna 16-feet on the *Grand Choeur* division, one of the most decisive voices in the tonal structure of the General Tutti of this 'super-Cavaillé' organ[26]. Rochesson was very enthusiastic about the new project, and most willing to collaborate, knowing that I should be unlikely to choose any but the best English builders, having made sure of *their* co-operation too.

On my return, the next step was to hold meetings with representatives of some organ-building firms who were shown the specifications to date and asked whether they would be willing to tender: the reactions of three of these groups varied between enthusiastic desire to co-operate, courteously amused incredulity, and severely admonitory correction. In the same order, their attitude to Rochesson's proposed participation was wholly favourable, mildly affirmative (presumably for a few special Solo stops), or frankly hostile and sceptical — and continued further communications from this last source (the same deceased Director I mentioned on page 77) were a constant embarrassment, evidently intent on, and largely succeeding in, shaking my confidence in the proposals!

The development which now took me completely by surprise came not from organ-builders but from the Acoustics Consultants, namely, the sudden appearance of a large orchestral canopy in front of the organ, in such a position as to impede its tonal egress to an alarming degree: while as a collateral calamity, the level of the main ceiling, where it reached the back of the organ, was now brought down to a level where the Spitzprincipal 16-foot pipes would disappear through it or be lopped off at three-quarter length!

As a product of all these circumstances (as well as other constantly changing dimensions in the platform and choir area), a long series of vacillations began, regarding the organ-specification. True, everyone had accepted the notion of exposed pipes, but their strategic arrangement became an increasingly controversial issue, not simplified either by the open hostility to organs in general on the part of the Acoustics team: "Your huge pipes shaking the place to pieces," feelingly observed the late Mr. H. Bagenal!

Meantime there was the target-date of 1951, and the specifications *must* be finalised without delay so that tenders could be obtained. But there were also great difficulties over the supply of raw materials in these post-war years — especially metal and suitable timber — and even with the powerful help of the LCC, such difficulties might at times be insuperable within the time-scale. It was not surprising therefore that one organ-building firm regretfully *withdrew*, emphatically declaring, when pressed, "We are not going to be stampeded into any hasty action which will endanger our reputation." As it became increasingly clear that nobody could absolutely guarantee completion by the target-date, some greater flexibility crept into the situation, so that this firm was once more invited to reconsider — and as a matter of fact they actually received the contract in the end. (They were the *second* firm referred to in the account of preliminary consultations mentioned above; from which it can be deduced quite easily that neither they nor I would have an easy time of it, once the project began to materialise: but more of this anon.)

So, a new layout had to be made immediately to meet the new conditions, with corresponding changes in the list of stops. One important feature had been safeguarded, namely, the wide and (comparatively) shallow organ-chamber or recess — the classically accepted ideal location for a concert hall organ, also corroborated by such authorities as G. A. Audsley, F. Webb, etc — only the presence of the canopy seemed set for disaster: for, of course, the whole concept of the organ was based on the use of what were then regarded as low wind-pressures and unforced voicing which, for success, demanded a completely open and unimpeded aspect for the pipes.

Since it would no longer be practicable to place the great Organ centrally, behind and above the Positive, my next move was to divide it into Great and Grand divisions (controlled by the second and fourth

PORTENTOUS INTERLUDE

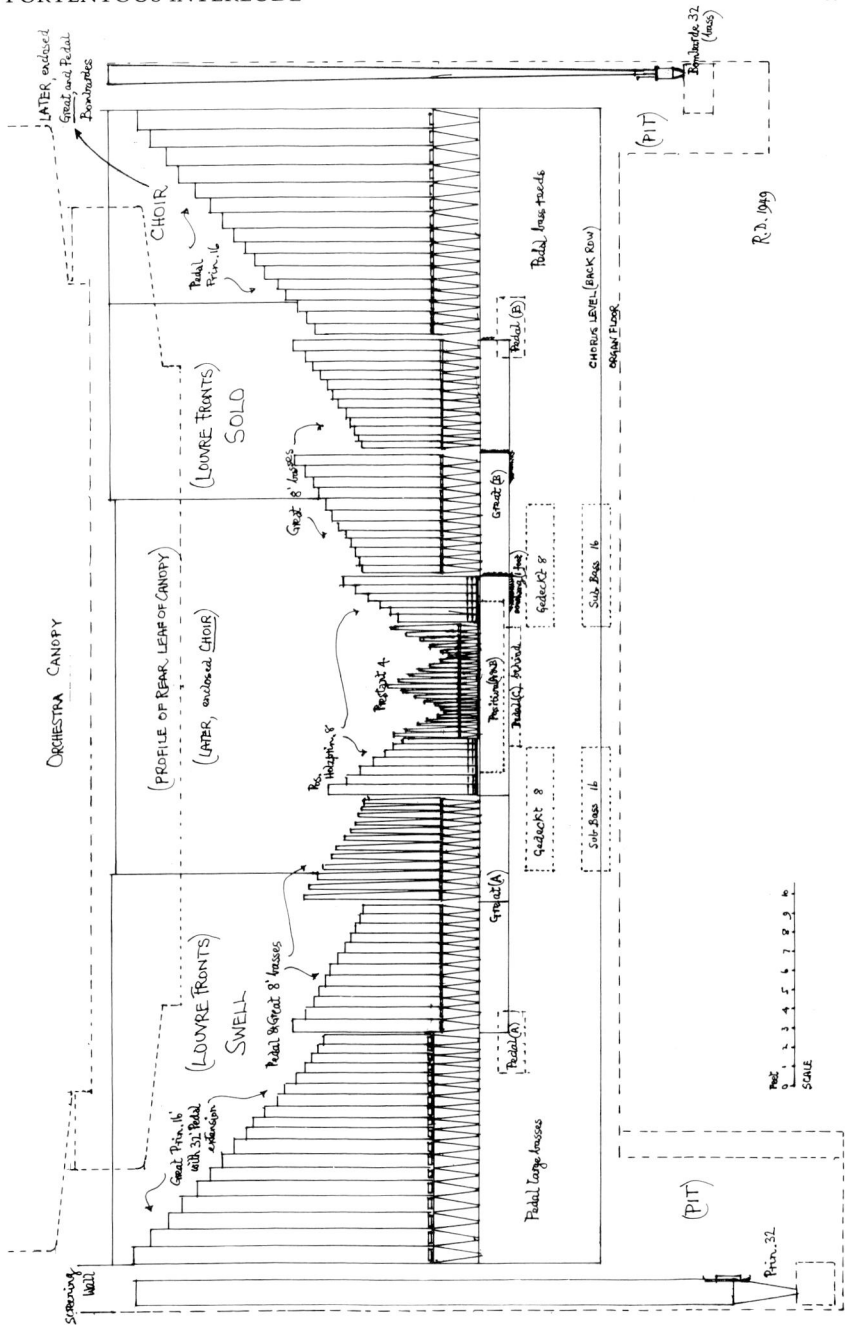

PLATE X *Royal Festival Hall, revised front elevation, 1949.*

manuals respectively) along the front of the organ and astride the Positive division. Most of the longer pipes would now be ranged along the front, atop the 'podium', where greater height was available, and so as to screen the interior pipes from view. The Pedal division would be divided at the right and left: and the enclosed divisions, now Swell, Solo and Choir Organs, would be ranged along the rear wall (Plate X). The new stop-list as follows:

GRAND ORGAN 3¾-inch wind
1 Principal 16 (front)
2 Bourdon 16 (24 wood)
3 Major Diapason 8 (12 on front)
4 Gemshorn 8 (12 on front)
5 Quint 5⅓
6 Octave 4
7 Tierce 3¹/₅
8 Septième 2²/₇
9 Rauschpfeife IV (12, 15, 19, 22)
10 Grand Cornet III-V (Bédos)
Enclosed in Solo box, 5-inch wind:
11 Bombarde 16
12 Trumpet (harmonic) 8
13 Clarion (harmonic) 4

SOLO ORGAN (enclosed, behind Grand, 5-inch wind)
14 Violon 16
15 Flûte majeure 8 (wood)
16 Violoncello 8
17 Violons célestes 8
18 Orchestral flute 4 (wood, harmonic)
19 Spitzgamba (Fugara) 4
20 Zauberpiccolo 2 (stopped, metal, harmonic)
21 Tertian II (24, 26 etc)
22 Cor anglais 16
23 Corno di bassetto 8
— Tremulant
24 French horn 8 ⎫
25 Tuba major 8 ⎬ (15-inch wind)
26 Tuba clarion 4 ⎭

GREAT ORGAN 3¾-inch wind
27 Principal conique 16 (front)
28 Diapason 8 (12 front)
29 Spitzflute 8 (12 front)
30 Harmonic flute 8 (12 open wood)

31	Bourdon	8 (12 wood)
32	Octave	4
33	Rohrflute	4
34	Nazard	2⅔ (conical)
35	Doublette	2
36	Quarte	2
37	Tierce	1³⁄₅
38	Fourniture	V (15, 19, 22, 26, 29)
39	Cymbale	IV (26, 29, 33, 36)
40	Trumpet	8 (medium)
41	Clarion	4 (medium scale)

SWELL ORGAN (behind Great, 4-inch wind)

42	Quintatön	16 (12 wood)
43	Geigen	8
44	Gedeckt	8
45	Viole de gambe	8
46	Voix célestes	8
47	Octave geigen	4
48	Flauto traverso	4
49	Fifteenth	2
50	Cornet de récit	III-V (Bédos)
51	Mixture	IV (19, 22, 26, 29)
52	Terz zimbel	III (29, 31, 33)
53	Bombarde	16 (½-length bass)
54	Trumpet	8
55	Hautbois	8
56	Voix humaine	8
57	Clarion	4
—	Tremulant	

POSITIVE ORGAN (front section, 3-inch wind)

58	Bourdon à cheminée	8 (12 wood on front)
59	Spitzflute	4 (front)
60	Nazard	2⅔ (metal, chimneys)
61	Octave	2
62	Tierce	1³⁄₅
63	Larigot	1⅓
64	Sifflöte	1
65	Petite cymbale	IV (33, 36, 40, 43)
66	Cromorne	8

POSITIVE ORGAN (back section, unenclosed, 3-inch wind)

67	Holzprincipal	8 (oak, 24 on front: metal from c')
68	Octave	4
69	Waldflute	2

70	Sesquialtera	II (12, 17)
71	Scharff	IV (22, 29, 33, 36)
72	Regal	8

CHOIR ORGAN (enclosed, 3½-inch wind)

73	Dulciana	16	
74	Hohlflute	8	(wood)
75	Salicional	8	
76	Vox angelica	8	(A sharp)
77	Gemshorn	4	("old English")
78	Nason	4	("old English")
79	Flageolet	2	(large scale)
80	Clochette	III	(19, 21, 22)
81	Bass clarinet	16	
82	Orchestral oboe	8	
—	Tremulant		

PEDAL ORGAN (3½- and 4-inch wind)

83	Principal	32	(12 wood, beards)
84	Major bass	16	(open wood)
85	Principal	16	(front)
86	Sub bass	16	
87	Violon	16	(No. 14)
88	Dulciana	16	(No. 73)
89	Quintatön	16	(No. 42)
90	Quint	10⅔	(open wood)
91	Octave	8	(front)
92	Flute	8	(wood, front)
93	Bourdon	8	(extension 86)
94	Viola	8	(extension 87)
95	Tierce	6⅖	
96	Quint	5⅓	
97	Septieme	4 4/7	
98	Octave	4	
99	Tierce	3⅕	
100	Nazard	2⅔	(conical)
101	Blockflute	2	(conical)
102	Mixture	VI	(19, 22, 26, 29, 33, 36)
103	Bombarde	32	(4-inch wind)
104	Bombarde	16	(4-inch wind)
105	2nd Bombarde	16	(No. 11)
106	Bass clarinet	16	(No. 81)
107	Trumpet	8	
108	2nd Trumpet	8	(No. 12)
109	Regal	8	(No. 72)
110	Clarion	4	
111	Cornett (reed)	2	

COUPLERS AND ACCESSORIES

All as previously, less the hitch-down pedals for reeds, but plus the following "transfers":
Grand on great (off Solo manual)
Back Positive on Solo (off lowest manual)

The second (enclosed) 32-foot reed was omitted (by advice from Rochesson, "too heavy")

Certain console refinements are also included:
toggle-touch (simulated "tracker action") and inclined manuals, and the mounting of the whole on a 180-degree swivel platform (an idea borrowed from the Liverpool Philharmonic Hall, one of the concert organs I visited while making a brief survey of modern concert hall organs).

It will be noted that this scheme was more unwieldy and less integrated than either of its predecessors: in particular, the Positive section was losing significance. The one advantage, perhaps, was visual; Edwin Williams liked the long sweep downwards of the front, from the long pipes at the ends to the rather 'dinky', partly wooden-fronted Positive in the centre. The unrelieved rows of swell-louvres at the rear could only be described as 'triste'.

I myself felt uneasy, and it was for my good friend, Donald Harrison (Aeolian-Skinner), to pull me out of this misconception of a classical concert-organ: he was indeed a good friend, for he was one who had been pressed for an opinion on the specifications by the unsuccessful tenderer previously mentioned, and had replied that the designer was on the right tack but had 'missed the boat'. Answering my own frantic enquiry, he said of the Grand division, "Forget it!" Following this, I managed to produce a more simplified scheme, which actually became the final 'Tender Specification':

GREAT ORGAN (3¾-inch wind)

1	Principal	16	
2	Major principal	8	($2/7$ mouths)
3	Diapason	8	
4	Spitzflute	8	
5	Flûte harmonique	8	(12 open wood)
6	Bourdon	8	(metal)
7	Grosse octave	4	
8	Principal	4	
9	Koppelflute	4	
10	Nazard	2⅔	
11	Octave	2	

12	Blockflute	2 (cylindrical)
13	Tierce	$1^{3/5}$
14	Fourniture	V (15, 19, 22, 26, 29)
15	Cymbale	IV (26, 29, 33, 36)

Enclosed section:

16	Grand Cornet	III-V (1, 8), 12, 15, 17)
17	Bombarde	16
18	Trumpet	8
19	Clarion	4

SWELL ORGAN (4¼-inch wind)

20	Quintadena	16
21	Principal	8 ($^{2/7}$ mouths)
22	Rohrgedeckt	8
23	Viole de gambe	8
24	Voix célestes	8 (from A)
25	Octave	4
26	Waldflute	4 (conical)
27	Nazard	$2^{2/3}$ (conical)
28	Octave	2
29	Nachthorn	2
30	Tierce	$1^{3/5}$
31	Octave	1
32	Mixture	IV (26, 29, 33, 36)
33	Zimbel	III (40, 43, 45)
34	Bombarde	16
35	Trumpet	8
36	Hautbois	8
37	Voix humaine	8
38	Clarion	4
	Tremulant	

POSITIVE ORGAN (2¾-inch wind)

39	Principal	8 (wood, 12 on front)
40	Gedeckt	8 (metal)
41	Prestant	4 (conical, 24 on front)
42	Rohrflute	4
43	Rohrnazard	$2^{2/3}$ (chimneys)
44	Octave	2
45	Tierce	$1^{3/5}$
46	Larigot	$1^{1/3}$
47	Sifflute	1
48	Plein jeu	III (22, 26, 29)
49	Zimbel	II (33, 36)
50	Regal	8

CHOIR ORGAN (4-inch wind, enclosed)

51	Salicional	16	(conical)
52	Violin diapason	8	(conical)
53	Concert flute	8	(harmonic treble)
54	Scharfgeige	8	(inverted cone)
55	Scharfcelestes	8	(inverted cone, from A)
56	Salicional	8	(conical)
57	Vox angelica	8	(conical, from A)
58	Harmonic flute	4	
59	Fugara	4	
60	Piccolo	2	(very large scale)
61	Tertian	II	(31, 33 etc)
62	Dulzian	16	(½-length)
63	Trumpet	8	
64	Cromorne	8	
	Tremulant		

SOLO ORGAN (5- and 15-inch wind, enclosed)

65	Flûte majeure	8	
66	Violoncello	8	
67	Viole céleste	8	(from A)
68	Orchestral flute	4	(wood, harmonic)
69	Cor anglais	16	
70	Corno di bassetto	8	

Heavy wind:

71	French horn	8	
72	Tuba major	8	
73	Tuba clarion	4	
	Tremulant to light wind		

PEDAL ORGAN (3¾-, 4¼- and 5-inch wind)

74	Principal	32	(20 from No.1)
75	Major bass	16	
76	Principal	16	
77	Sub bass	16	
78	Quintadena	16	(No. 20)
79	Salicional	16	(No. 51)
80	Flûte ouverte	8	(metal)
81	Gedeckt	8	(metal)
82	Principal	8	(conical)
83	Quintadena	8	(No. 20)
84	Rohrquint	5⅓	(koppelflute type)
85	Octave	4	
86	Koppelflute	4	
87	Tierce	3⅕	

88	Nachthorn	2
89	Rauschpfeife	II (19, 22)
90	Mixture	VI (26, 29, 33, 36)
91	Bombarde	32 (20 from No. 92)
92	Bombarde	16
93	Dulzian	16 (No. 62)
94	Trumpet	8
95	Regal	8 (No. 50)
96	Clarion	4
97	Regal	4 (No. 50)
98	Cornett	2

The Bombardes, 91 and 92, enclosed with Great reeds, on 5-inch wind.

The front display was virtually unchanged from that shown in Plate X.

This stop-list, like its predecessor, displayed an obvious desire to appease the already articulate critics of so un-English a classical scheme — note the presence of large-scale wooden flutes, string-tones at four dynamic levels, and 'indispensable' orchestral reeds and Tubas, not to mention those important chorus Trumpets of the Great, stowed away 'under expression' — an American idea encountered in a fine Michell and Thynne organ in Germantown, Philadelphia, more effectively done than at Princeton. Other 'neo-classical' features were the Swell chorus structure, redolent of Gottfried Silbermann plus a Tierce-Cimbel and French reeds; the slightly American Positive retaining its wooden Principal 8-feet ('borrowed' from the Danish State Radio organ) and pro-German Regal (of unspecified type); and, of course, the American-oriented large Pedal division replete with duplexing of manual stops supplementing an already fully developed chorus. As the late W. N. Sumner (and recently, John Rowntree) observed, this was an eclectic design with a vengeance. What they did *not* appreciate was that when the actual organ was finished, by a subtle change near the end of the road, the eclecticism vanished, giving way to a new and completely integrated realisation: this will be studied later.

But to return: Donald Harrison liked the greater simplicity of this scheme, though he himself strongly advocated a fully fluework Great — as in his organs at Groton School, Symphony Hall, Boston, and Salt Lake City Tabernacle; and he once again cited his use of wide pipe-scales for his Mixtures, favouring the 'resultant' build-up of the quints with the unisons and achieving Principal sonority by keeping the mouths cut low; he *hated* narrow-scaled pipes, blown hard, and in theory I felt likewise. But when I listened to recordings of two of his organs — the Germanic Museum at Harvard, and Columbia University — I was less happy: the mixtures seemed to me to be too 'fifthy', too

English (in the Lewis sense) to fit into a French-oriented ensemble (or even into the German-Romantic sounds I had so far experienced). The scales were even sometimes wider than those of the 8-foot foundation-stops; this was against all historical precedent, and instinctively I felt that he was crossing the line into Cornet sonority (*above* the Töpfer Normal) but with a hardness of intonation absent from the original Methuen choruses which would have been intolerable if so voiced. Shortly afterwards I was encouraged by the receipt, from Rochesson, of Cavaillé's scale for the Plein Jeu, which ranged from -5HT in the bass to about Normal in the treble: this confirmed my own views, so I hung on.

Anyway, we now had a fairly neat 'paper specification' — as regards size and musical scope, most requirements had, I felt, been met, *theoretically*, and a number of *cognoscenti* praised it: but a very disturbing new element was its cleavage from the structural, positional and visual requirements now stipulated by the architectural design team — it was a scheme 'in a vacuum'.

Granted that the classically conceived Positive division must occupy a prominent central position, the Great must evidently be ranged around it in a kind of horse-shoe formation, and (for lack of head-room) on practically the same level, viz, the top of the podium, some 6 ft 6 in. above the back row of chorus seating. In accordance with the then accepted view that an organ needed maximum space above the pipes in order to sound at its best and fullest, all the unenclosed pipework was designed to be 'open' up to the ceiling: how, then, was the Positive sound to be differentiated from that of the other divisions, especially the Great? How could its identity be established aurally? Through Felix Aprahamian I appealed to André Marchal: "By its voicing," came his reply. Well, all right! But I did not feel convinced that this would work, and I began to think in terms of building a baffle behind the Positive soundboard, possibly surmounted by a small canopy to aim at forward projection of the sound. (With hindsight, this was clearly a move in the right direction — towards the concept of resonant casework.)

But now began a year-long conflict of priorities on the architectural plane, especially between the design team, the acoustical consultants and me. The main bones of contention were the size, shape and height of the orchestral canopy (especially at its rear, towards the organ frontage), the height of the podium, and the width of the opening into the organ-recess: and, of course, the still generally unaccepted visual frontage of the organ, an issue which remained unresolved until 1952! One important issue was, however, settled before the Tenders went out: owing to structural restrictions below the Concert Hall level, the idea of a moveable console on a lift was abandoned: now, thank goodness, the action of the organ could be a good electro-pneumatic (not direct electric) with mechanical swell-control!

The Tenders were sent out, and were for the most part received by the organ-builders with a good grace. Donald Harrison had pointed out to me that the tight control the Architects and I were imposing on them could be highly offensive, almost reducing them to the level of common contractors: yet, as he admitted, there was scarcely any alternative, and he (and I) shuddered to think what they would make of such a specification without such control, since their contemporary practice was along such very different lines to what was being proposed, even if their electro-pneumatic technology was excellent.

The Tenders came back, and in May 1949 the firm of Harrison & Harrison (the most expensive) was chosen expressly on my recommendation: not that I liked their recently built organs — I did not; neither did I foresee that they would easily adapt to my tonal conception — I knew they would not, and indeed they made a final effort to obtain acceptance of one of their normal schemes. But I had managed to get inside one of their larger organs, and observed their execution of trivial details (which nobody but the tuner would ever see) in a manner which plainly spelt Perfectionism, no less: that was all the evidence I needed, and later events proved me right; everything in the new organ was an exemplary model of proud craftsmanship — soundboard construction, cabinet-work, electro-pneumatics, pipe-making; no detail was skimped anywhere.

When it came to 'the crunch', the Managing Director finally agreed to build my specification in all respects: "This is marvellous," he said, with the air of accepting a challenge, as we left the Architect's office together!

CHAPTER FIVE

The Study of Pipe-Scales (1) More Ill-Fated Empiricism

Among the causes of unsatisfactory blend and over-inflated power which I had encountered when performing on large contemporary organs (especially with orchestra and/or chorus), over-large diapason scales and excessively high wind-pressure were prominent in my diagnosis: from the start I had been determined to avoid these evils in the new concert-organ, and I had laid down what I felt were reasonable limits. But here I was in a quandary, as long as no organ-builder had been chosen: yet it was necessary to write a condition of conformity into the organ contract so that effective control could be maintained over the organ-builder's performance and policy. My ever-faithful friend, Reginald Davidson, counselled early consultation with the chosen firm on the question of scaling; and both he and Walter Goodey (of the Walker firm) gave me helpful demonstrations of 2-foot and 1-foot C 'principal' (diapason) pipes of different scales on different pressures. All very perplexing! A scale of, say, 3 HT under Normal gave a delightfully fresh quality, perhaps on the 'light-weight' side with a pressure of, say, 3 inches WG. A pipe about 4 HT wider sounded broader — a little 'opaque' — but if the pressure were increased to 3½ inches, it too gave a fresh sound, but with greater weight and drive! After this first difficult choice (made in a small voicing-room, too), the further question of the *progression* of the scale, upwards and downwards, had to be settled.

After a good deal of reading, discussion, listening, "belly-aching" — as the Americans say — and the exercise of all the imagination I could bring to bear, I gulped and fixed the scales for the main stops in the Tender specification as now shown in graphical form in Figure 9, plotted as before against the Töpfer Normal scale. The 'dipping' curves will easily be recognised as derived from the Dom Bédos procedure, with a corresponding over-width at both ends, especially the trebles: the straight lines are Töpfer's simple logarithmic progressions, halving on the 17th, 18th or 19th pipe. Some variety might be imagined to result from this interplay (analysed in Figure 9E), but since it was rather accidental than deliberately calculated, its value must be

100   BAROQUE TRICKS

Figure 9

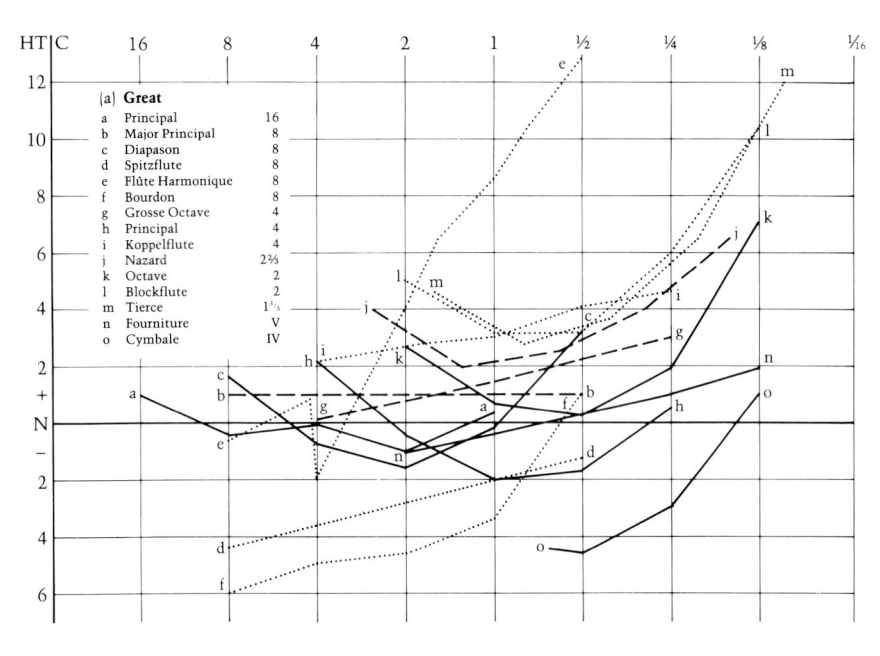

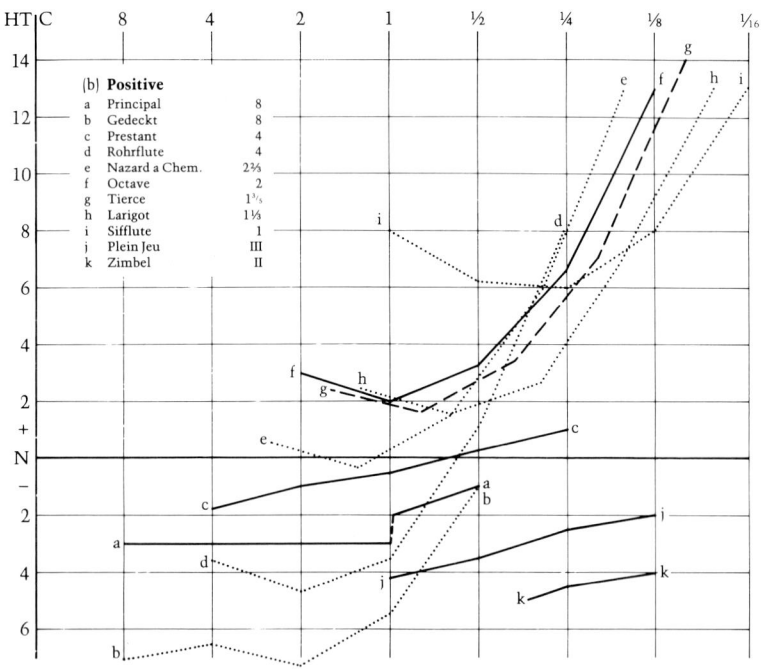

(a) **Great**

a	Principal	16
b	Major Principal	8
c	Diapason	8
d	Spitzflute	8
e	Flûte Harmonique	8
f	Bourdon	8
g	Grosse Octave	4
h	Principal	4
i	Koppelflute	4
j	Nazard	2⅔
k	Octave	2
l	Blockflute	2
m	Tierce	1³⁄₅
n	Fourniture	V
o	Cymbale	IV

(b) **Positive**

a	Principal	8
b	Gedeckt	8
c	Prestant	4
d	Rohrflute	4
e	Nazard a Chem.	2⅔
f	Octave	2
g	Tierce	1³⁄₅
h	Larigot	1⅓
i	Sifflute	1
j	Plein Jeu	III
k	Zimbel	II

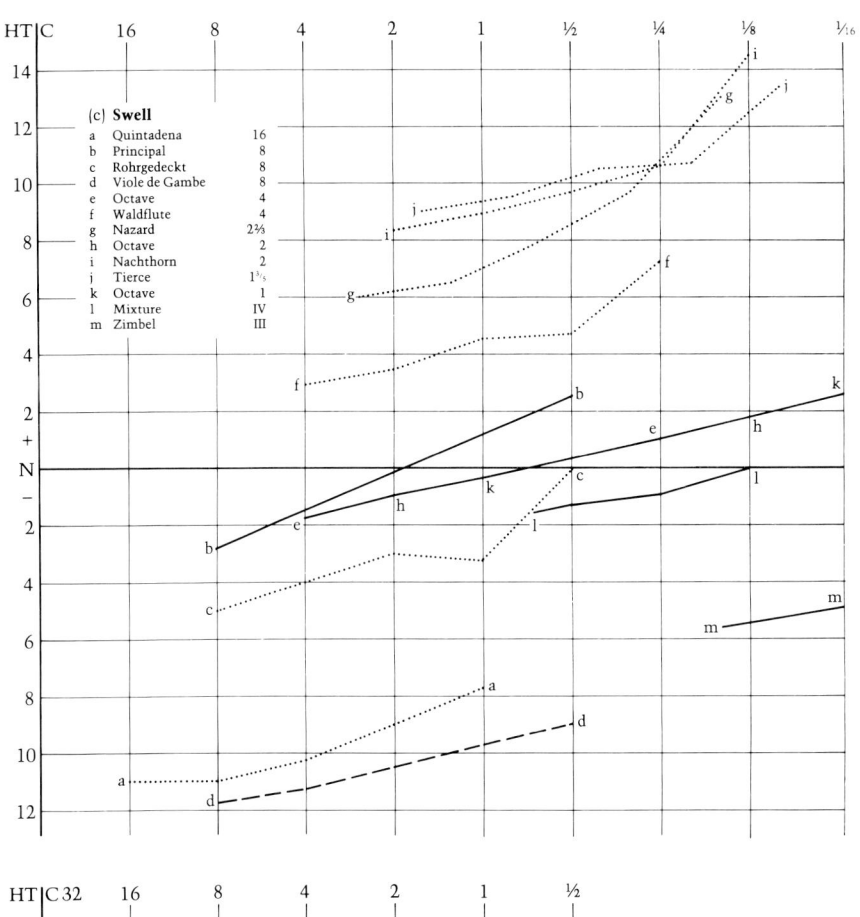

THE STUDY OF PIPE-SCALES I

(c) **Swell**

a	Quintadena	16
b	Principal	8
c	Rohrgedeckt	8
d	Viole de Gambe	8
e	Octave	4
f	Waldflute	4
g	Nazard	2⅔
h	Octave	2
i	Nachthorn	2
j	Tierce	1³⁄₅
k	Octave	1
l	Mixture	IV
m	Zimbel	III

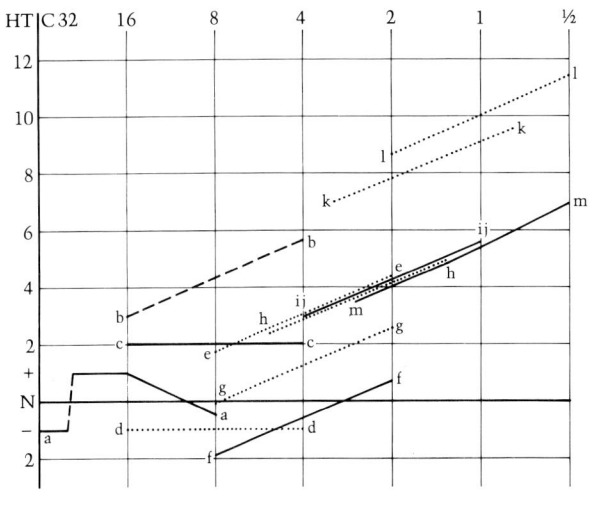

(d) **Pedal**

a	Principal	32
b	Major Bass	16
c	Principal	16
d	Sub Bass	16
e	Flûte Ouverte	8
f	Principal	8
g	Gedeckt	8
h	Rohrquint	5⅓
i	Octave	4
j	Koppelflute	4
k	Tierce	3¹⁄₅
l	Nachthorn	2
m	Mixture	IV

(e) **Analysis**

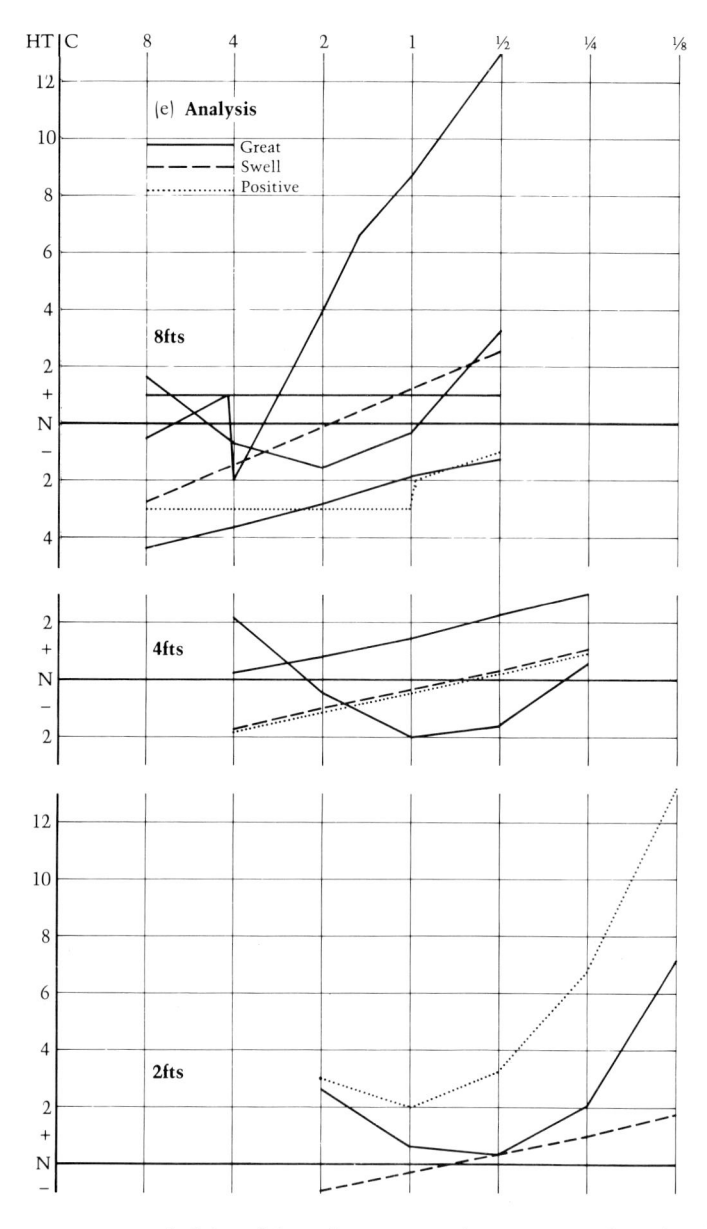

——— Great
– – – Swell
······· Positive

8fts

4fts

2fts

suspect, and this I felt subconsciously. In more detail, with hindsight the entire Pedal section was too wide, and followed an identical progression — thus dull and obviously monotonous: the 8-foot flute scales, especially the stopped and half-stopped varieties, were mostly narrower than the Principals; the mutations of Principal type were over-wide, particularly at the bass end. The main Mixtures of Great and Pedal had obviously been affected by Don Harrison's warning, and were too wide, but according to his conception, the 8-foot Principals were too wide, and the 4-foots too narrow! The uniform curves of all the mutations of the wide-scale group (all à la Bédos) would again make for monotony of effect.

The burning question before me was, "Would it work? How would it all sound?" Now that the builder was at last chosen, I lost no time in seeking full discussion, if not actual *confirmation* of my figures, sending him in addition a complete exposé of my conception of the organ, which I quote in full:

> "The idea behind the scheme is to be able to perform music of all styles and periods with a high degree of faithfulness. A compromise is therefore necessary, between the true classic ideal and the demands of later Romantic music. But this need not be to the detriment of either.
>
> "For Bach, and the pre-Bach masters of all nationalities, there is needed the low-pressure chorus (2 or even 3 manuals) of Principals and Quint Mixtures, so as to ensure contrapuntal clarity, especially by means of the mixture breaks: this is for music of three parts and more, played all on one manual or passing from one manual to another with both hands, as in the fugue episodes, played on 'Oberwerk' or 'Positiv'. Then one needs the 'wide-scale' chorus of mutations, for trios, etc, for two manuals and pedals. Both ideas call for complete pedal independence — extension never accomplishes this satisfactorily.
>
> "The masters of the eighteenth century in France need very much the same treatment, but in addition the characteristic reed timbres — the Trompettes and Clairons on Great and Positif, the Cromorne, and of course the manual and pedal Bombardes for the great climaxes.
>
> "There is also the true Romantic organ style of César Franck, and his pupils and descendants, calling for mellow, full foundation tone, fuller though softer than the modern English diapasons, the characteristic broad Célestes and Unda maris, the Harmonic flutes, and the solo and chorus reeds (especially Swell) of Cavaillé-Coll.
>
> "Lastly there is the modern music of Germany (which, however, fits into the classic structure best): modern American music, and modern English. As *music*, I think one has to admit the extreme paucity of both, when it comes to real quality — works, that is, not merely written by organists for organists!
>
> "Then of course there is the use of organ as a bolstering-up of orchestra, in, say, *Cockaigne, Enigma Variations, 1812 Overture*, and so on, in which massive tone, mainly 8-feet and 4-feet without reeds, is the best recipe. But I feel that one should be able to use Full Organ for quite long periods, if needed, without fear of overwhelming an orchestra or a chorus. (This can seldom be done, though it often *is* — with lamentable results.)
>
> "To come back to the specification [27], there are two Principal groups on the Great, (1) a pure classic one, though with scales slightly increased so as to counteract the deadness of the hall: stops 1, 3, 8,

11, 15; and (2) a 'modern' classic chorus, stops 1a, 2 (big Schulze-type), 4, 7 and 14. The Swell (corresponding with 'Oberwerk') has a 'sharper'-toned chorus, stops 20, 21 (Schulze 'Armley'-type), 25, 28, 32, (33). Positive has 39 (or alternatively 40), 41, 44, 46, 47, 48, (49); Pedal 74, 75, 76, 80, 81, 85, 89, 90.

"There are mutations series on each manual: built up of bourdons, open flutes and conical and half-stopped pipes: the Great of fairly big scale, the Swell (Cornet de récit, 22, 26, 27, 29, 30, with 31 making it into a carillon) of very big scale:" *(No. 31 had been changed from an Octave to a wide-scaled Flageolet)* "the Grand Cornet with scales getting very big in treble: and a more brilliant and delicate series on Positive. The same holds good for Pedal.

"With regard to tonal blend, the upper octaves of all classic stops have all been given larger scales than now usual, while tenor octaves are whittled down a little. The idea is to give enough body to trebles so that they can be kept up without getting too stringy or forced, and to keep tenor register clear and free of modern 'tubbiness'." *(With hindsight, this was a serious miscalculation; the Royal Festival Hall's acoustics gave undue prominence to trebles and tended to fade out the entire tenor and bass ranges!)* "(Donald Harrison, as you probably know, has abandoned Töpfer scales for this reason, and with good results.) Then again, the scale of upper work is (in case of Principals) a trifle larger than the lower voices, so as to make for fullness without scream, and greater adaptability, eg, so as to be able to use 4-foot and 2-foot Principals supported by bourdons or flutes 8-feet only, and so as to bind 8-foot tone into mixtures. The scale of upper mutations is *much larger*, in accordance with old principles, so that pitch of quints, tierces, etc, *disappears completely*, and produces pure synthetic organ tone.

"By large scales, you will understand that I do not mean 'loud tone'. Hence, though I would encourage letting the 8-foot stops go pretty well 'all out', I should feel that the 4-foot should be slightly softer, the 2-foot softer still, and so on right up into the mixtures. The very high ranks in bass of the Zimbels would probably be the softest pipes in the organ, but will probably be heard in full-organ with reeds, because their pitch is so far from the fundamental. It should be possible then to get an ensemble in which every note on the keyboard is plainly audible *at its own pitch*, no matter what registration or style is used. For this, I am sure that one of the essential conditions is very low cut-up, not more than ¼ of mouth-width for the ¼ mouth, and even less in trebles and in the stops with $2/7$ mouths of the Schulze type. In the 8-foot stops, there will then be enough harmonics to absorb mixture and mutation tones, and in upper-work there will be a good margin to soften down without the tone losing vitality and steadiness.

"I feel I must next say a word about the character of the individual departments: Great, is of course, in addition to the English Great with Diapasons I, II and III (Spitzflöte), the corresponding Hauptwerk, or Grand Orgue, with broad scales and voicing. Swell, is also the French Récit, or classical Oberwerk, more 'sharp' or 'brilliant' than Great, though not by forcing up the trebles, or at the expense of perfect clarity all through the compass. Positiv is the equivalent of Brustwerk (or French Positif) with smaller scales, more charming effect, but the low pressure is compensated by *ample volume* of wind, so that by this means, and by its prominent position and high pitch of ranks, this division should be able to hold its own against Great or Swell, either *en masse* or in trio playing on two manuals and pedals. Choir and Solo are modern divisions, but they also look in the direction of perfect ensemble, and should not be contrasted too strongly with the unenclosed parts: in other words, it has to be *one* organ.

"I have avoided the customary large pedal scales for 16-feet and 32-feet, because I am convinced that they are of no musical value: but with the addition of upper mutations of 16-foot and 32-foot series, *voiced to blend*, and of larger scales, I look for a clear melodic line from the pedals in all circumstances. I am convinced that quality always tells, and that even in modern orchestral music, a good ensemble of bass stops will be as telling, and much more effective musically, than one or two booming wood opens of no particular pitch!

"Regarding reeds: I have come to the conclusion (reached by your namesake in the USA) that the French type of chorus reed, when well voiced and artistically scaled so as not to predominate over the flues, gives a much better blend than the modern smooth type with weighted tongues. One reason is that the basses are much freer, and if well done, the speech has an explosive promptness, on even low pressures, which is of great musical value, giving vehemence and attack like the playing of a fine orchestra: and this, right down to the bottom notes of the 32-foot Bombarde. By using low pressures also, one ensures that the reeds will not sound too loud for the flues *at a distance*, and the freer harmonic development makes for absorption of upper work, even the high mixtures into the reed tone, so increasing the *unity* of effect. I suppose the quality of the Tubas will need to be slightly modified also to mix in. I am not keen on the type with fiery trebles and stifled basses.[28] It seems to me that the Tubas should add (harmonically, ie, *in chords*) a climax to all the organ, but I don't see any value in being able to hear single Tuba notes above everything else. I don't know any music for the organ which calls for this, except Norman Cocker's piece. Greatly as I admire him, I don't think we can take that sort of thing — a pastiche, after all — too seriously as organ music, by the side, say, of Liszt, Franck, Reger, Hindemith, Vierne, Messiaen, etc? I don't think any Tubas have surpassed the Willis types used at Salisbury or the *Chancel* Tubas at St. Paul's. These, even, are inclined to 'honk' in the tenor, but I suppose that is inevitable. I regret to say that the reeds are the only things I really do not admire (from the musician's standpoint, that is) at Westminster Abbey, Royal Albert Hall, West London Synagogue, Redcliffe, Durham Cathedral, etc.

"I must apologise for going on at such length: my only aim is to be helpful by clarifying matters at once, on which there could easily be serious misunderstandings. If (as I hope you don't) you have any feelings of resentment at being 'lectured' by an amateur, I apologise, but once again feel I must say that I approach all this as a professional musician with a strong personal interest in the organ as a means to an end, not as an end in itself. I cannot see that anything is to be lost by the musician putting his point of view clearly and frankly to the master craftsman who makes his instrument. Without descending to personalities, I do not need to remind you of the unspeakably low standard of criticism and taste regarding organ music generally in this country, as compared, say, with the orchestra, the piano, violin, etc. There are even large bodies of organists whose tastes one may hope to improve by a lead in the right direction, but upon whose opinions one cannot rely for sound musical judgement in these matters. On the other hand, I do know that there are many non-organist musicians who are very interested in the kind of thing I am trying to do, and these people accept even the best of our modern instruments with a shrug of the shoulders!

"Well, I do wish you good luck in this great venture, and I am very glad that the Council have had the foresight to recommend your firm for the job, and am sure they will not regret their decision."

WHEW! Well, so far so good, from my point of view: but thinking over it now, I can find it hardly surprising that the immediate brief, polite acknowledgement of all this mass of material had for me the air of stunned silence, although cheerfully enough phrased. Again, speaking with hindsight, I have little doubt that the variations and interplay of the quoted pipe-scales seemed confused, if not totally incomprehensible, causing much rueful shaking of heads in Durham. The Director's covering written affirmation of support and wholehearted co-operation seemed to carry the whole issue into the sphere of personal loyalty — an admirable sentiment in itself, but highly dangerous when applied to artistic principles and procedures: any form of discussion could only too readily tend towards putting the ball back firmly into the Consultant's court — "We will give you what you want," so to speak. Supposing one could not be absolutely sure in one's own mind! And I was, by turns, most unsure and in need of discussion of the problems, especially with the actual craftsmen involved: after all, the as-yet-unbuilt hall itself was an acoustically unknown quantity; one could only be sure that it was intended to be very 'dry'·— Mr. Bagenal even suggested that music made in it would sound as if played in the open air!

Drawing the curtain for a moment on this scene, I return to the situation at Buckfast Abbey and the Oratory. At Reginald Walker's suggestion, with an eye to Buckfast plans, Walter Goodey came to Brompton to see and hear what I had achieved there. He was evidently not too disapproving, even though he must have disliked the reeds as altered by Davidson and me. An unforeseen development at Buckfast arose from the Abbey authorities' disposal of the old Great and Swell chorus reeds and the entire Large Open Diapason to some party who wanted to put them into another organ, it seems for sentimental, nostalgic reasons! So far as I was concerned, this was "good riddance" and opened the way to improvement of the Great chorus, based on a new spotted metal 8-foot Principal, and in view of his presence already in London, I recommended that Rochesson be engaged to design and voice new reeds, 8- and 4-feet, for the Great, and also to rebuild the Pedal Trombone unit with new French shallots and tongues as a Bombarde, Trumpet and Clarion. Walkers' were keen on exploring a new style, and readily agreed.

So Rochesson came in June (1949), pausing in London to voice the manual Trombone for the Oratory (in Davidson's workshop), and then to inspect the Buckfast site; and lastly, to finish the Oratory Pedal Bombarde (already voiced) in the organ. Meanwhile, Mr. Davidson delivered the pipes of the latter at the church, and while Rochesson was voicing the Trombone trebles, Davidson's tuner agreed to tidy up the organ for a broadcast recital, having already inserted the bottom octave of the Bombarde 16-feet. I could not resist the temptation to try them on their new reduced presure of 4½ inches: bottom A would have been useful, but was flat even when turned to the sharpest limit of the tongue. I persuaded the tuner to try and bring it to pitch by cutting about 1 inch off the top of the resonator. As the metal was thick hard baked zinc, his comments were not helpful to my morale, especially as the effect on the pitch was disappointingly small — it was still flat! Eventually we found that 12-foot F would come practically into tune, and I drew it on the final pedal note of a Buxtehude Toccata in that key. It fairly 'raised the roof'. (This was noticed in the broadcast by one of my radio 'fans' who reproved my lack of purism.)

Rochesson came the next day, just as Davidson was securing the rest of the pipes to their stays. The latter had asked me to "keep him out of the way for a while" until this operation was complete, and was attempting to get the basses roughly into tune. Said Rochesson, down in the church, *"C'est moi qui doit faire cela!"* and he could hardly be restrained from rushing upstairs at once. But all was settled amicably in the end: he cut slots in the pipes, one full diameter from the top — for auxiliary tuning — and of course the pressure had to be reduced, to a bare 4 inches. There was still plenty of tone and to spare, and I understood then in retrospect the import of Rochesson's grimace when he had first seen the pipes: I myself could not have credited the tremendous increase in output caused by the substitution of open French shallots for the normal British type in conjunction with these large-scaled resonators, on a wind-pressure reduced from the original 10½ inches to 4½ inches!

With the new Trumpet 8-foot extension, the Pedal, and indeed the ensemble of Full Organ was for the first time really good — a classic sonority, as Rochesson remarked, and not unlike that of Andreas Silbermann at, say, Ebersmünster. The Oratory organ never sounded better than this — the later completion of the Choir mixtures was not happy: I had made the mistake of stipulating both narrow mouths and low-cut lips and (as I had still to learn) what was really a rather *high* pressure of 3¼ inches — we then thought it *low* — and the tuner's observations as he tried to put the pipes 'on speech' were not personally flattering, though he did not actually walk out! Similar discoveries were made the next year at Buckfast, where the new Positive on a similar pressure was horribly strident: and once again I had miscalculated the volume of a French Bombarde, even though the scale was a moderate 7 inches or so for low C: partly owing to position in a narrow and very reverberant aisle, the new stop turned out to be so appallingly loud that nothing short of a hardboard baffle built over the pipes could reduce it to within reasonable limits. A tuner working in this covered and restricted space was absolutely deafened!

Let it not be thought, however, that only amateurs in the field make such errors of judgement: I could quote two instances in more recent years where a most distinguished firm rebuilt organs, parts of which turned out to be impossibly loud: in one case, the installation of a large impeding baffle was likewise the only, if lame, solution; in the other, the new division had to be left unacceptably loud — there was no cure, and there it remains!

To close this chapter, and as a companion-piece to the Royal Festival Hall scale-plan to date, I will quote (again in graphic form) my revised scales, as of July (1949) for the Buckfast Positive division — likewise now largely adapted from Töpfer's ratios, which Walkers' accepted as at least rational (Figure 10). No work was yet being done on the Abbey organ apart from planning the soundboards, which, it had been agreed, would be of the sliderless type which the firm now regarded as more stable than the slider construction in varying climatic conditions: extra capacity was being allowed for a copious supply of low-pressure wind, as we then regarded it.

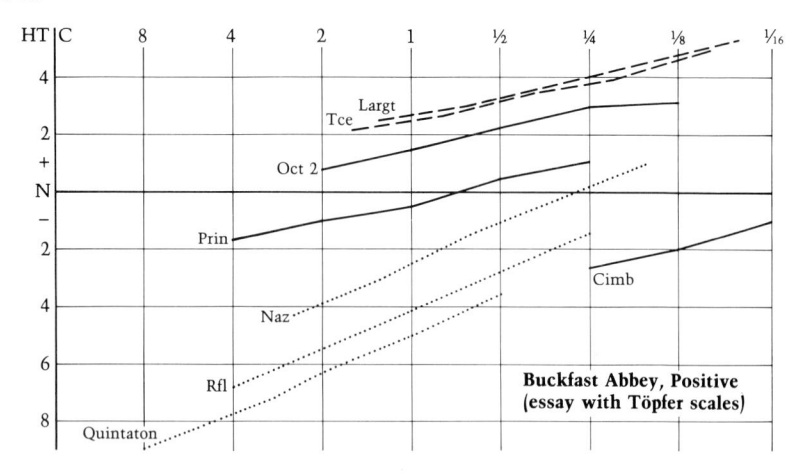

Figure 10

CHAPTER SIX

Illumination

I have already cited Susi Jeans' interest in my endeavours, and the assistance she frequently gave me — acquainting me with the important writings of Christhard Mahrenholz, for instance, and thus paving my way for more considerable research among the organ authors available in the British Museum Reading Room (now the British Library), such as Hans Klotz, Paul Smets, Rudolf Quoicka, etc: I also possessed Jean Huré's *L'Aesthétique de l'Orgue*, a sensitive musician's view of organ design and its commonly encountered shortcomings especially in France. Late in 1948 my old friend, the distinguished organist (and now organ-builder), Robert Noehren, came over from the USA to research on European organs of the seventeenth and eighteenth centuries, pausing in London *en route* for France, his first sphere of activity. ("A waste of time, my boy," said Mr. Henry Willis III: "when you've heard one, you've heard them all" — a remark which occasioned us a little quiet mirth). I received a rather glowing account of his findings when he got home again: and he was back on a similar more extensive programme in 1949. Now, he wrote in greater detail, and when he had left France for Holland (having seen and praised in particular the splendid intact Clicquot 4-manual at Poitiers, as well as organs at Souvigny and St Maximin, which were *not* in such good order), he waxed really enthusiastic about the old Dutch instruments, not least those which showed the Schnitger influence from North Germany. (In fact, he *had* experienced some of the musical indigestion forecast by Mr. Willis, and had almost walked out of a recital in Ste. Clothilde, Paris, having become quite satiated with the Cavaillé sonority of *fonds* and *anches* — as rebuilt in the 1930s). He dwelt on the wonderful 'freshness' of the Schnitger tone, the remarkable blend of all the stops, and the immense variety of colour not only in the 8-foot, 4-foot and 2-foot, but also in the mutations (wide- and narrow-scale), the narrow-scaled Mixtures and compound-stops, and the Baroque reeds: all of them on low wind-pressure and all mild and unforced, even though 'lively' — yet capable of a breath-taking synthesis. He pressed me — as did Susi — not to fail to see these organs before finishing my South Bank specification — which meant "IMMEDIATELY", for Harrisons' were already pressing

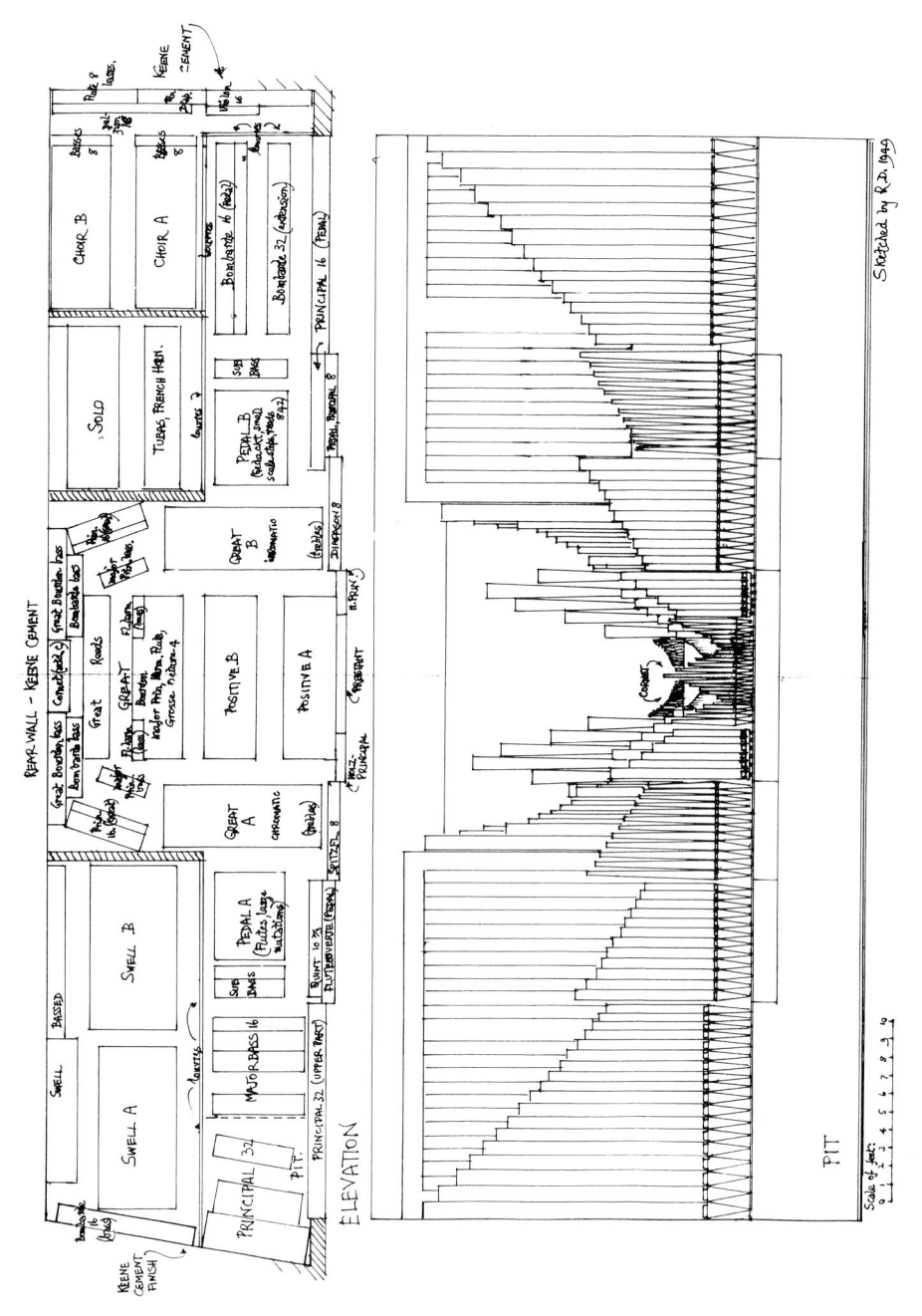

PLATE XI *Royal Festival Hall, plan and front elevation drawing, 1949.
A further elaboration of the 'Tender' scheme shown in plate IX.*

me for final details of the console layout, so that they could begin making it and the combination-piston machines.

Meanwhile, the seemingly endless struggle went on for priorities upheld by Architects, Acousticians, Organ-builders and me, over the organ's visual and acoustical aspects: the bones of contention were still the over-60-foot width of the organ-opening (I refused to countenance the word 'chamber'); the height of the podium or impost level; the further height of the organ ceiling, and the relation of the rear of the orchestral canopy to it; the internal placement of soundboards and pipes, and the consequent front-display — all of which had a bearing on the stop-list, and would be vitally affected by any significant change in that. As fast as the acousticians, or the organ-builders, or I, produced a scheme, it was 'downed' by one or both of the others: the Architect (and principally the Deputy, Dr Leslie Martin) had the ungrateful task of trying to decide each issue fairly while having regard to the wishes of his own 'backroom' aestheticians as well as his own overall conception of the hall's interior. Plate XI was a further elaboration of my elevation for the 'Tender' scheme, and formed the basis of one of two scale models made by Harrisons' (Plate XII). But it was not completely acceptable to him: the stalemate continued!

Still, we *must* get on with the organ itself.

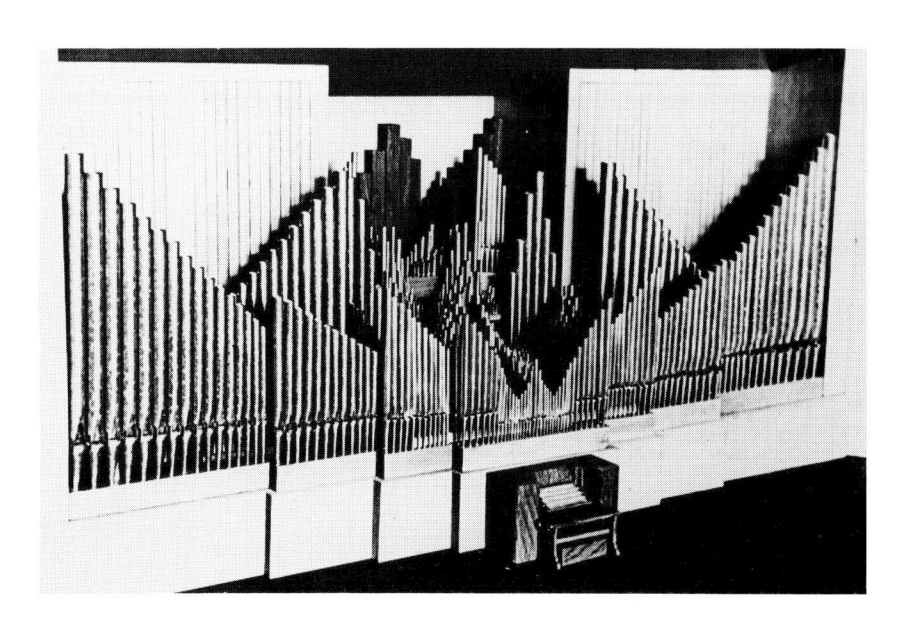

PLATE XII *Royal Festival Hall, scale model by Harrisons' based on the 1949 scheme shown in plate XI.*

I had already studied Professor Klotz's analysis of Schnitger's work [29], its essentially logical principles of design as reflected in its casework, eg, *Hauptwerk* 8-feet, *Rückpositiv* 4-feet, *Brustwerk* 2-feet, Pedal 16-feet, as the respective sizes and pitch of a typical 'prospect' of Principal pipes: its strategic opposition of wide and narrow scales, eg, wide Nazard 2⅔ feet *vis à vis* narrow Sesquialtera 2⅔1³/₅ feet: its comprehensive plan of a complete Principal chorus in each division, with the usual inclusion of one narrow-scaled Tierce-register, eg, Tertian, Sesquialtera, Cimbel: and a suitable allocation of reeds, full-length in *Hauptwerk* and Pedal, half-length in *Rückpositiv*, and quarter-length in *Brustwerk*. But I had not seen or *heard* this in actuality, and I could not therefore speak with sufficient certainty to integrate such ideas into a new organ 'out of the blue'. My first visit to Holland was thus a complete revelation.

Not that all the Dutch organs I saw were of great merit: the first two, a nineteenth-century one in The Hague (on which Noehren was to give a recital), and the (rebuilt) older organ in the Pieterskerk in Leyden, left me utterly unimpressed. Later, left to my own resources, I managed to get at the organ in the (round) Marekerk in the latter city — a 2-manual, actually partly pneumatic but containing many old pipes in its elegant case of two storeys — *Hoofdwerk* and *Bovenwerk*. Here I was captivated by the fresh sound of the case-Prestants — there was something magical in this free natural speech, inviting the player to improvise at length. There was no Swell, but it did not matter. The few reeds were of little consequence: the fluework was everything, and always fascinating in some indefinable way. Of course the acoustical properties of the octagonal cupola were very helpful to this galleried organ.

Next day Robert and I visited the Old Church and New Church in Amsterdam, both containing large 3-manual organs from the eighteenth and seventeenth centuries respectively, with minor nineteenth-century modifications. At the New Church the old 'spring-chests' remained — every stop when pulled (with some strength of effort) needed to be notched in, or it would return with a terrific bang. The *Rugwerk* (Positiv) stops were behind one, at the back of its own case. But the consequent impracticability of lightning kaleidoscopic changes of registration '*à la mode*' was not missed! Each combination, in both these organs, was completely satisfying and could easily last out a movement, if need be. Again, there were no Swells, nor were they missed: of course one was not so indiscreet as to attempt Franck!

At the Old Church Robert drew my attention to the finely keen (but not loud) ringing brilliance of the upper Mixtures — Scherp, Cimbel, Sesquialtera. The *Rugwerk* was if anything louder than the *Hoofdwerk* (Great) — a complete refutation of the current concept in England and even the USA, of a soft, innocuous Choir-organ division with a few 'synthetics' to ape the 'Baroque' so-called — and of course the boldness arose largely from the prominent position of the case at the base of the organ-structure. The Prestants, Flutes and Quintadenas could be quite beefy, but were acoustically matched most agreeably to their surroundings. The organ cases, both here and at the New Church, were a perfect joy to behold, and were a perfect expression of their internal content: one could see at a glance the number of manuals, framed, so to speak, by the majestic Pedal towers. Susi Jeans more than once said that the builders of this period had no truck with the idea of a *Werkprinzip*: I agree that they did not talk or write about it, but here it was plainly visible. Actions speak louder than words! (Plate XIII)

I preferred the sound of the New Church *Rugwerk* with its flute-mutation series, a little more French in character than that of the Old Church, as comparison will show:

NEW CHURCH (1650-70)		OLD CHURCH (1724-39)	
Praestant	8	Praestant	8
Octaaf	4	Octaaf	4
Octaaf	2	Quint	2⅔
Quartane II	2⅔	Octaaf	2
Mixtuur III-VI	2	Mixtuur V-VIII	2
Sesquialtera II	2⅔	Scherp IV-VI	1⅓
Holpijp	8	Sesquialtera II-IV	2⅔
Quintadena	8	Roerfluit	8
Openfluit	4	Quintadena	8
Quintfluit	2⅔	Gemshoorn	4
Spitsfluit	2	Woudfluit	2
Quintfluit	1⅓	Cornet V	8
Cornet V	8	Carillon (modern) III-IV	⅖
Trompet	8	Trompet	8
		Dulciaan	8

Of course, all actions were mechanical-tracker, and the key-touch universally *rather heavy*, the *Rugwerk* usually lightest. Coupled manuals in a Grand-Pleno called for relaxed weight and strong fingers!

Our next joint excursion was to the celebrated Schnitger-rebuilt organ at St. Laurens, Alkmaar, just restored (1949) by D. A. Flentrop, who met us at the station. Being invited to try the Prestants (8-feet), of which there was one to each manual — *Hoofdwerk, Rugwerk, Bovenwerk* — I noted their different sonority, but without as yet digesting what I heard. Later we went down into the long church while other members of our party played: and again Robert pointed out the astonishing scintillating brilliance and 'sharpness' of the Scherps and Cimbels — there were two of the latter, of identical composition

PLATE XIII *Oude Kerk, Amsterdam. Organ by Christian Vater, 1726, casework designed by Juriaan Westerman.*

(containing the Tierce), one on the *Bovenwerk*, and the other on the *Rugwerk*, with ranks 38, 40, 43, at C. One noted, moreover, the generally distinguished sonority of this instrument in its large and imposing west-end case designed by the architect, van Campen (as was that of the New Church, Amsterdam).

Robert Noehren said, as we left, that this was as fine an instrument as that at Notre-Dame, Paris, to which I agreed: but this remark was received with marked, if amused, disapproval by our Dutch hosts. (It was still some years later that I was able to appreciate their reaction.)

Mr. Flentrop wanted to take us to see some of his own organs — Noehren was frankly disinclined, having come expressly to study *old* instruments, and some of the modern Dutch work was even more unworthy than some of their so-called restorations. However, it was impossible to decline without positive rudeness, so we went. The smallest and best of three which we saw was at Driebergen (1948), a 3-manual of 21 speaking-stops with minimal casework but a *Rugwerk* and a Swell: mechanical action throughout, of course. Specification:

HOOFDWERK		*ZWELWERK*	
Prestant	8	Baarpijp	8
Holpijp	8	Gamba	8
Octaaf	4	Koppelfluit	4
Fluit gedekt	4	Openfluit	2
Mixtuur IV-VI	2	Sesquialter (treble)	II
		Trompet	8
RUGWERK		*PEDAAL*	
Quintadeen	8	Subbas	16
Roerfluit	4	Prestant	8
Octaaf	2	Octaaf	4
Scherp IV	1	Ruispijp III	2⅔
Dulciaan	8	Cinck (reed)	2

Noehren played the Bach big G minor Fugue with the very simple Pleno registration on two manuals (*Hw* and *Rw*). We were amazed: the clarity was remarkable, yet everything harmonised. "See how you can hear the music," he cried, as he repeated the famous last entries of the fugue subject with their compelling dissonances in the inner voices: it was *extremely* good, and the touch most sensitive, every device of articulation and phrasing came out crystal-clear.

On our way home I showed my RFH specification to Flentrop, who discussed it there and then with the Dutch organist, Cor Kroonenberg, who had come with us. As might be expected (with hindsight) they at once pounced upon the Choir and Solo divisions and their Romantic flabbiness with disapproving gestures which set me thinking once more. During my visit I had not heard a single modern 'string' stop, and only two Swells, both by Flentrop — and *had not missed them:* they seemed musically irrelevant. Of course, most of the music played had been Bach's, or very effectively improvised in a modern idiom.

Apart from a visit to the large 3-manual Bätz organ in the Utrecht Dom — a proof that fine Dutch baroque organs were still being built in the 1830s — my last experience was crucial. Noehren had left, and had warned me of many old organs which had been cleaned and partially revoiced since World War II, losing their distinguished character in the process. As a fine intact survival, he instanced the *Rugwerk* division (only) at the New Church in the Hague, and I gained access to it and played it at length. I drew the (*Rugwerk*) Prestant 8-feet and played single notes, listening intently. What *was* it that made it so distinguished, as it certainly was? Would it give up its secret? I listened again and again but could get no further — I had been told that most of the fluework in these organs had un-nicked languids, or nearly so, and of course I had never encountered this phenomenon in England: 'nicking' was done as a matter of course (just as bass reed-tongues were all weighted) "to remove speech-defects" [*sic*]. Noehren had told me that the tone of the un-nicked pipe had much greater vitality owing to the retention of the natural 'attack' sound of the airstream on the upper lip as well as many high partial-tones; and also that the speech could be made 'quicker'. Well, I sat and listened in near desperation: but in fact I was unconsciously making a valuable mental photograph which could be used to identify and match when the appropriate time arrived.

In general, apart from the wide Nazards and 2-foot stops, two other particular sonorities much impressed me — they were nearly always found together in the *Bovenwerk*: namely, Baarpijp and Quintadena 8-feet. The former was a species of Spitzflute with a taper (inwards towards the top) varying from ⅔ to ½ and generally a wide scale (around +2 to +5 or +6 HT over Normal). The other was a stopped rank of narrow scale, (± 10 to 14 HT *under* Normal) with a wide mouth cut low and voiced somewhat 'slow' to prevent its actually overblowing, so that it gave the fundamental and its own 1st harmonic (the 12th) in equal strength. The particular attack produced in these un-nicked pipes on 'full wind' gave them immense value in delineating contrapuntal voices especially in bass and tenor registers, performing a like function with the keen-toned plucked strings of a spinet or harpsichord in the same musical range. In addition to being beautiful solo stops, the Baarpijp and Quintadena could provide useful alternative foundations for a Mixture or mutational combination; they would also go well together, even with the addition of the 8-foot Prestant, largely because of their widely differentiated scale progressions.

Naturally, on my return to London, I went straight to the Oratory organ: the Diapason chorus sounded disappointingly devitalised, and in every sense lacked *lustre* compared with what I had been hearing. The following months were spent in vainly trying to improve this; but there were too many obstacles — the pipes were heavily nicked, mouths too high, tin-content of the pipe-metal too low, etc, etc.

Turning once again to the South Bank scheme, I could at once see room for improvement, and I obtained leave to incorporate new ideas, mainly in the design of the Positive and Choir divisions. Flentrop and Noehren had both given me some Dutch scale-measurements, of which I made what use I could. (Flentrop in a subsequent letter impressed on me that pipe-scales were only one important detail: the whole conception of an organ, the design and placement of soundboards, the wind arrangements, the mechanical action, the casework, must *all* be right. However, he agreed to look at my scale-scheme: his comment on this was that too many of the scales "went the same way", ie, followed the same progression — more food for thought!) I had now produced the following amended stop-list (the scales are indicated in Figure 11):

Figure 11

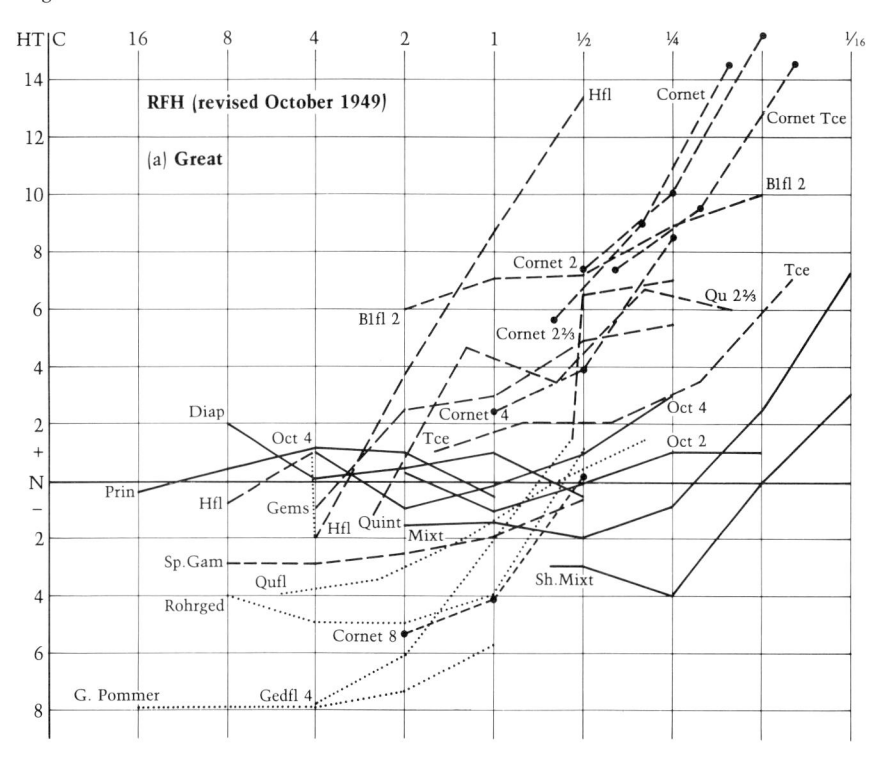

(b) **Positive**

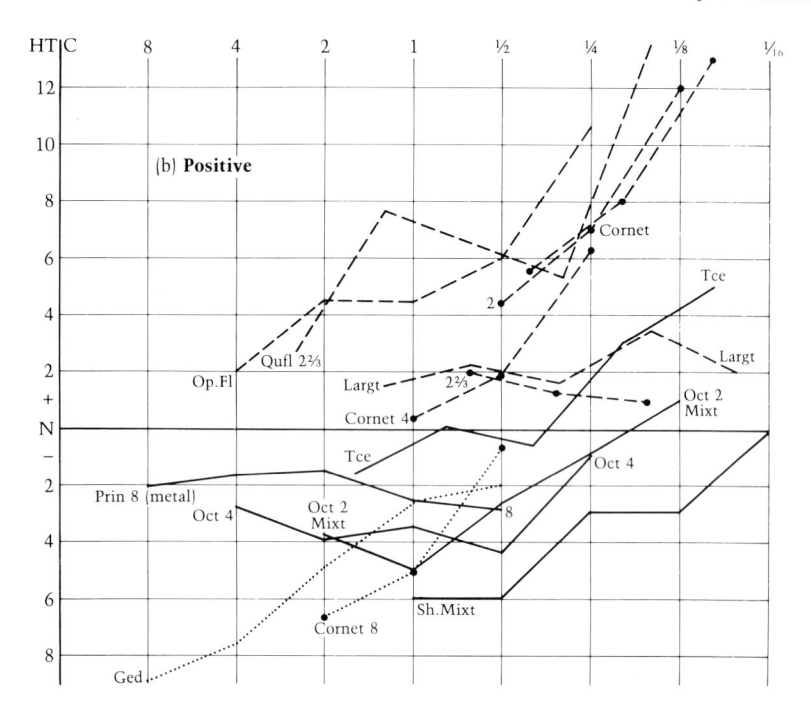

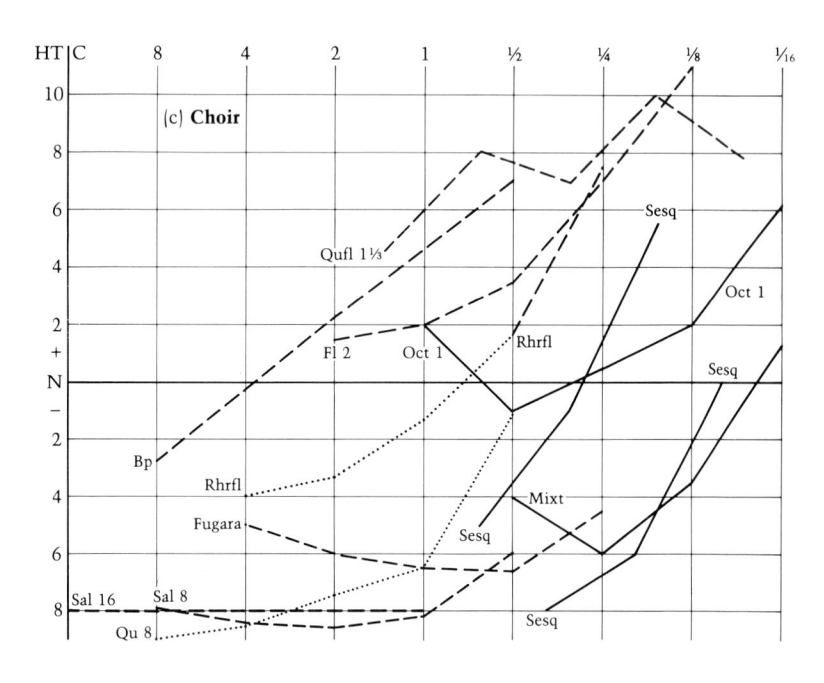

(c) **Choir**

ILLUMINATION

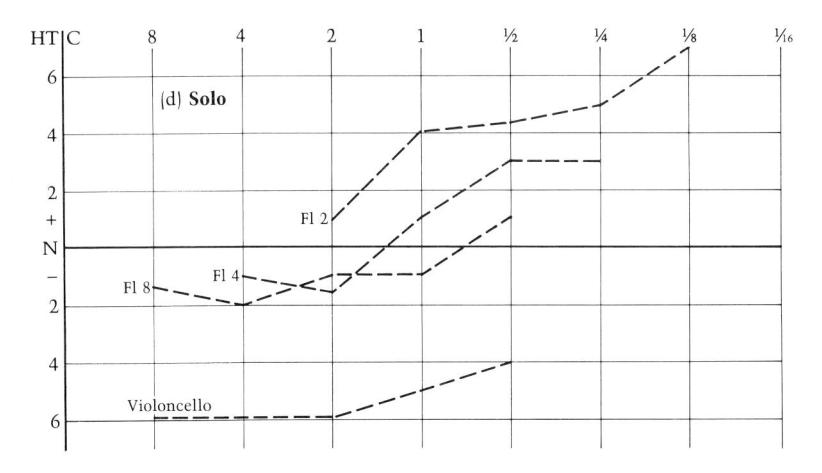

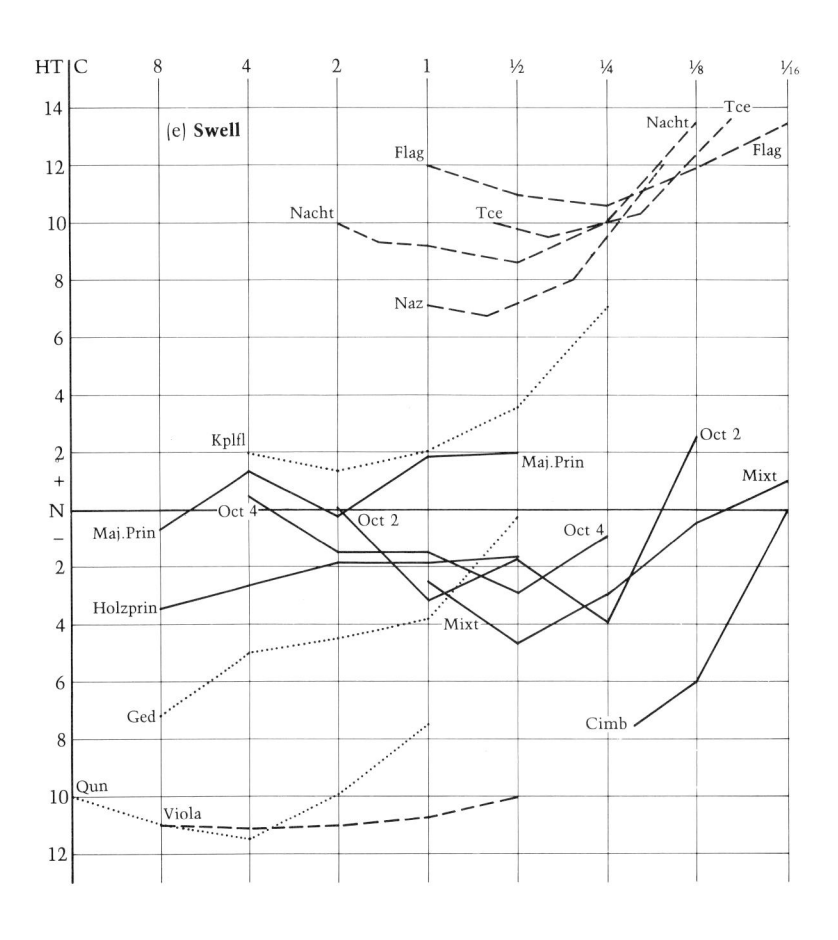

(d) **Solo**

(e) **Swell**

(f) **Pedal**

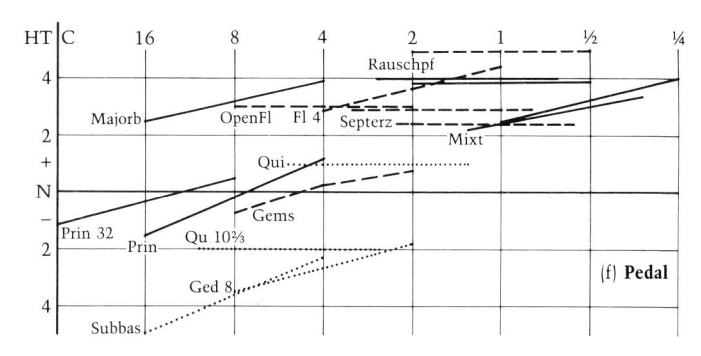

GREAT ORGAN (3½-inch wind)
1. Prestant — 16
2. Bourdon — 16 (24 wood)
3. Diapason — 8
4. Flûte harmonique — 8
5. Spitzgamba — 8 (conical)
6. Bourdon — 8 (12 wood)
7. Quintflute — 5⅓
8. Octave — 4
9. Gemshorn — 4 (conical)
10. Gedacktflute — 4
11. Quint — 2⅔ (conical)
12. Octave — 2
13. Blockflute — 2
14. Tierce — 1³/₅ (wide-scale)
15. Mixture — V (15, 19, 22, 26, 29)
16. Scharf — IV (26, 29, 33, 36)
17. Cornet (middle c) — V (1, 8, 12, 15, 17)
18. Bombarde — 16
19. Trumpet — 8
20. Clarion — 4

Reeds and Cornet on Solo

SWELL ORGAN (3½- and 4-inch wind)
21. Quintadena — 16 (24 wood)
22. Majorprincipal — 8 (²/₇ mouths)
23. Holzprincipal — 8 (wood)
24. Rohrgedackt — 8
25. Viole de gambe — 8
26. Voix célestes — 8 (from A)
27. Octave — 4
28. Koppelflute — 4
29. Nazard (from f) — 2⅔ (conical)

30	Octave	2
31	Nachthorn	2
32	Tierce (from f)	1³/₅
33	Flageolet	1
34	Mixture	IV-VI (22, 26, 29, 33)
35	Zimbel	III (38, 40, 43)
36	Hautbois	8
37	Voix humaine	8
	Tremulant	
38	Bombarde	16
39	Trumpet	8
40	Clarion	4

Octave (16-, 8- and 4-foot stops only)

POSITIVE ORGAN (2¾-inch wind)

41	Prestant	8
42	Gedackt	8
43	Prestant	4
44	Openflute	4
45	Quintflute	2⅔
46	Octave	2
47	Tierce	1³/₅
48	Larigot	1⅓
49	Cornet (middle c)	V (1, 8, 12, 15, 17)
50	Mixture	V (15, 19, 22, 26, 29)
51	Scharf	V (22, 26, 29, 33, 36)
52	Trumpet	8
53	Regal	8

CHOIR ORGAN (3¼-inches flue, 3¾-inches reed) (enclosed)

54	Salicional	16 (slight taper)
55	Barpyp	8 (conical)
56	Quintadena	8
57	Salicional	8 (conical)
58	Unda maris	8 (from A), (conical)
59	Fugara	4
60	Rohrflute	4
61	Waldflute	2 (conical)
62	Quintflute	1⅓
63	Sifflöte	1
64	Sesquialtera	II (26, 31: 19, 24: 12, 17)
65	Mixture	IV (29, 33, 36, 40)
66	Dulzian	16
67	Cromorne	8
	Tremulant	

Octave (16- and 8-foot stops only)
Choir on Solo

SOLO ORGAN (enclosed)
(4-inches flue, 7-inches trumpets, 12-inches wind, horn)

68	Flûte majeure	8
69	Violoncello	8
70	Violes célestes CC	8
71	Flûte harmonique	4
72	Piccolo	2
73	Corno di bassetto	8
74	Orchestral oboe	8
	Tremulant	
75	Trompette harmonique	8
76	Clairon harmonique	4
77	French horn	8

PEDAL ORGAN (3-, 4- and 4½-inches wind)

78	Prestant	32 (5 wood, bearded: 7 zinc, rest from No. 1)
79	Majorbass	16 (wood)
80	Prestant	16
81	Sub bass	16 (stopped wood)
82	Salicional	16 (Choir, No. 54)
83	Quintadena	16 (Swell, No. 21)
84	Quintflute	10⅔ (stopped, 17 wood)
85	Openflute	8
86	Gemshorn	8
87	Rohrgedackt	8 (metal, chimneys)
88	Quintadena	8 (Swell, No. 21)
89	Openflute	4
90	Nachthorn	2
91	Sesquialtera	II (12 17)
92	Septième	$2^{2/7}$
93	Rauschpfeife	II (19 22)
94	Mixture	IV (26 29 33 36)
95	Bombarde	32 (20 from No. 96)
96	Bombarde	16
97	Dulzian	16 (Choir, No. 66)
98	Trumpet	8
99	Regal	8 (Positive, No. 53)
100	Clarion	4
101	Regal	4 (extension, No. 99)
102	Kornett (reed)	2

Unison couplers over the whole organ, as before: full supply of combination pistons, all instantly adjustable on the capture system.

This list was accepted by Harrisons' as the basis of a brochure printed later in 1949. Although it immediately provoked a storm of criticism from the Establishment, they refused to be alarmed thereby but stood firm behind what they had undertaken, though naturally they publicly placed the responsibility on my shoulders. Sad to relate, it was *I* who (in addition to the Architect's design team) from then on made life really difficult for them.

For of course this last stop-list was still conceived largely in a vacuum, since no decision had emerged as to the organ's front design. In fact, Harrison was already beginning to moot the idea of installing a total grille behind which the organ could be constructed on "normal good organ-building lines", everything to stand where most generally convenient, for access, for maintenance, for structural stability. In fairness, it must be added that he had accepted the need for some 'terracing' of the divisions, so as to provide some sound-reflecting 'backing' for all the unenclosed pipework.

I myself now took up firmly an idea put forward by Dom Bédos [30], namely, that when conditions were unfavourable for construction of a *Rückpositiv*, the Positive could be placed in sideways opposition to the Great: indeed, in the present circumstances this was a godsend; the main Pedal soundboards could stand in the centre with Great and Positive on either side. (This also fitted in with a further new conception of the Architects, incorporating large (16-foot) Pedal pipes as a central 'frontispiece': but after the setting up of a full-size 'mock-up' with some old pipes at Durham, they became undecided as to its suitability, and it was dropped until too late to be revived. This added further cogency to the idea of the total grille.)

The revised stop-list was now more 'eclectic' than ever — a vaguely Dutch flavour pervaded the Choir division, which nevertheless (with hindsight) still had no very clear structure or even *raison d'être*, apart from the presence of the mild undulants and the enclosed reeds. True, it was additionally playable from the Solo manual (perpetuating theoretically Donald Harrison's American ideas already incorporated in the Oratory and Buckfast schemes) but not in any way relating to the actual Solo division when added to it. The Solo section was still as (*c* 1930) Anglo-American as could be: the Positive now rather more Dutch in style than French or German.

At this point another *'deus ex machina'* arrived, in the form of a letter from Susi Jeans: her neo-baroque organ (tracker action by Norman & Beard, pipes by Eule of Bautzen) was due for some refurbishing at the hands of its original voicer, the genial Fritz Abend, who was coming for this purpose from Lich, Oberhessen, after Christmas 1949. Abend was known as an authority on Silbermann, and was working as a 'free-lance' as well as with the firm of Förster and Nicolaus (who had just completed a new 3-manual organ for Helmut Walcha's church in Frankfurt). She felt sure that at her instigation he would help me by 'vetting' the pipe-scales and other details for the new organ: this, in fact, he gratuitously consented to do.

Cuthbert Harrison was interested, and a meeting between us all was tentatively planned. A helpful turn in this direction arose from Susi's wish to acquire a Sesquialtera: there would be difficulty at that time in importing new tin pipes from Germany, and I suggested that Harrisons' be asked to make them, with the *arrière-pensée* that Abend might then go to Durham to voice them, within sight and earshot of their chief voicer, (the late) Thomas Austin, and possibly demonstrate his methods additionally on one or more specially made test-pipes for the South Bank organ.

This was all arranged and agreed, and we journeyed North. As might have been expected with the exercise of a little imagination, in actual fact Mr. Austin went his own way and paid little or no attention to Abend's activities — beyond extending the normal common courtesies!

Abend voiced a 1-foot Principal pipe for me — quickly dealing with the mouth-height, foothole, languid and flue: the pipe, 'chirped' very musically (and, as it were, *in German*!). "*Natur*," said Mr. Abend with obvious satisfaction — it was a well-made pipe. This impressed on me an idea which I had *met* already but which until then had not really sunk in: the pipework of a good organ must be so scaled and constructed as to enable every individual pipe to speak its optimum natural, 'un-retouched' tone in its surroundings or ambience. Of course, there was room for some begging of the question here — the voicer must set the wind-pressure and adjust the cut-up and speech to suit local circumstances: but (and a big BUT), with un-nicked pipes speaking naturally on 'full wind' and with unfaked voicing, the actual margin of adjustment is very restricted; thus the scaling and mouthing were of paramount importance. Any attempt to 'fiddle' the voicing (eg, by giving superimposed 'fluty' tone to principal-scale pipes — through the use of nicks and high-cut upperlips — or 'diapason' (principal) tone to pipes of wide flute scale) could only produce a characterless hybrid sonority, typified in the vast majority of modern English 'Clarabellas' and diapasons too. True flute character could only properly result from proper wide scaling with appropriate mouth-width and height, so that good flute tone was actually the optimum natural uninhibited speech of the pipes in the ambience in which they were set. Likewise, good Principal sonority could only result from true principal-scale, usually narrower than Normal, with only some 4 HT plus or minus as tolerance, made with normal mouths, about a quarter of the circumference in width, and cut up about a quarter to two-sevenths of the width, winded by a generous foothole and narrowish flue — "*NATUR!*" Of all this, more anon.

I did not despair of Mr. Austin: a few weeks later I got him to come to Broadcasting House in London to listen to a playback of Geraint Jones's playing on the restored Schnitger organ at Steinkirchen. But despite the low wind-pressure known to exist in that organ (64 millimetres Water Gauge) and the appropriately moderate scales of the Principals, he found the tone *"very hard"*! (Of course a recording was not — never is — a fair test: his reaction might have been different had we heard the organ itself in the church: though it must be added that Geraint, who had gone there half-expecting Baroque *sweetness*, told me later that he had been surprised to find the Pleno "bloody loud"!)

A little later still, I visited Mr. Austin (by invitation) at a south-London church where he was 'finishing' a new Harrison & Harrison organ. He was regulating an 8-foot Gamba (or perhaps a Salicional). Holding treble e, he proceeded *legatissimo* to f, and was only finally satisfied when the upper pipe 'followed' perfectly and exactly, aided by various voicing procedures. The whole stop? It sounded smooth and in a way sweet; but musically speaking, characterless. Every vestige of 'personality' had been scrupulously removed: it was absolutely free of harshness! This in any case was contrary to nature: in a real musical instrument, whether string or wind, and even when modern makers have *tried* to 'smooth them out', the timbre alters completely as one plays through its tonal range: consider the flute, clarinet, bassoon, trombone, viola, for instance, when played straightforwardly, *p*, *mf* or *f*. Hence the utter futility of trying to give an organ-stop a uniform tone-colour throughout its compass — but this was, at the time, the unquestioned ideal of a *perfectionist* voicer.

So I knew we were set for a difficult course!

My reaction to Dirk Flentrop's opinion of my proposed scale-progressions had been to introduce some deviations, especially in the Principals, largely based on Professor Klotz's observations on Schnitger practice — but again, rather theoretically; we had no pipes to play with: *that* was what I needed! The scale-plan drawn in Figure 11 is what I showed to Mr. Abend.

His general opinion was that the Principals were too wide — (What? Even for a rather 'dry' modern hall holding 3,000? But yes: there were limits which must not be exceeded) — particularly in the tenor and bass, where he suggested one or two variations.

Moreover, he found the Positive division too repetitive of the Great plan, and he proposed a quasi-Brustwerk type, to contain the following flue-stops (centrally placed, of course):

Gedackt	8	(medium scale)
Quintadena	8	(narrow scale)
Principal	4	(narrow scale)
Spitzflute	4	(medium scale — tapered ½)
Quint	2⅔	(narrow scale)
Octave	2	(narrow scale)
Octave	1	(narrow scale)
Tertian	II	(17, 19) (narrow bass, wide treble)
Mixture (from 26th)		(narrow)

(Scale graph as in Figure 12)

He wanted this section to be sprightly, bright, energetic, not too solid but prominently commanding attention: all else as before.

I dallied with this for a while, but was not finally convinced that it would do — it did not promise to combine well with the Choir, and it seemed too far differentiated from the Great with its 16-foot Prestant.

Meanwhile, through Dr. Klotz's account of the St. Marie organ at Bernau, and the publication of details of the organ in the village church at Mittelkirchen, I became aware of two of Arp Schnitger's *Brustwerk* schemes, and I was greatly taken with them: basically they were identical:

BERNAU			MITTELKIRCHEN		
Gedackt	8	(older)	Quintadena	8	
Rohrflute	4	(older)	Principal	4	
Quint	2⅔	(older)	Blockflute (wood)	4	
Octave	2	(older)	Octave	2	
Octave	1	(older)	Quint	1⅓	
Tertian (17, 19)	II	(narrow-scale)	Octave	1	
Mixture	IV		Sesquialtera	II	(26, 31: 19, 24: 12, 17)
Hautbois	8		Mixture	III	(29, 33, 36)
			Krumhorn	8	

The Mittelkirchen scheme struck me as exactly right for the foundation of our *Choir* division: I also saw the need to revise and refine the existing Positive design, increasing its tonal scope, dovetailing it into the Choir, as well as setting it into greater contrast with the Great. The little Carillon II-III (now replacing the redundant second Cornet V) could add a charmingly piquant, spicy brilliance

Figure 12

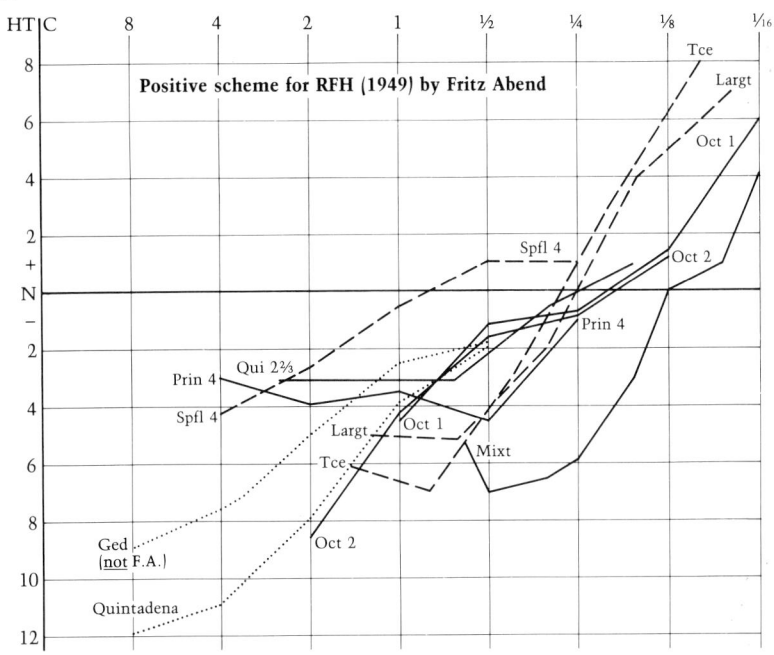

[Figure: Positive scheme for RFH (1949) by Fritz Abend — chart with horizontal axis labeled HT|C, 8, 4, 2, 1, ½, ¼, ⅛, ¹⁄₁₆ and vertical axis from +8 to −12 around N. Labels on curves include: Tce, Largt, Oct 1, Spfl 4, Oct 2, Prin 4, Qui 2⅔, Prin 4, Spfl 4, Largt, Oct 1, Tce, Mixt, Ged (not F.A.), Oct 2, Quintadena.]

reminiscent of both nineteenth-century Dutch (Amsterdam, Old Church; Gouda, St. Jan) and Cavaillé-Coll examples, also combining well in the Pleno with a bright little Trumpet 8-feet to be enclosed, with the Dulzian, at the front of the *Choir* box. After further slight modification, the revised stop-list was published in a Council memorandum in the Spring of 1950. Now Great, Positive, Swell, Choir and Pedal each had a complete Principal-chorus of characteristic pitch, with appropriate allocation of wide-chorus stops and reeds — the whole neatly interlocking: only the Solo section remained totally 'Romantic'.

Other subtle but significant changes included the strengthening of the Principal family: in the Great by the addition of another 8-foot Principal (tin) replacing the Spitzgamba; in the Pedal by dropping the Openflutes in favour of Principal sonority — Octave 8- and 4-feet, and by lowering the pitch of the Pedal Mixtures; also the Tierce was separated from the Nazard 5⅓ feet, but combined with the Septième to make a 'Septerz II'. All these changes were in the first instance suggested by Don Harrison, who was always most generous with his advice, "for the good of the cause". The 4-foot flutes on Choir and Positive were also transposed, and the Positive 2-feet became a Spitzflute which contrasted charmingly with the Blockflute on the Great. This left the main tonal structure as follows:

GREAT ORGAN

Principal	16
Gedacktpommer	16
Diapason	8
Principal (tin)	8
Flûte harmonique	8
Rohrgedackt	8
Quintflute (stopped)	5⅓
Octave	4
Gemshorn (conical)	4
Gedacktflute	4
Quint (principal)	2⅔
Superoctave	2
Blockflute	2
Tierce (principal)	1³/₅
Mixture V	2
Scharf IV	⅔
Cornet (middle c) V	8
Bombarde	16
Trumpet	8
Clarion	4

SWELL ORGAN (enclosed)

Quintadena (metal)	16
Scharfprincipal	8
Barpyp (conical)	8
Quintadena	8
Viola	8
Celeste (CC)	8
Principal	4
Koppelflute	4
Nazard (conical)	2⅔
Octave	2
Nachthorn	2
Tierce (from f) (wide)	1³/₅
Flageolet (wide)	1
Mixture IV-VI	1
Cymbel III	⅕
Bombarde	16
Trumpet	8
Hautbois	8
Vox humana	8
Clarion	4
Tremulant	

POSITIVE ORGAN

Principal	8
Gedackt	8
Quintadena	8
Octave	4
Rohrflute	4
Rohrnazard	2⅔
Spitzflute	2
Tierce (wide)	1³/₅
Larigot (wide)	1⅓
Mixture V	2
Scharf V	1
Carillon II-III	½
Trumpet (choir box)	8
Dulzian (choir box)	8
Tremulant	

PEDAL ORGAN

Principal (ext from Great)	32
Majorbass (wood)	16
Principal	16
Sub bass (wood)	16
Dulciana (from Choir)	16
Quintadena (from Swell)	16
Quintflute (stopped metal)	10⅔
Octavebass	8
Gedackt (stopped metal)	8
Quintadena (from Swell 16 ft)	8
Nazard (conical)	5⅓
Superoctave (tin)	4
Spitzflute (conical)	4
Nachthorn	2
Septerz II	3¹/₅, 2²/₇
Mixture IV	5⅓
Scharf III	2
Bombarde (extension)	32
Bombarde	16
Dulzian (from Positive, ext)	16
Trumpet	8
Cromorne (from Choir)	8
Clarion	4
Schalmei (from Choir)	4
Cornett (reed)	2

CHOIR ORGAN (enclosed)	
Dulciana	16
Holzprincipal (wood)	8
Holzgedackt (wood)	8
Salicional (conical)	8
Unda maris (conical)	8
Spitzoctave (conical)	4
Openflute	4
Principal	2
Quint (narrow)	1⅓
Octave	1
Sesquialtera II	⅔
Mixture IV	½
Cromorne	8
Schalmei	4
Tremulant	

A notably organised feature here was the alternation of wide- and narrow-scale stops, especially among the mutations, as, for example, the wide Flageolet (Swell) versus the narrow Octave (Choir), the Principal Quint and Tierce (Great) against the wide Nazards and Tierces (Swell and Positive) and the narrow Sesquialtera (Choir), etc.

There were two significant happenings in the Spring of 1950: Cuthbert Harrison, the current head of the Durham firm, made the sagacious decision to come with me to Holland to see what it was all about; and the (still unfinished) organ at the Oratory was completely wrecked by fire. Without doubt there was an act of arson, which some attributed to my enemies in the organ world, others to *me*! I had certainly become very unhappy about the halting progress of the rebuilding: the new components for the console had never arrived, the scheme to put the unenclosed Solo division in the transept arch had foundered, and the soundboard was being crammed into the main case, already too deep and too full despite the recent discarding of the Bishop monster-scaled Open Wood 16-feet: and now compromises were being made in the siting of some Pedal pipes on small, scattered chests around the bottom of the organ. Worst of all, much of the older material was by now, frankly, so much *junk*. After the first shock of deprivation, I did frankly welcome the opportunity of clearing the decks, and the prospect of designing a new organ, largely paid for by the insurance claim. J. W. Walker & Sons were re-engaged, once the site was cleared: this was a considerable advantage since technical information gleaned during experiments could be passed about from one organ to another — Buckfast Abbey, The Oratory, and the Royal Festival Hall — for the benefit of all concerned. This development will be noted in a later chapter.

Harrison's visit to Holland with me was mutually profitable: he turned my pages and helped pull stops on the three large organs on which I made recordings for the BBC: thus he had a front-seat experience of registrational effects in the Baroque style of instruments. I learned later that he was deeply impressed by the fine ringing intonation of the Dutch flue choruses. When we went to Alkmaar, Dirk Flentrop met us, and took my breath away as I sat below in the church while he demonstrated the organ to Harrison upstairs, playing on the uncoupled *Pleno* of each of the three manuals: suddenly he added the manual couplers, and the enhanced output of the General *Tutti* was simply hair-raising, and proved all that Don Harrison had told me about the cumulative effect of many well-voiced but mild stops, skilfully arranged and scaled. (With hindsight I could now observe that not a little of this synthesis was due to the 'tone-cabinet' effect of the casework.) I had just received a copy of the Alkmaar scales, and set to work to study them in detail.

Flentrop had looked at my latest scale-plan for the Festival Hall, noting with some concern how often the Principal ranks still crossed the Normal line into Openflute territory. In his view a diameter of 145 millimetres was the practical maximum for 8-foot C in Dutch and German classical organ-building: he cited wider-scaled examples recently made by a French firm, with a concomitant flutiness and poor carrying power. (It is worth noting here that Cavaillé-Coll — like Father Willis — frequently employed wide Diapason scales; but — also like Father Willis — he slotted his pipes, thus imparting to them a kind of horny string-sonority which passed for Principal tone in the ensemble. Of course it was a hybrid which I rejected on principle, along with all other forms of 'superimposed voicing'.) Flentrop helped us further by presenting us with newly obtained copies of the scales and mouth-treatment of the Schnitger-rebuilt organ now in Cappel, an organ whose sound was well known to me through the many excellent recordings of Helmut Walcha. Here were shown very clearly the separate paths followed by the Principals *vis-à-vis* the wide- or flute-scales (see Figure 13). Upon my citing the quotation that much larger Principal scales (even wider than Normal) might be necessary in a very large or acoustically dead building, he replied that though the C pipe ideally should still not exceed 145 mm to 148 mm in diameter, the scale might widen rapidly towards the 2-foot pipe (middle c'), narrowing again towards the ½-foot pipe (c'''). However, the Schnitger Principal scales studied so far exhibited such variety that, like Don Harrison a few years previously, I despaired of getting much further on any such basis for the time being. It would seem simplest and best to adopt Harrison & Harrison's normal diapason scaling, reducing or increasing the same by one or more pipes — beginning, in other words, at D or B according to need, as Gottfried Silbermann was said to have done, and even using their modern voicing methods, as

ILLUMINATION

Figure 13

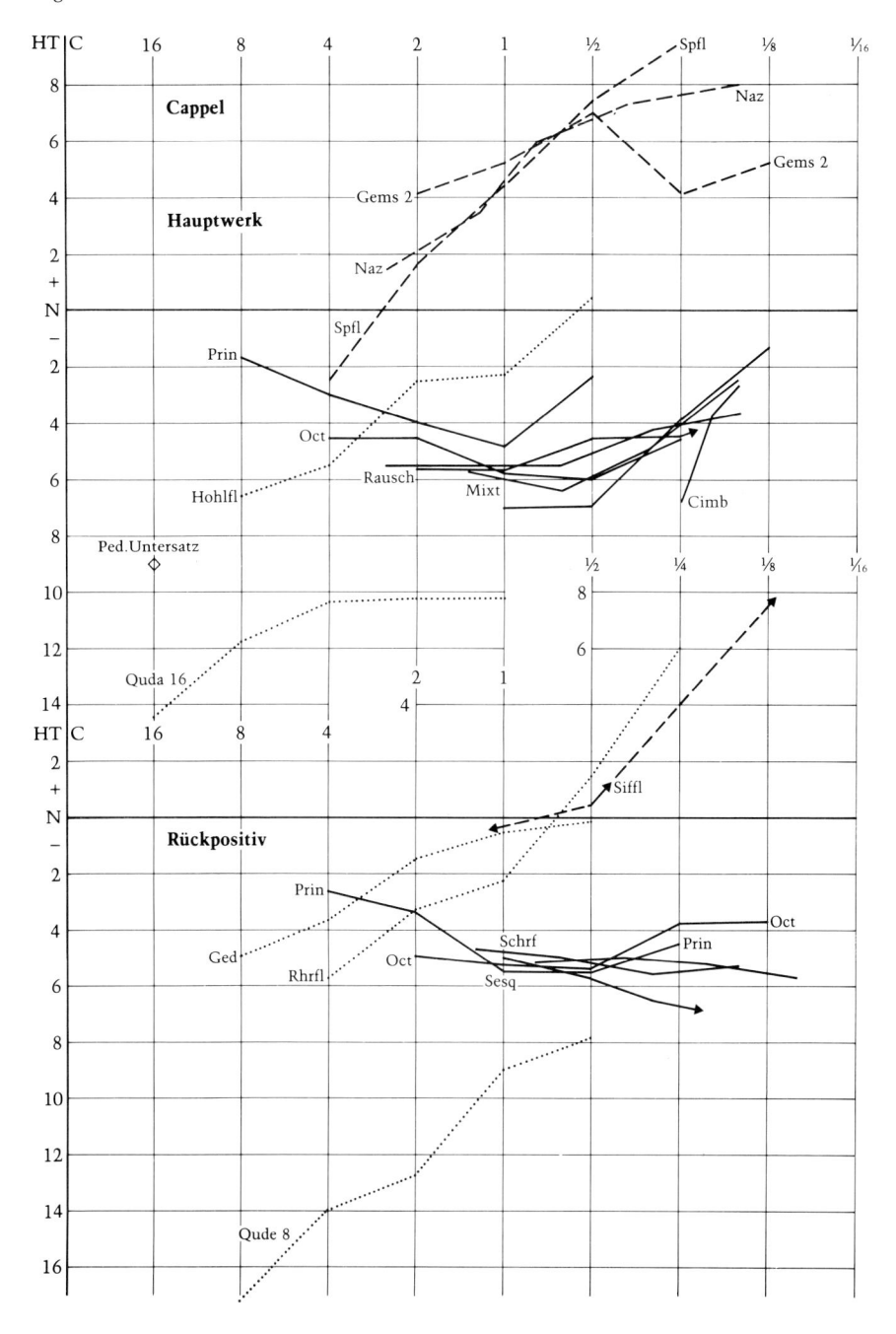

observed in their many existing organs. But no! I was sure this would not succeed: and the dilemma remained. If one opted for 'variability', where to begin? A prototype, a precedent, was surely needed as a starting point.

Of course there were English organ-builders who pooh-poohed the whole idea of variable scales: "unscientific" — or even more caustically, "due only to crude methods of pipe-making, and therefore accidental". In the case of Cappel, this view might appear to have some validity: all the Principal scales are (superficially) identical. Those of Alkmaar, however, show a subtlety which put it out of court. For instance, the scales of C (8-feet) and c''' (½-foot) of the unison Principals of *Hoofdwerk* and *Rugwerk* are identical — as Flentrop pointed out to us: but *between* these limits there is a deviation of from 1 to 3 HT, and this can not only be *heard*, it can also be justified, as will be shown later. (For the complete diagram of the Alkmaar scales, see Appendix B.)

However, the crowning evidence came from studying the scales of the Schnitger organs of Steinkirchen and Mittelkirchen, both moderate-sized 2-manual organs, and both incorporating earlier pipework. Though the progression of the Principals of these organs shows considerable deviation, each contains on its Hauptwerk a Rohrflöte 8-feet, and graphic comparison of them gives an interesting result which is plainly *not* accidental (Figure 14).

Figure 14

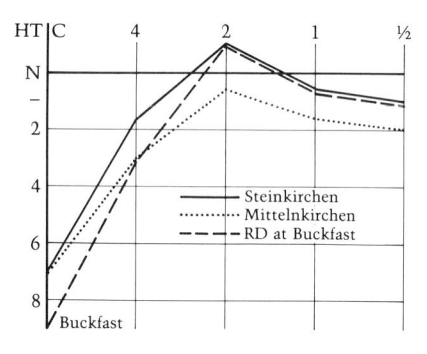

To prove the point, I specified a compromise between the two for a new stop for the Buckfast Abbey Great. The result was a most lovely stop which everyone praised. It was, of course, voiced with practically no nicking, on a pressure of 3¼ inches (82.5 mm), with feet fairly well open.

However, the variability issue was not as yet clear enough for me to be able to employ it creatively: as I wrote to Cuthbert Harrison, "I am rapidly coming to the conclusion that for present purposes, variable scales will only be desirable if arrived at aurally ..." and again, "It *must* come down, sooner or later, to 'fiddling with pipes', and I think the sooner the better..." I saw the futility of merely *prescribing* something for which the organ-builder would take no responsibility, and I felt the need to get down to discussion with the actual voicers, with whom I had not achieved any considerable contact as yet.

Meantime, another circumstance led me to modify the stop-list in such a way as actually to arrive at its final form which neatly eclipsed the 'eclectic' feature; it became thenceforth an integrated whole. This circumstance was the formulation of an official protest against the 'untraditional' character of the scheme — one eminent personality spoke of the unsuitability of a "delicately voiced Baroque organ" as orchestral backing for Elgar's *Enigma Variations* — and ridiculous comparisons were made with the obligatory use of a harpsichord for piano concertos! The lack of modern powerful Diapason stops and high-pressure reeds was what really alarmed these people. Well, they unconsciously raised a valid point: if the organ would at some time have to accompany massed singing, there *could* be some measure of doubt of its tonal adequacy. I decided to scrap the Romantic Solo Organ, substituting a fifth Pleno of Principal character. In spite of his loyal adherence to my design in the face of official opposition, even the organ-builder disagreed with this: but by this time it was the only option left open; the soundboards of all the other divisions were already cut out and about to be assembled.

SOLO ORGAN (enclosed)	
Diapason	8
Rohrflute	8
Octave	4
Waldflute (conical)	2
Rauschquint II	2⅔
Tertian II	1⅓, 1³⁄₅
Mixture VI	1⅓
Basset horn	8 (later changed to 16)
Harmonic Trumpet	8
Harmonic Clarion	4
Tremulant	

It surprises me that even nine years after the organ's final completion, a critic like Mr. Cecil Clutton described the inclusion of five complete manual diapason choruses as seeming "wasteful in a concert instrument" [31], whereas I, as a professional concert organist, know very well how this final modification clinched the organ's success in practice. (Other criticisms made by Mr. Clutton in the same context seem to me to reveal a lack of appreciation of the instrument's capabilities even if they contain a grain of truth here and there.)

At all events, the official Committee of the Council recognised that I had modified the specification to meet the objections of the critics, and gave their blessing to the amendment (not realising, or at least *countenancing*, the fact that these critics were thereby positively outraged!) So the new Solo division was adopted; but the scales remained an exasperatingly open question in an almost daily exchange of letters. Thus the atmosphere of uncertainty continued throughout much of 1950: indecision from the Architects, about the frontal design and even the console siting: indecision about the pipe-scales and voicing in relation to the supremely unknown actual acoustic properties of the hall, and even about details of the stop-list: while Cuthbert Harrison and his team who wanted to get on with the job were held in suspense. He wrote by turns approvingly, reprovingly, enthusiastically, despairingly: no sooner was some detail settled than I would have a change of mind as some unforeseen facet presented itself. One thing was increasingly clear to me, namely, the absolute necessity of trials of test-pipes, and as soon as possible actually in the hall, before the main Principal scales could be finalised. Only certain wide flutes were likely to be unaffected; moreover it *was* possible to establish certain maxima even for the Principal basses so that soundboards could be cut out and construction could begin.

And of course work was proceeding apace with the console — frame, keys, stops, pistons, etc: at least the *number* of all these was settled. On hearing that a new console for Manchester Cathedral was available for inspection at Durham, I went up at once to view the new curved (concave) stop-jambs: and thus I met Bob Wood, the Works Manager, and a man of the most exacting standards of craftsmanship and finish, down to the last detail. As soon as I opened my mouth he said, "Now don't make any hasty judgements; a great deal of trouble and thought has been put into this." It certainly looked very fine, but I persuaded him to slew round the whole jamb fractionally so that the ivory stop-heads all exactly faced the player. This was, and was acknowledged to be, an improvement: it was fixed there and then.

CHAPTER SEVEN

The Voicers: Study of Pipe-Scales (2)

My anterior and now simultaneous involvement with Buckfast Abbey was a great convenience: the interim specification there was settled by the beginning of 1950, and pipes and experiments were already being made by Walkers' with varying degrees of success. By the time I returned to Holland for a recital at Haarlem (August 1950) and yet another BBC recording in the Old Church, Amsterdam, they had received the order for a new organ for the Oratory: so on this visit I was accompanied by their Head Voicer, Walter Goodey, a youngish man of considerable practical experience, trained partly by Fred Eagle and W. C. Jones, the 'wizard' reed-voicer already mentioned. Not less significantly, Harrison sent his two men in the same bracket, Thomas Austin (diapasons and flutes) and Fred Howe (strings and reeds, also trained in his early days by Mr. Jones).

Being generally conservative in their outlook, Austin and Howe were not greatly impressed by what they heard: not so Mr. Goodey, who responded at once to this experience, and played enthusiastically on all the organs we visited: on his return home he spread what he had absorbed with the rapidity of an infectious disease, among his assistants, chief of whom at the time was Dennis F. Thurlow — notable Hi-Fi practitioner and founder of the Ruislip Gramophone Society: he was immediately thrilled by the lively tone obtainable from un-nicked pipes, and on the crest of this wave he soon mastered the art of voicing them, and did some excellent work for Buckfast and later at the Oratory. (Progress on those organs will be reported anon.)

Messrs Austin and Howe were rather put off by the uneven intonation (according to their standards) of the Dutch flue-ranks, old and new: well do I remember the ever-obliging Mr. Flentrop's pointing out to them that with un-nicked pipework on "full wind", ie, speech-regulated at the flue (or *embouchure*), every pipe was an individual, and one could not obtain the superlative smoothness from note to note which nicking and other such Romantic devices imparted to the speech of a whole stop. This was a price which had to be paid for greater musical liveliness in the tone: the pipes of a stop, like human beings, could be clearly recognisable as members of the same family in spite of small divergences in their individual features.

The initial difficulty in working with un-nicked pipes, and the bone of contention, was the presence of what was nicknamed the 'scrape' in their tone-production.

To put the clock back a little: under the influential patronage of the amateur connoisseur, Colonel George Dixon, Arthur Harrison's *beau idéal* of "first-class voicing" (often cited by Colonel Dixon in his writings) rested heavily on the elimination of 'harshness', which meant anything offensive to what was deemed a *cultivated ear*. For the louder registers this called for the nicking-tool, liberally applied even if with considerable *finesse* — there was nothing slip-shod about anything he touched — it also meant very heavy pipes, even leathered upper lips, for the fluework, and well-weighted tongues for the reeds. What was then lacking in vitality was compensated by wind-pressures raised to the required power. The firm's ultimate achievement in this direction was typified in the No.1 Diapason, the Pedal Open woods, and the unenclosed Tubas and Trombas at the Royal Albert Hall — reaching a decibel output more than equal to the largest orchestra's *fortississimo*, but so robbed of harmonic development as to become musically 'deadweight', and therefore only loud and rather vulgar in actual effect: but it was undeniably an example of "first-class voicing", in which great care had been expended to realise the ideal. In this context, the 'scrape' of un-nicked pipes would come out as highly offensive, especially to the ears of the identical voicer, even twenty years later: for the firm's style had changed but little in that time. (Admittedly their secondary diapasons and Solo trumpets sometimes reached a degree of stridency in the middle and treble ranges which contrasted sharply with the smoother sound of the more powerful stops: but in this case too, the stridency was 'controlled': wind-pressures were still inordinately high, and the resulting forced tonality had not very much to do with music, and *nothing at all* in common with the 'fresh' (if raw) sound of un-nicked pipes on copiously supplied low-pressure wind.

The 'scrape' (with hindsight) was largely due to insufficient cut-up of the upper lip and necessary 'slowing' of the speech to prevent overblowing to a harmonic: a nicked pipe needs a lower mouth so as to catch the partly dissipated energy of the 'fluted' windstream caused by the nicking: the windstream from an un-nicked flue is a simple 'ribbon' of air, aimed directly at the upper lip, and ideally split in half by same. If the languid edge is too high, more wind comes out of the pipe than goes in (causing 'slow' speech) : if too low, too much goes inwards (causing 'quick' speech, fluty tone and possibly overblowing).

Some of the 'scrape' can be removed by narrowing the flue (pressing the lower lip inwards towards the edge of the languid): but this may impoverish the tone and lead to instability of tuning; the only true remedy is, (having set the languid straight and on the low side, and having opened the flue to a moderate extent) to cut the upper lip up just far enough for the pipe not to overblow when put on its wind. Great care has to be taken not to overdo this, for once a shaving has been carved off, it cannot be replaced — the pipe will have to be remade and may then be too short for its pitch! Thus there is little margin of adjustment, and all must be done empirically according to experience. Any organ-builder who habitually cut up all the mouths of a rank of new pipes to a set proportion of the mouth-width before starting to voice them would find nickless voicing a bugbear, far too costly in time and labour to be commercially viable.

By the end of 1950 the Festival Hall auditorium, now roofed over, was sufficiently finished for acoustic tests to be on the way, and Cuthbert Harrison agreed to slip in with me beforehand with his voicers, equipped with a small electrically-blown soundboard (like a voicing-machine) on which we could try out a few well-chosen pipes, to hear what we should hear. The Director of the acoustics team was invited, out of courtesy, together with the indispensable Edwin Williams, and as a happy afterthought the violinist, Maurice Clare, with whom I was playing at the time. Memorably, we heard 2-foot and 1-foot C Principal pipes of substantial scale, and, I think, 2-foot and 1-foot C of the wide-scale Gemshorn ('*Baarpijp*') for the Swell. I was appalled: firstly, because it really did sound as though we were out in the open air (as had been predicted); the hall had no perceptible ambience whatever: and secondly, because the Gemshorn pipes had not the sound of a flute but rather that of a forced Principal. Worst of all, the 'scrape' seemed even more offensive than when heard at close quarters on the voicing-machine in the works. The Principal pipes sounded 'hungry' and rather unmusical: tolerable, perhaps, as a sharp-toned *Rückpositiv* type, but unacceptable as a Great stop. Only Maurice Clare's playing was a bright spot in that discouraging experience; but its near-naked beauty was entirely comprised in his instrument and his handling of it. The hall's 'reception' of it was a dead negative.

We had three casualties that night: two pipes, and, alas, one human being. Mr. Austin had not been well when we met in Holland, and while there I had hospitably and unwittingly fed him with all the good Dutch victuals best calculated to aggravate a heart-condition. On his way back from the hall to King's Cross he nearly collapsed, and was ordered to bed when he reached Durham. I never saw him again. God rest his soul, he had sterling qualities both as a man and a member of his craft! Henceforth Fred Howe took over the responsibility for the whole of the flue-voicing. Fred was a voicer of wide experience, and an immaculate craftsman. After his early training at Durham he had actually intended to work in America for Robert Hope-Jones: but this trip was abortive, and later he returned to Durham. In consultation with W. C. Jones (already mentioned) he was largely responsible for the voicing of the reeds at the Royal Albert Hall.

There was a subtle irony of fate in his selection to voice a large organ on lines so far removed from his normal practice: only more remarkable than his mastery of this new style was his swing back to habitual methods in his next organs, notably at Colston Hall, Bristol, and Harrow School.

Having assessed all that we had heard in the hall, we soon met again in Durham, as I was determined to settle the scale-variability question (and indeed the scaling as a whole) without delay. As a preliminary test I had asked for two sets of Principal pipes to be made, sounding c', c'' and c''', three pipes in a fairly wide scale, and the other three in a series about three pipes smaller. The three wide c's played as a series gave the impression of a stop of rather opaque tone-quality; the narrow ones (at the same loudness) sounded thinner and clearer. Taking now the wide c' and c''' in a series with the narrow c'', one did *not* get an impression of incongruity, but rather of a new stop with a particular tone-character: conversely, the narrow c' and c''' plus the wide c'' gave the impression of another stop of a different character, not just a haphazard collection of pipes; and this character was complementary to the first series.

This result demonstrated the advantages and feasibility of variable scaling within a Principal group: but much more was to follow. In his excellent small treatise, *Neuzeitlicher Orgelbau*, Paul Smets defines the Absolute Scale — the basic width necessary to give to 'Principal' sonority sufficient carrying power in a given building. In one reprint he cites the former English and American scaling practice as having flagrantly exceeded rational limits by making overwide Diapasons for this purpose — frequently the widest scales in an organ: and he quotes the more musical procedure — well known to the builders of the Baroque era — of employing 'acoustic coupling' of wide-scale *soft* flutes and narrow *penetrating* principals; the latter as it were 'energising' the former.

Arriving at exactly this most propitious moment, the complete scales of a fine Dutch baroque organ of 1839, sent to me by Dr. M. A. Vente, demonstrated not only the practical application of this principle, but also a practical example of widening the Principal scales at strategic points without forfeiting their character or vitiating the above basic philosophy. (An important feature of Baroque practice, especially of the Schnitger school, is the immense freedom in the scaling procedure: thus a wide-scale register may well be narrow at some point, and *vice-versa*!)

The 8-foot C pipe of the *Hoofdwerk* 'Octaaf 8-foot' — the unison diapason in fact — had a diameter of 130 mm: 4-foot c measured 80 mm; c' was 54 mm; c'' had 27 mm; c''' 17 mm. Figure 15 expresses this graphically, as usual in deviations from the Töpfer Normal, in

THE VOICERS: STUDY OF PIPE-SCALES II 139

Figure 15

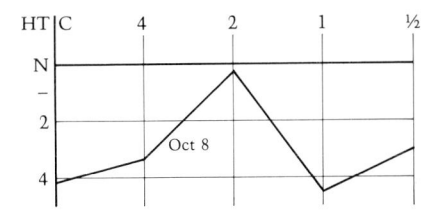

half-tones. The most significant phenomena here are the wide 2-foot c (with slightly narrower mouth), spelling a broad sonority, not overloud: and the narrow 1-foot c (with wider mouth), giving a 'keener', more singing tone. The tenor range was of moderate scale, with a good ¼ mouth.

The 8-foot Roerfluit had diameters of 138, 92, 54, 33 and 23 mm for the C's, and was thus mostly *wider* than the open 8-foot stop. (In contemporary English work, the opposite was universally true: the stopped ranks tending to become more and more *'lieblich'* as the diapasons became more inflated!) Even at Alkmaar (Franz Caspar Schnitger), the Gedackt ('Holpijp') and the Roerfluit were narrower than the Prestants, though the 8-foot Baarpijp had a generous wide scale; but at Cappel, the middle and upper ranges of the Gedackt of the *Rückpositiv* have the widest 8-foot scale in the organ, with the 8-foot Rohrflöte of the *Hauptwerk* coming a close second.

Figure 16

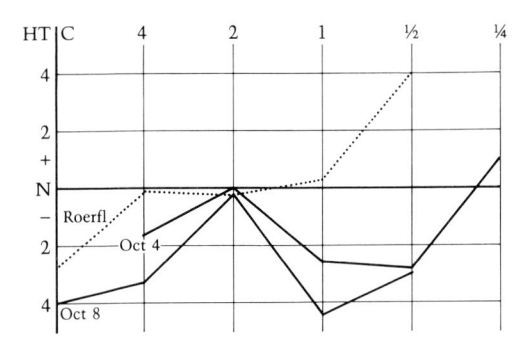

The 4-foot Octaaf (*Hoofdwerk*) had for C a scale of 86 mm, and for tenor c 54 mm (thus wider than the 8-foot tenor octave), but at middle c (c′) the diameter was 29 mm (thus narrowing in the Töpfer scale where the 8-foot is wider, and therefore imparting brilliance to the latter). At treble c (c′′) the 4-foot measured 17 mm (thus relatively wider where the 8-foot narrows, though still narrow enough to continue the brilliant sonority upwards into the treble). Figure 16 shows the mutual relationship of all these registers.

I therefore asked Harrisons' to make some more C test-pipes at Durham, the Opens following the compound-scaling of Figure 17 (black line), and the Stopped (with chimneys) at the wider scale (dotted line). Fred Howe voiced these on about 3¼ inches pressure, on 'full wind' (open foot-holes), and it became obvious that with the further addition of a wider-scaled 8-foot Diapason and a wider doubled rank of the 4-foot Octave (broken lines), the tonal output would be sufficient for a large Great Organ in normal circumstances, and the sonority crystal-clear. At the end of a full morning's work on these pipes, Fred described the experience as "thrilling", and he really had warmed to the task. In later months, as various snags began to appear, he and Cuthbert Harrison spent a number of evenings extending these researches when the works were closed and silent — all this was to bear abundant fruit later, for it is eventually *in the ear of the voicer* that the character of the organ takes shape (or fails to "get off the ground", as the case may be!) Of course I gave Fred all the scales and diagrams as they developed, and he much appreciated this visual guide, and said so.

Figure 17

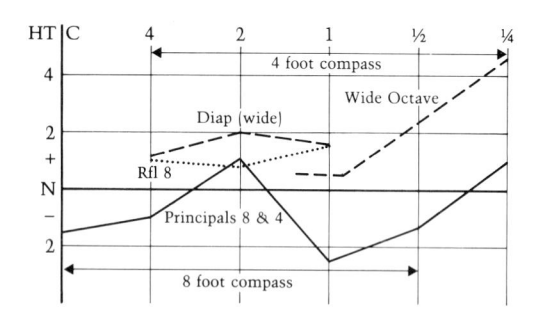

While deliberating on the scale of the Gemshorn 4-feet, I was very interested to find that in the Dutch instrument under review, this stop had almost exactly the same scale and scale-progression as the Spitzflöte 4-feet on the Great of the Cappel organ (allowance having been made for the pitch of the latter being one half-tone higher). The two scales are shown graphically in Figure 18, and it will be noted that they differ fundamentally from English nineteenth- and twentieth-century practice: the German and Dutch trebles were much wider, and from beginning at the bass end as something bordering on string tone, the register became more and more fluty towards the treble end. By the application of my established standard of *equality*, the top range was pure flute; and it is important to note that this progression from medium to very wide scale was entirely responsible for this treble fullness. I have encountered a modern imitation in which the voicer merely obtained flute *tone-colour* in the treble, probably by cutting the

Figure 18

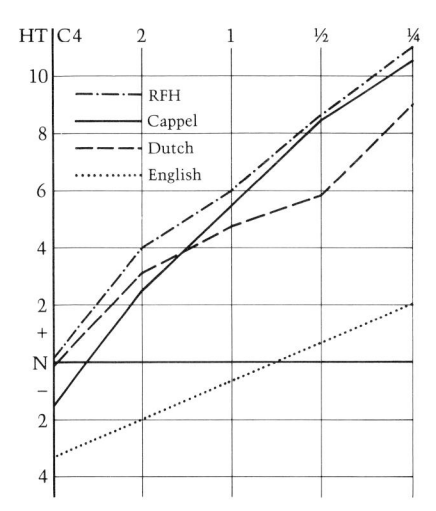

mouths higher, and certainly without the necessary widening of the scale: it failed miserably for want of amplitude, the tone was insubstantial, and did not carry.

The rest of the Great fluework developed logically from these beginnings — for good measure (as just noted) I had included a wide Principal scale for the second open 8-foot register ('Diapason'), and of course the second rank of the Octave 4-feet, which began at tenor g, was likewise wide, with narrower mouths and somewhat fluty intonation (what the Germans incorrectly termed an "Italian Principal"), coupling acoustically with the narrow, wider-mouthed first rank's more penetrating sonority, especially from the middle tenor range to the top. Figure 19 is a diagram of the main scales of the Great fluework. The very wide-scaled Cornet, V ranks, (Dom Bédos' *'Grand Cornet'*) has not been included, but is drawn separately in Figure 20.

The Swell was conceived as an *Oberwerk*, with sharp-toned 8-foot Principal (medium and narrow scale), *wide* Principal 4-feet and Octave 2-feet, both diminishing in scale and thus 'sharpening' in character, into the treble range where the 8-foot stop widened out (as at Alkmaar) and similarly capped by a fairly narrow sharp Mixture IV-VI ranks and a very high-pitched Tierce-Cimbel beginning 38, 40, 43. Alongside this there was to be a well-developed chorus of wide flutes (based on a wide Baarpijp and narrow Quintadena 8-feet) in true *Oberwerk* style, including also a wide *'Cornet décomposé'* — Quintadena 8-feet, Koppel flute 4-feet, conical Nazard 2⅔ feet, Openflute 2-feet, and Tierce 1³/₅ feet (the *Cornet de récit* of Dom Bédos) — and Flageolet 1-foot (very wide) which supplied the final ingredient for a Carillon of Cavaillé-Coll type. Figure 23 shows the Swell scales (see page 175).

Figure 19

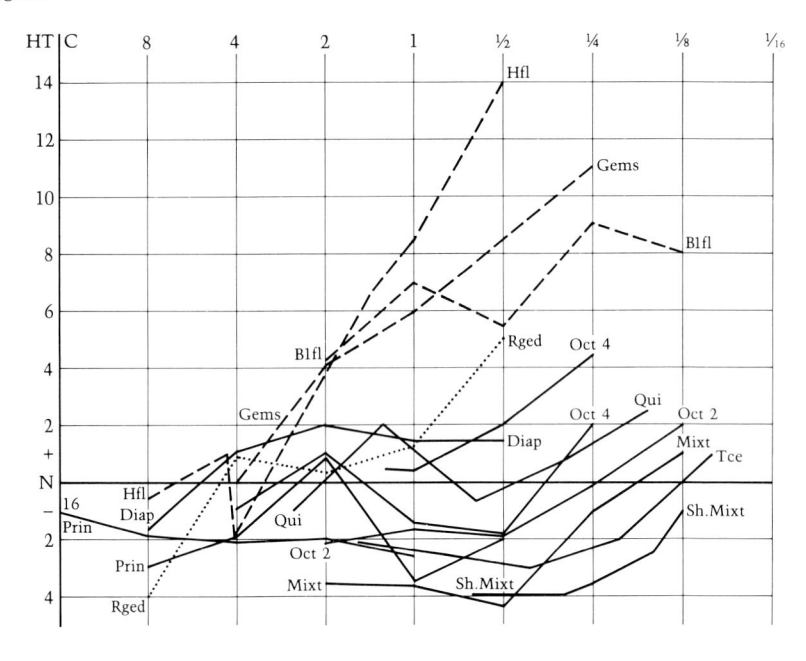

Figure 20

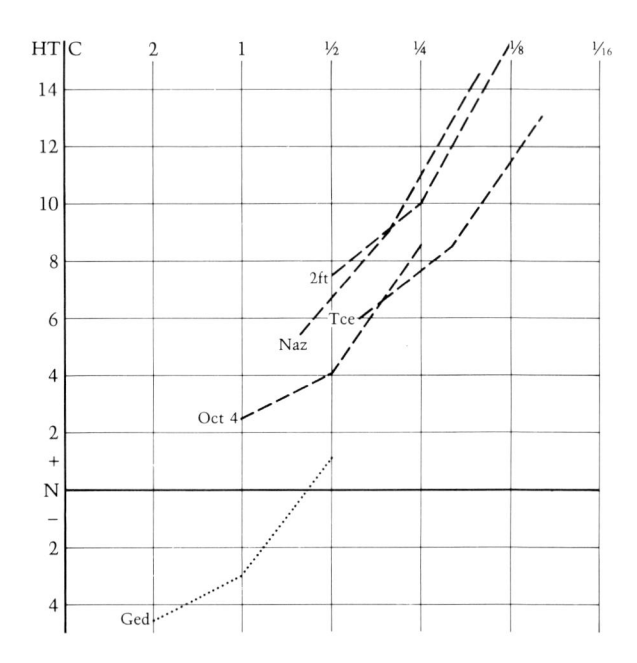

The scales for the main stops of the Pedal division were soon mapped out, and it was agreed that the soundboards, actions and much of the fluework of Great Swell and some Pedal should be set up in Harrisons' works for a more comprehensive trial, about the middle of 1951.

In the meantime the hall was sufficiently advanced for a trial concert to be held, as an acoustic test. Almost the entire population of the County Hall, and many other guests (including myself) were seated on the unfinished concrete floor, and we listened alternately to pistol-shots and musical selections (including the acoustician's "joy", the *Coriolanus Overture* by Beethoven with its convenient, breathless silences) played by a students' orchestra from the Guildhall School of Music.

The experience was *dire:* timpani, played *fortissimo*, were almost reminiscent of those large, square Jacobs' biscuit-tins! Inwardly, though I groaned as a musician, I breathed a fervent prayer of thanksgiving that it was not the organ but an orchestra that we had heard first in this astounding ambience: something would *have* to be done: and it was, speedily. In short, a good deal of the eliminated natural reverberation was recovered, by filling up cavities, and removal of absorbents, though the large span and ingenious suspension of the ceiling absolutely forbade the addition of considerable weight to its fabric: at the very best, therefore, dryness would have to remain a characteristic of the hall's acoustic properties.

CHAPTER EIGHT

The Study of Pipe-Scales (3) An Acoustical Somersault

This is an appropriate point for bringing up to date the progress at Buckfast Abbey.

As a direct consequence of my first Dutch visit in August 1949, important changes had been made in the stop-list, with further modifications after subsequent visits: as finally noted in the Autumn of 1951, when tonal regulation on site began, it stood as follows:

GREAT			CHOIR (enclosed)		
Subprincipal	16	(old)	Lieblich Bourdon	16	(old)
Principal	8	(new)	Hornprincipal	8	(old)
Gross Flute	8	(old)	Quintatön	8	(old)
Rohrflöte	8	(new)	Spitzgamba	8	(old)
Octave	4	(old)	Vox angelica (tc)	8	(old)
Gedacktflöte	4	(new)	Claribel	4	(old)
Quint	2⅔	(old)	Koppelflöte	4	(new)
Octave	2	(old)	Rauschpfeife II	2	(new)
Tierce	1³/₅	(new)	Sesquialtera III	2	(new)
Fourniture IV	1⅓	(new)	Corno di bassetto	8	(old)
Cymbal IV	⅔	(new)	Enclosed Choir on Swell		
Posaune	8	(new)			
Clarion	4	(new)			

ECHO (enclosed)			POSITIVE		
Rohrflöte	8	(old Swell)	Gedackt	8	(new)
Salicional	8	(old Swell)	Principal (conical)	4	(new)
Unda maris (tc)	8	(old Swell)	Nazard	2⅔	(new)
Dulciana	8	(old Echo)	Octave	2	(new)
Flauto traverso	4	(old Swell)	Tierce	1³/₅	(new)
Lieblich flute	4	(old Echo)	Larigot	1⅓	(new)
Salicetina	2	(old Swell)	Sifflöte	1	(new)
Echo sesquialtera	III	(old)	Scharf III	⅔	(new)

THE STUDY OF PIPE-SCALES III 145

SWELL			PEDAL		
Gedackt	16	(old)	Sub Bass (EEEE)	32	(old)
Geigen	8	(old)	Contrabass (wood)	16	(old)
Gedackt	8	(old)	Principal (Great)	16	(old)
Harm. flute (bass grooved)	8	(old)	Bourdon (ext)	16	(old)
Viole de gambe	8	(old)	Dulciana Bass	16	(old)
Violes célestes (tc)	8	(old)	Gedackt (Swell)	16	(old)
Octave	4	(old)	Flute ouverte	8	(old)
Concert flute	4	(old)	Viola (ext)	8	(old)
Octave viole	4	(old)	Gedackt (ext)	8	(old)
Flageolet	2	(old)	Octave Bass	4	(part old)
Sesquialtera II	2⅔	(old)	Flute (ext)	4	(old)
Mixture III	½	(new)	Gedackt (ext)	4	(old)
Cymbal III	⅕	(new)	Bombarde	16	(old tubes)
Contra clarinet	16	(old)	Clarinet	16	(Swell)
Clarinet (ext)	8	(old)	Trumpet (ext)	8	
Trumpet	8	(old)	Clarinet (ext)	8	
Clarion	4	(new)	Clarion (ext)	4	
Tremulant			Clarinet (ext)	4	

Figure 21 shows the scale-plan of the main fluework, old and new together. There will be little difficulty in recognising, in the Positive section, the main lines of Fritz Abend's design for the Royal Festival Hall Positive, which I had discarded in that context. Plates XIV and XXI give a rough plan and elevations, of the layout as made by the builders' draughtsman.

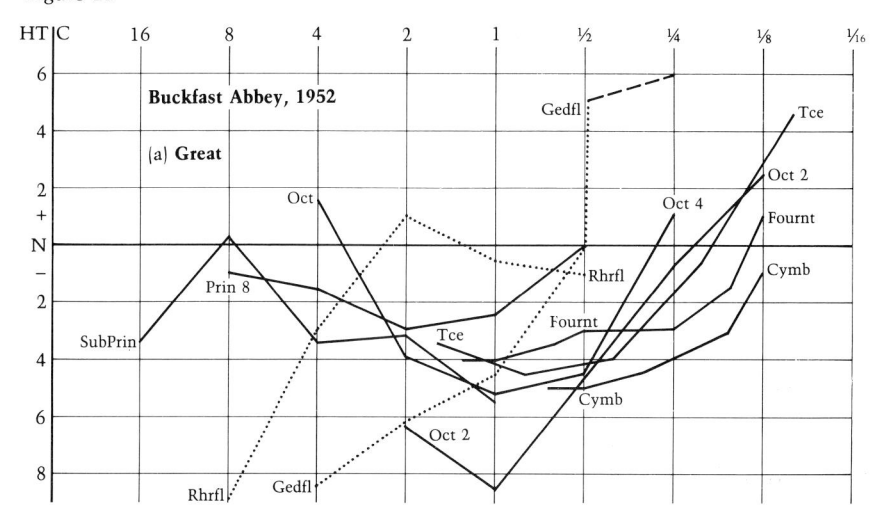

Figure 21

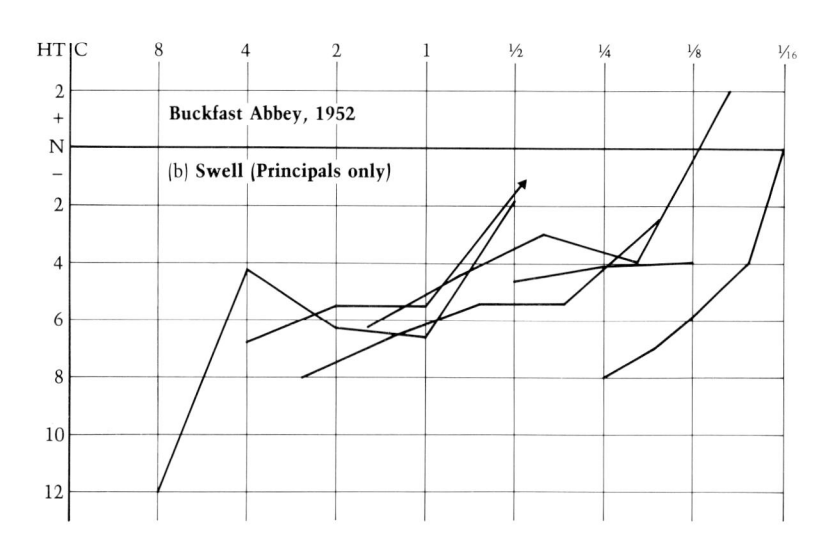

Buckfast Abbey, 1952

(b) **Swell (Principals only)**

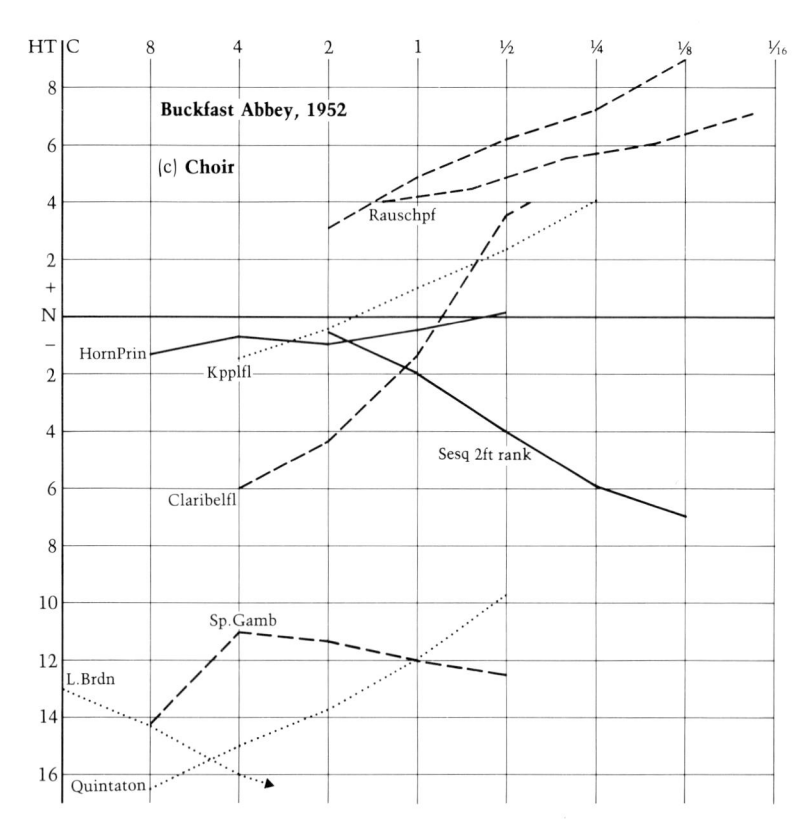

Buckfast Abbey, 1952

(c) **Choir**

Rauschpf
HornPrin
Kpplfl
Claribelfl
Sesq 2ft rank
Sp.Gamb
L.Brdn
Quintaton

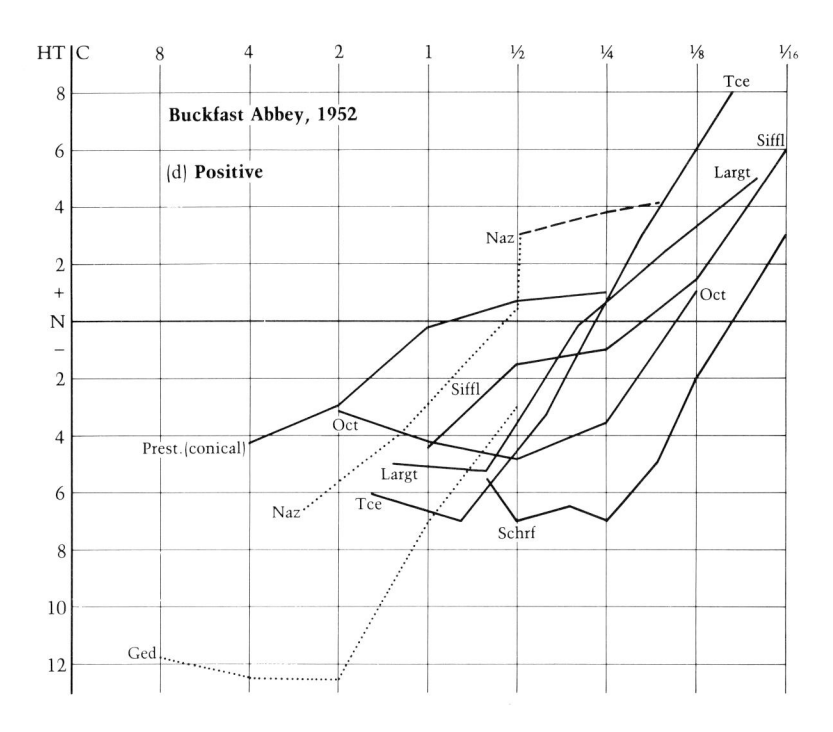

THE STUDY OF PIPE-SCALES III

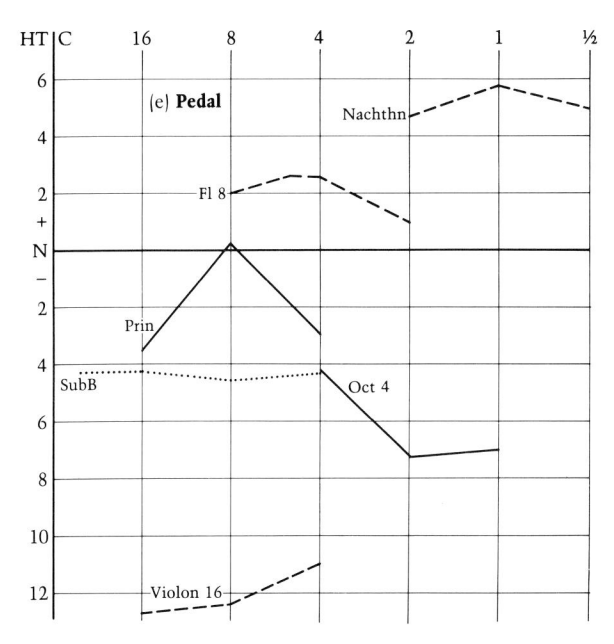

Buckfast Abbey, 1952

(d) **Positive**

(e) **Pedal**

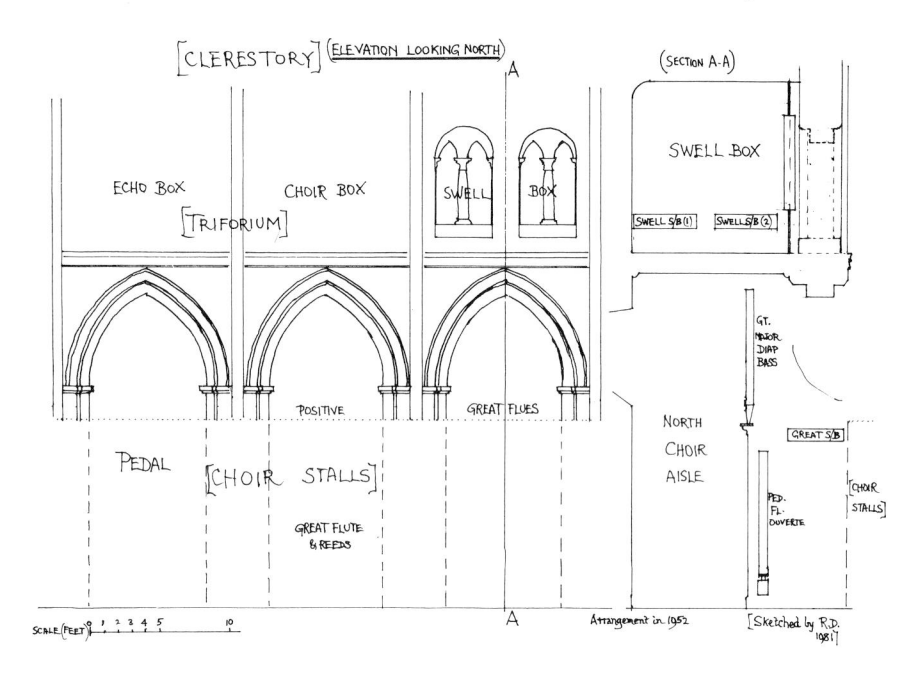

PLATE XIV *Buckfast Abbey, elevation and section through organ.*

Pipe-making had gone on throughout 1951 at Ruislip, and the following reduced wind-pressures were finally agreed there:

Great:	flue (except Grossflute) 3¼ inches: Flute and reeds, 3½ inches
Choir:	4¼ inches
Swell:	±5 inches
Positive:	3 inches
Pedal:	3½ to 4 inches

The voicing of the new pipes was to be on 'full wind' (with open feet) as recommended most strongly by Mr. Flentrop, who visited both Harrisons' and Walkers' works with me in that summer. I lost no opportunity of stressing three prerequisites, viz; *low* cut-up everywhere, equal power everywhere, and lively tone with no nicking of languids or lips. (With hindsight, this was a good programme to lay before the pipe-*makers*, but it oversmacked of standard theory, or, at best, a rule-of-thumb approach.) Mr. Goodey had some fun with the Koppelflöte, for instance, while trying to keep within this 'iron cage' of restrictions. He rang me up on the telephone, to let me listen to one of the pipes, which was making a most extraordinary noise! It was greatly to his credit that although he discovered empirically the practical impossibility of complete conformity, he had the imagination and *savoir faire* to get these pipes speaking acceptably and entirely in the spirit of my requirements, and our joint impressions of the Dutch pipework we had heard (even though this had not included the particular stop in question). Of course the mouths had to be cut up higher. I have already mentioned the enthusiastic response of Dennis Thurlow, who also rapidly developed the newly required technical skills.

However, it was when we actually got to Buckfast and began the tonal regulation there that we encountered really serious snags. True, the remote upper, enclosed divisions — Swell, Choir and Echo — came out acceptably; and though the Pedal stops were still an ill-assorted collection, their sound was already familiar enough: but with the Great and Positive (which was the last to arrive), things were painfully otherwise.

Even though the old pipework of the Great had stood on a nominal pressure of over 4 inches, the nicking of their languids, and reduction of the footholes, might well have halved that figure (as measured inside the pipe-foot) at the initial tonal impact: the ensuing slow build-up to the full pressure would correspond to the highish cut-up of the mouths, thus ensuring a steady note, once it was established.

The reduction of pressure to 3¼ inches (even with wider foot-holes) reduced this firmness, and the Octave 4-feet — all-important structural and *tuning* rank — was a chief offender here: with hindsight again, the obvious practical expedient should have been the scrapping and replacement of this stop and all others like it; but in the order of priorities I then envisaged, no money could be spared for such an expensive remedy.

But the output from the new, almost un-nicked 8-foot Principal and Mixture pipes with open feet (and hence a full initial pressure-impact of 3¼ inches) was most unpleasantly loud and rough, completely lacking the necessary blending capacity to go with the old work. With the best will in the world, the voicers had to admit that they could do little to remedy this disappointing situation, which was aggravated still further by the violent impact of the wind supply, as released through the individual valves of a sliderless chest. The 'scrape' effect in the new pipes was appalling: reduction of the flues (by tapping in the lower lip with a hammer or chisel) only made the tone 'hungry' and 'lean' and unstable as to pitch. Another most unfortunate contributing factor to the general effect was the actual planting of the pipes, with the 8-foot Principal at the *rear* of the soundboard (in the choir aisle) and the upperwork and Mixtures at the front (over the choir-stalls). Even though the latter pipes were choked off to a practical limit, they were sure to predominate because of their prominent, exposed position, sited in an aisle surrounded by flat, hard stone surfaces and a stone floor, and roofed over by individual transverse stone barrel-vaults which corresponded to the main arcading of the choir.

As an immediate expedient, the languids had to be raised and nicked somewhat, the foot-holes being reduced slightly — any reduction in the wind-pressure might have incapacitated the pneumatic part of the action.

If the Great proved difficult, the new pipework of the Positive, when it arrived, was far worse. Similarly placed in the next bay westwards, its mutations and mixture had an incredible stridency, even though by contemporary standards its wind-pressure was accounted low — 3 inches (76 mm). The same causes were operative; but the high pitch of all these ranks, plus the over-reverberant acoustics, made the whole division a blatant caricature of a classical Positive. Even the narrow-scaled 8-foot Gedackt (which I had intended for accompaniment of a single voice or small group) came out as far too loud even for the whole monks' choir in plainsong. Almost worst of all, the very *raison d'être* of a classical chorus was defeated: far from being contrapuntally clear, its effect was irritatingly noisy, uncouth and confused. Walter Goodey and Dennis Thurlow made the best of the situation as far as the Great was concerned, and obtained a fairly plausible result. But, as mentioned earlier, when M. Rochesson arrived with the new reeds (Great 8- and 4-feet, Pedal Bombarde 16-, 8- and 4-feet — all with new tongues and shallots, but only the Great with new, spotted metal, pipes), the whole trouble broke out again: in their acoustical situation in the choir aisle, west of the Great, they were far too loud and "angry" (as Roger Yates expressed it when he heard them — he was a good friend of mine, building organs in Bodmin, Cornwall). The Pedal stop had to be literally stifled, under a huge baffle: the Great stops were actually under the Positive soundboard, which reduced them to a barely endurable intensity. Yet the wind-pressure, again, was only the supposed moderate — even, in those days, *low* figure of 3½ inches (89 mm). What *could* be the matter? It was evident that the free, open speech coming from the long, unweighted tongues and fully open parallel shallots, was the cause; plus an acoustic at this low level in the building which would inevitably enhance and magnify this kind of uninhibited tone.

News of this kind of happening soon gets around, via what is vulgarly termed "the grape-vine" or "the bush telegraph". On my next visit to Durham, Fred Howe could not resist making the jibe, "I have got a friend living near Torquay — he says your new organ at Buckfast is a washout!" (There was little I could say in reply: but Fred did not abandon me, as some organ voicers would have done at that point!)

The monks themselves were not offended, by and large: in fact the general effect of the whole organ had been notably improved, if one chose one's registration with care, avoiding the 'sore spots'. Only the contrapuntal *un*clarity remained for me a tantalisingly inexplicable disability. The Organist (the late Dom Gregory Burke) agreed, but he also continued to support me in my quest for a better outcome: in fact it was only after ten years' further research and experience that it was finally achieved in a comprehensive replanning of the interior, coupled with renewal of some key-actions, and a final re-voicing of the unenclosed divisions on lower wind (by the original team, Goodey and Thurlow). The organ then really 'arrived' and was successfully put on record by Nicolas Kynaston. Details of these operations will be given later.

CHAPTER NINE

Operation Phoenix

At the Oratory, when the wreckage was removed from the organ-gallery and I stood against its rear wall and looked out into the church, I was completely amazed: I seemed to be looking into a distant railway-station from inside a long approach-tunnel! (Plate XV) The old organ had always the reputation of being 'buried', but *this* was simply astounding. The situation was further complicated by the shape of the gallery ceiling, a flattish saucer-dome of hard plaster, with deep spandrels running down into the corners. It was obvious that any new organ would need to be flattened out against the side wall of the building to a minimum practicable depth so that the side-openings (into the transept and the adjoining aisle-chapel) could be adopted as additional means of tonal egress. There was really no workable alternative to this: the organ and the choir *must* stay together; a west-end site for the organ would have involved the building of a new large gallery, for which available funds were quite insufficient, even had it been possible to obtain a building-licence for the work in the post-war period of shortages which still existed: and, of course, blower-room space, means of access, storage and toilet facilities for the choir would have been impossible to arrange at the west end, whereas all these things were available in the present sideways-on location. Added to this, the organ and choir would have been much too far away from the Fathers in the sanctuary, who at Vespers traditionally sing the alternate verses of psalms, hymns and canticles, the organ supplying a common accompaniment for all.

Naturally I was anxious to apply classical principles to the building of the new organ: however, a *Rückpositiv* was effectively ruled out by the need to preserve the traditional arrangement of choir-singers and conductor, the latter standing at the front of the gallery, where a Positive organ-case would have been an unwelcome encumbrance. Similarly, *at that date*, tracker action had not been developed in this country to the point where sideways twists could be accommodated; and the lack of height, plus the saucer-dome, made a 2-storey structure the maximum which could be accommodated; and even so, the console would have to be detached, the Great soundboards having to be set too low to admit of an *en fenêtre* arrangement: in fact, a sideways position was indicated, and proved better than the old reversed position of the Bishop organ, centrally located in front of the old Great.

As usual still at this period, one began somewhat inconsequentially with a list of desirable stops: needless to say, on this occasion I did *not* begin with a large diapason and a Tuba. I suppose that in general terms I was realistic enough about height and depth not to make absurd suggestions, such as a reversion to the old couple of 32-foot stops; in any event these were luxuries we should be unlikely to be able to afford: even a fourth manual had to go.

The specification for which the order was first officially given by the Oratory Fathers was as follows:

GREAT ORGAN		POSITIVE ORGAN	
Gedacktpommer	16	(unenclosed)	
Principal	8	Gedackt	8
Rohrflöte	8	Quintadena	8
Octave	4	Principal	4
Gedacktflöte	4	Rohrflöte	4
Superoctave	2	Rohrnazard	2⅔
Rauschpfeife II	2⅔	Octave	2
Tertian II	1³/₅	Waldflöte	2
Mixture IV	1⅓	Larigot	1⅓
		Cornet III-V	2⅔-8
SWELL ORGAN		Sesquialtera II	1⅓, 2⅔
Quintadena	16	Scharf V	1
Barpyp	8	Dulzian	8
Quintadena	8	Tremulant	
Viola	8		
Céleste (tenor c)	8	PEDAL ORGAN	
Gemshorn	4	Principal	16
Nazard	2⅔	Sub Bass	16
Principal	2	Octave	8
Mixture IV	1	Gedackt	8
Cymbel III	1/5	Rohrquint	5⅓
Trumpet	8	Octave	4
Hautboy	8	Nachthorn	2
Vox humana	8	Mixture IV	2⅔
Clarion	4	Bombarde	16
Tremulant		Bombarde (ext)	8
		Clarion	4
Electro-pneumatic action		Six unison couplers	

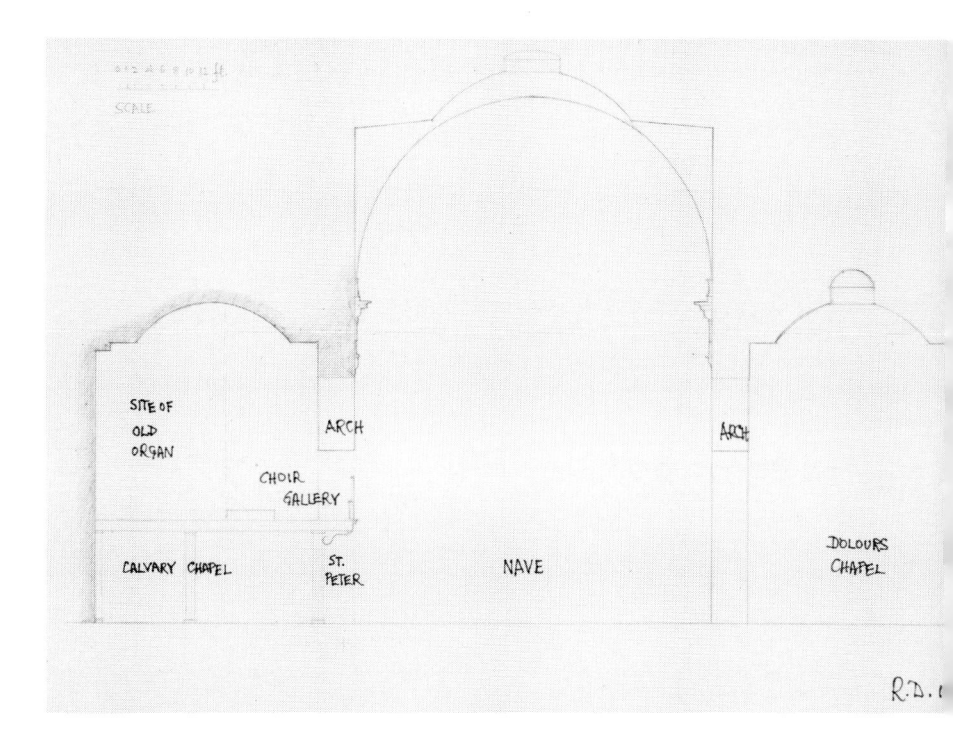

PLATE XV *Brompton Oratory, sectional diagram across nave through centre of choir gallery, 1951.*

With hindsight it does not take much perspicacity to detect a good deal of 'Dutch fever' here: natural enough for its date, July 1950. In the course of the next year, and under compulsion of reducing costs which a new wage-award for organ-builders had pushed up, the final scheme was agreed as follows. The over-developed Positive (renamed CHOIR) was brought into a better relationship with the Great; the excess of Quintadenas was corrected; the confused tonal structure of the Swell was righted by the substitution of a proper 4-foot Principal for a hybrid 'Gemshorn', etc.

No provision was being made for any kind of 'case' (which also, at that time, only actually meant 'façade'), on account of its addition to the cost: but clearly there would have to be *something*, for the gallery was brilliantly illuminated during services, for the singers' sake. Henry Washington mooted "Corinthian pillars" — really not a bad idea. But *I*, freshly back from Holland again, felt (under the spell of the Schnitger school) urged to copy that approach, willy-nilly!

Eventually, and as the stop-list was revised, a layout and a fairly presentable front array were devised in consultation with Albert

Collop (Walkers' Managing Director in succession to the late-lamented Reginald Walker, and a man of great practical organ-building experience), and Peter Goodridge (supervising Architect for the Oratory). A light structure, in aeronautical plywood, braced to the main members of the new building-frame of the organ, and painted in a suitable manner, turned out to be relatively inexpensive, and was installed as shown in Plate XVI. So the final specification was:

GREAT ORGAN		CHOIR ORGAN	
Quintadena	16	(unenclosed)	
Principal (front)	8	Gedackt	8
Rohrflöte	8	Principal (front)	4
Octave	4	Rohrflöte	4
Gemshorn (conical)	4	Octave	2
Quint	2⅔	Waldflöte (conical)	2
Superoctave	2	Larigot	1⅓
Tertian II	1⅓	Sesquialtera II	1⅓
Mixture IV-V	1⅓	Scharf IV	⅔
Trumpet	8	Cromorne	8
		Tremulant	
SWELL ORGAN			
Barpyp (conical)	8	PEDAL ORGAN	
Quintadena	8	Principal (front)	16
Viola	8	Sub Bass (wood)	16
Céleste (AA)	8	Quintflöte (st metal)	10⅔
Principal	4	Octave (part on sides)	8
Gedacktflöte	4	Gedackt (metal)	8
Nazard (conical)	2⅔	Rohrquint	5⅓
Octave	2	Octave	4
Gemshorn (cylindrical)	2	Nachthorn	2
Tierce	1³/₅	Mixture IV	2⅔
Mixture IV	1	Bombarde	16
Cymbel III	⅕	Trumpet (extension)	8
Echo Trumpet	8	Trumpet (separate)	2
Vox humana	8		
Tremulant		Approximate wind-pressures:	
		Great: $3^{1}/_{16}$ inches	
Unison couplers,		Choir: $2^{11}/_{16}$ inches	
Great Suboctave		Swell: 2¾ inches	
Manual compass C-a''', 58 notes		Pedal: 3⅝ inches	
Pedals C-g', 32 notes			

Figure 22 shows the final scale-plan.

BAROQUE TRICKS

Figure 22

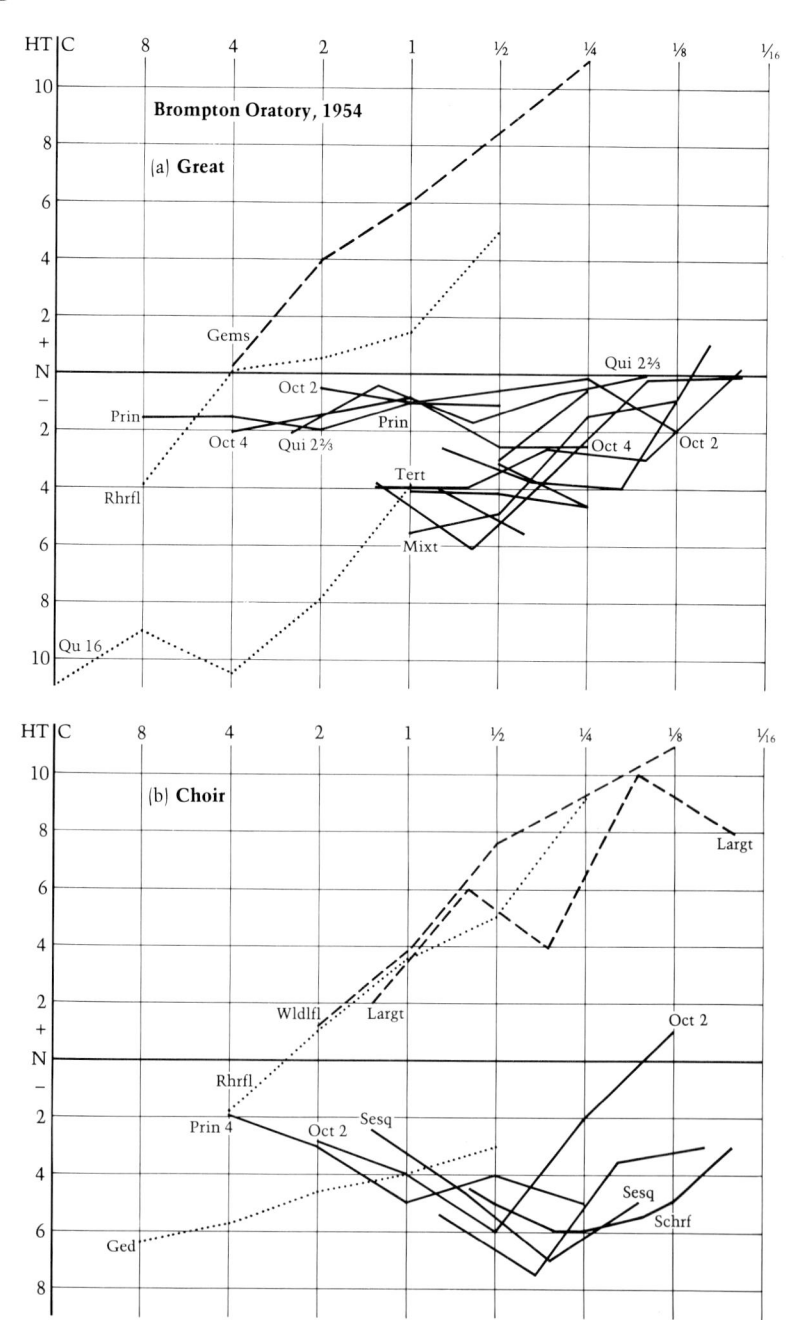

Brompton Oratory, 1954

(a) **Great**

(b) **Choir**

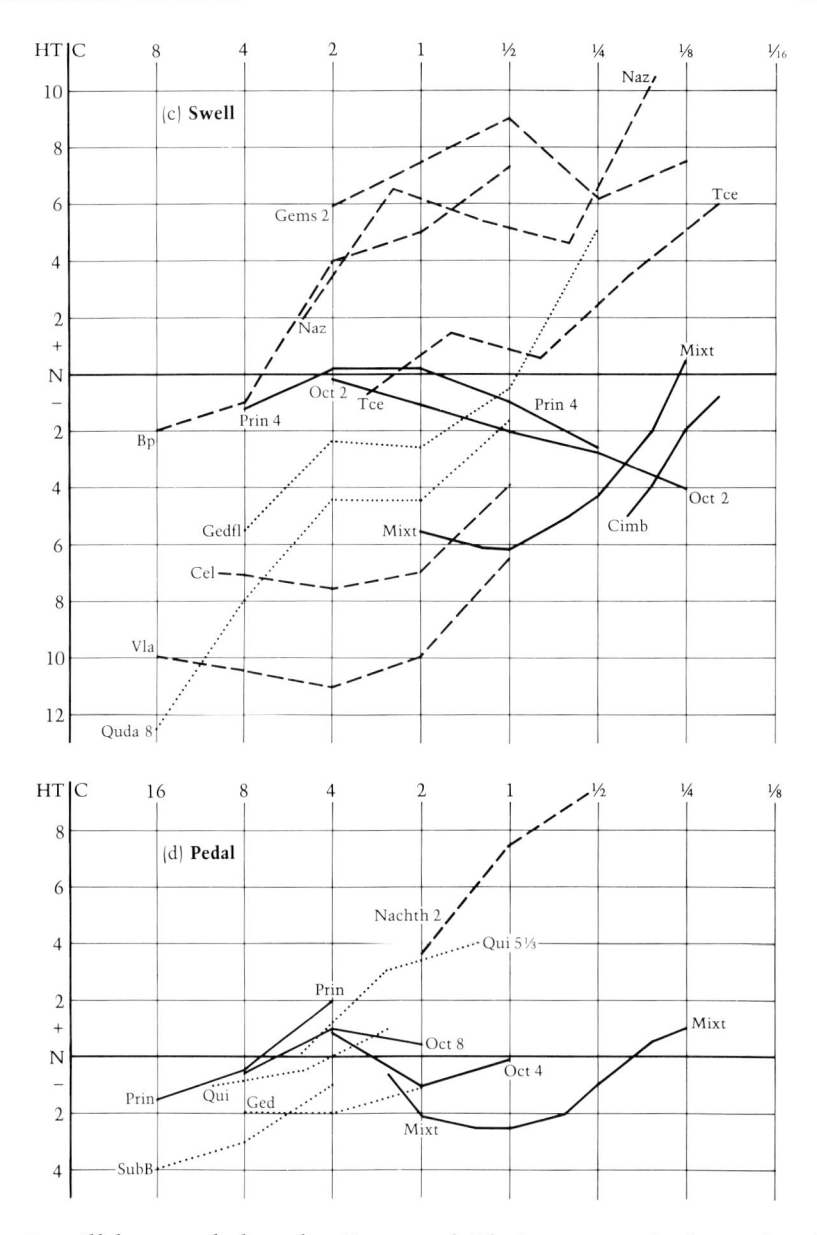

It will be noted that the Great and Choir occupy the lower level, with their soundboards end to end; while the two soundboards of the Swell, also end to end and raised to a second storey, make a real and effective *Oberwerk* or *Bovenwerk*, dominating the whole building with the reflective help of the saucer-dome.

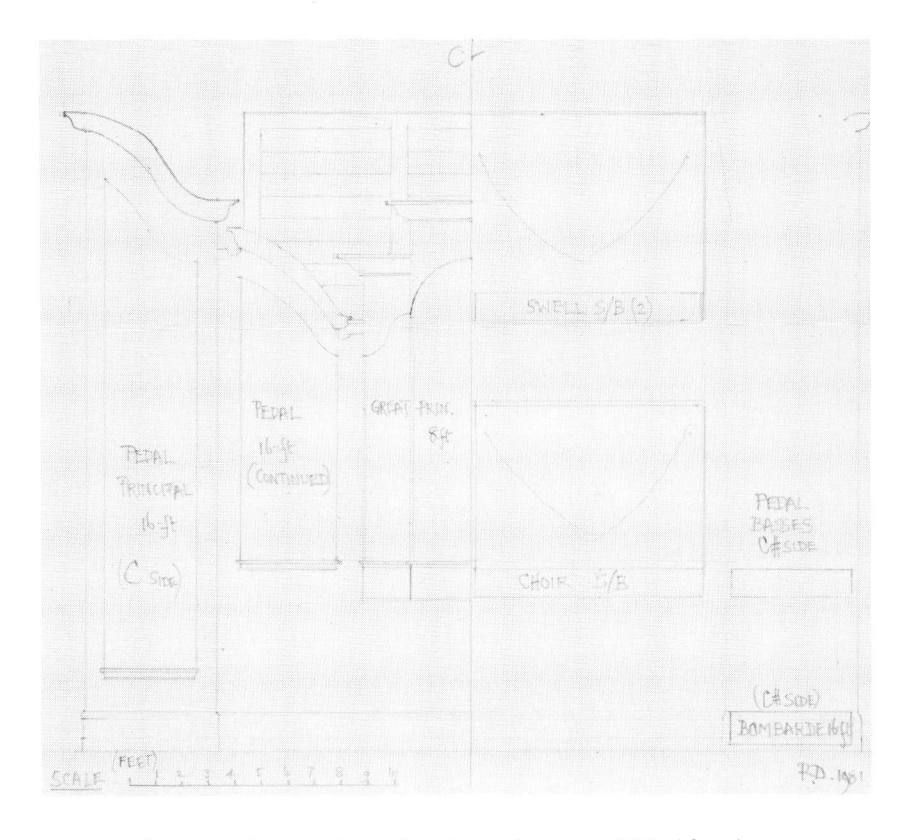

PLATE XVI *Brompton Oratory, front elevation and section, 1954. (above)*

PLATE XVII *(right) Brompton Oratory, section and plan of choir gallery and organ.*

The main Pedal basses are divided into C and C-sharp sides, with most of the 16-foot Principal and the bass half of the Octave 8-feet providing the main front-display. To these are added the lowest 19 pipes of the Great 8-foot Principal, and the lowest 6 of the Choir 4-feet as a symmetrical centre-piece. All the Pedal trebles and stops of less than 8-foot length are planted on a small chromatic slider-chest located behind the Choir (Plate XVII). By great good fortune, a set of excellent slider-soundboards by Lewis were at this time thrown out of organs at Harrow and a church in Ealing, and were offered by the builders as likely to prove superior to any of new manufacture. Thus, with the further provision of five good-sized double-rise reservoirs, the winding arrangements promised to be adequate and stable. As at the Festival Hall, under-actions were designed, working on high wind-pressure — this time about 7½ inches — to pull down the pallets of the main soundboards.

OPERATION PHOENIX

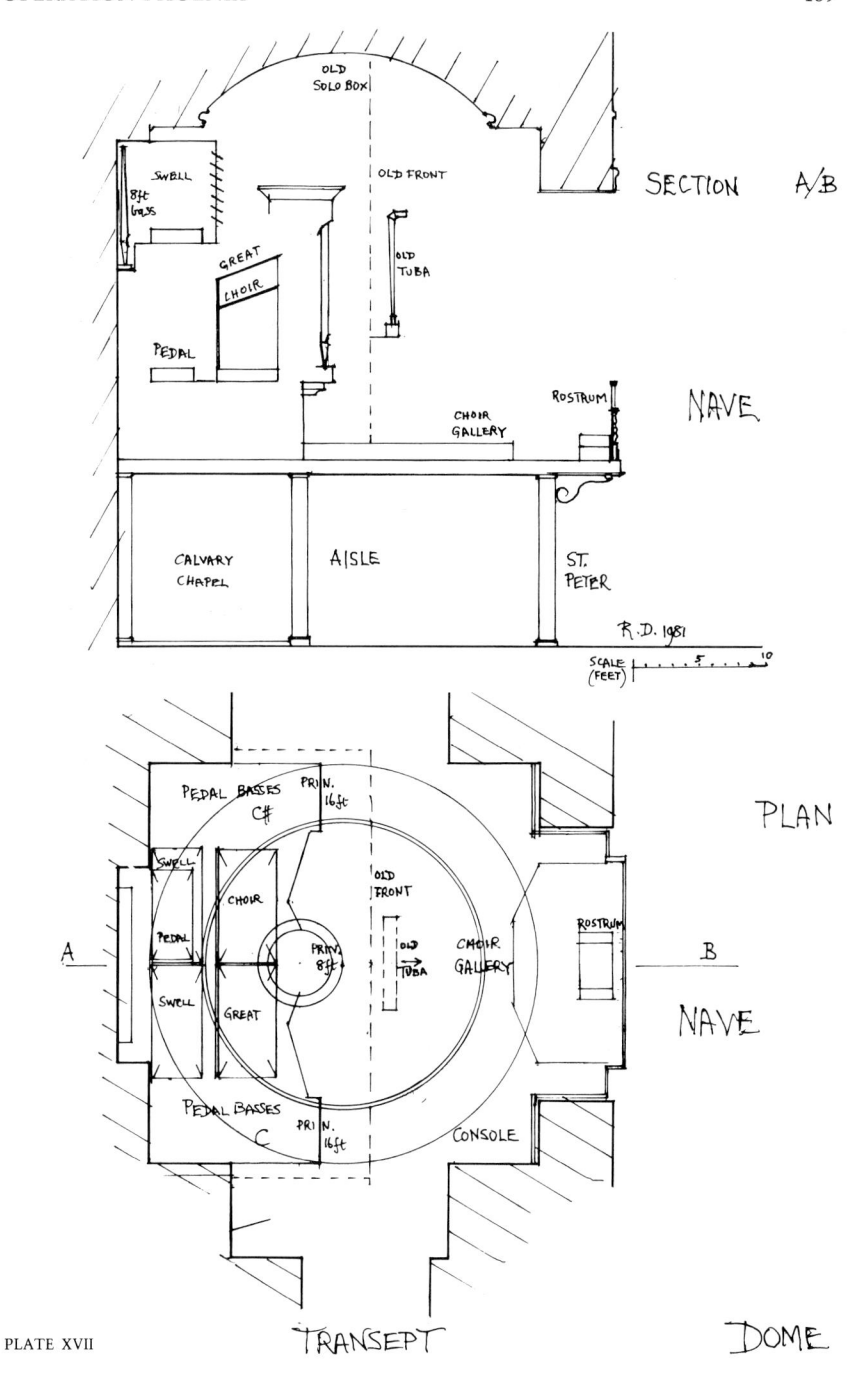

PLATE XVII

As the new pipes began to arrive — 8-feet and 4-feet on the Great and Swell, and two 16-feet and one 8-feet on the Pedal — our feeling was naturally one of relief after two years of electronic organ-substitutes: even so, the tone of the individual pipes came as an unpleasant surprise — the Swell Viola speaking 'wheezily' and unsteadily; the Quintadena 8-feet very 'sour', and much of the rest producing an objectionable 'fizz' in the steady note, especially in the middle compass of the 8-foot Principal and of the Pedal 16-feet front pipes, which started me thinking about the true function of an organ-case, which above everything must be solidly constructed in order to avoid loss of tone through resonance-absorption: I asked Mr. Collop to reinforce the structure with cross-braces and stronger supports for the small soundboards holding the 16-feet and 8-feet front pipes, and he took the point, with a noticeable improvement in the effect. The Pedal Principals 16-feet had been put on their wind in the factory, voiced according to Walkers' normal practice: I had found the tone bluff and almost brutal in its attack. I wanted a sweeter, more singing sound. Mr. Collop again conceded the point; but Mr. Goodey said, "Oh well, if you want *Dulcianas*, we shall have to lower the mouths", and this was confirmed in a pipe whose mouth had not yet been finally cut up. I thought the sound of this pipe was more musical even though softer: but there was eventually a sequel to this, which will be recounted anon.

The arrival of still more pipes of the new manual divisions, an action check-up (including the insertion of new, more lively pallet-springs), and some slight adjustments in wind-pressures — all these gave the voicers more to work on, and they began to grasp the new techniques: it soon became clear that the margin of adjustment in the un-nicked pipes was very much smaller than in the normal nicked ones; and I was to begin to learn then that the cut-up of the individual pipes was a most sensitive adjustment coupled with an equally precise adjustment of the relative positions of upper lip, languid and the width of the flue. All of these operations had to be carried out *in the organ*, with the pipes standing in their final position on the soundboards; for the effect of the speed and force of the release of wind supplied could be crucial in determining the musical speech. If the cut-up was too low, then the pipe would have to be 'slowed' (to prevent overblowing to the octave) by raising the languid or pressing in the upper lip: the pipe then might become unsteady, and if the flue were closed slightly, the tone could become impoverished and windy. With this state of things it would soon be obvious that the mouth would have to be fractionally higher; but it would be necessary to proceed very cautiously on an empirical basis — once a shaving had been removed from the upper lip, it could not be stuck on again!

All this demonstrated clearly that the effect of an organ depends completely on the aural sense of the voicer, a highly personal matter, depending partly on his knowledge of music and conception of musical balance between treble and bass: and this was where, as a musician, I could help the voicer to achieve the optimum result — that is, if he were disposed to follow my guidance — it being understood that I must reciprocate by listening carefully to his observations on how the pipes were responding to treatment. Walter Goodey and later, Dennis Thurlow, showed great enthusiasm; and the latter was responsible for what he called "The Oratory sound", the significant ingredients of which were the finally mellow, rich tone of the 8-foot Principal and the full-toned Rohrflöte of the Great, plus the wide-scaled conical Barpyp, the singing Viola and Quintadena in the Swell. He was very proud of this fine accomplishment, which seems admirably suited to the acoustics of that large vessel, the Oratory Church. Only the position of the organ in the building was far from ideal, far from clear, due to the effect of 'standing waves': and having heard a good deal from the Continent about the necessity of resonant casework, I persuaded Mr. Collop to provide solid wood backing (with removable doors) to the Great and Choir divisions — thus reducing their actual depth to something like 5 feet or less. There was undoubtedly a slight improvement. But about this time I was negotiating for the installation at the Festival Hall of two small canopies, over the Mixtures and upperwork of the Great and Positive divisions; why not apply this principle also at the Oratory? So in the end, the Great and Choir were completely boxed in, with a slightly inclined roof, and only the front left open (see Plate XVII): this had a damping effect on the tone, naturally, and necessitated a slight increase in the wind-pressure — about ⅛ of an inch: but a surprising increase in clarity resulted, especially in the effect of the mixtures inasmuch as the very high ranks of the bass range no longer went flying around the building and confusing the soprano lines.

As has been said, the soundboard action was of crucial significance in the tone-production: those pipes which stood directly over pneumatic valves were likely to suffer most — in this case it was mostly the front pipes which were so placed, and they gave a certain amount of trouble for some time: those on the slider-soundboards spoke better on account of the relatively gradual input of air from the opening of the long pallets, even though this was more 'explosive', due to the smart movement of the electro-pneumatic power-box, than would have been produced by tracker action. It was found possible to make all the flue pipes speak more 'quickly' — giving the sweeter effect of an emphasised *octave* partial-tone as opposed to the 'quinty' effect of slower speech — the final adjustment being a very slight raising of the mouths, one by one, to just a sufficient extent to prevent overblowing: and this, in fact, was the optimum recipe for natural, relaxed, resonant musical tone. This discovery gave the voicers greater confidence, and enabled them to create a fine musical effect.

The final touch to the fluework was applied to the large front pipes of the Pedal Principal, which Mr. Goodey cut up higher, though not as high as originally: after months of poor speech, slowness, 'quinting', etc, the effect of this carefully conducted operation was almost miraculous: as usual it was a question of steering a middle course between the objectionable 'cough' and slowness of the too-low mouth, and the equally unsatisfactory unsteady, woolly tone of a mouth cut too high — both of these tendencies being considerably increased by the absence of nicks in the languids. In desperation, I had once tried to persuade Mr. Goodey to nick these pipes slightly, in order to cure their manifest defects: but with a touch of pride in his voice he (happily) refused, and corrected the matter by raising the mouths. In fact there is not a nicked pipe anywhere in this organ — a considerable achievement at that time in England!

When the reeds arrived, we were in for more adventures: Rochesson had offered to voice them, but there were tactical obstacles, and Mr. Goodey decided to "have a go" in the French style — after all, we had all the necessary scales and other technical information already from Rochesson, who had already voiced (for the old Solo division) the 16-foot Trombone, with its half-length bass, which, for reasons of economy, we had to put into the Pedal as a 16-foot/8-foot extension. Rochesson had also supplied a very good scale for the Echo Trumpet, with very narrow bass. Here again the ear of the voicer held the secret of success or otherwise: it took some time to obtain the right kind of curve for the reed-tongues; a too flat curve produced a poor bassoon-like sonority in the Trumpets and especially the Pedal 16-feet. The Cromorne, a later arrival, went better: but my chagrin could be imagined when the pipes were actually put in, and I heard each one being treated so as to *remove* its excellent quick speech (reminiscent of a good wind-player's 'tonguing'). After about half of them were done — a hole had been bored in the boots — I could bear it no longer and said, "Let's go now" — it was about midnight. Next day I stuck adhesive plaster over the holes, and of course the natural speech returned. Mr. Collop, to whom I reported all this, talked it over with the voicing staff, and Mr. Goodey obliged by soldering up the offending gaps. As usual, he had been thinking along the lines of good maintenance and tuning margins: but we could see that something had been sacrificed in musical effect, and that the sacrifice was unacceptable in this case. The end-result was, and is, a fine stop.

The last important modifications to take place were the final substitution of a full-length bass for the Pedal 16-foot reed [33] — an immense improvement: and an increase in the cant of the roofs over the Great and Choir, which were being reflected at too low an angle so as to lose a good deal of tone in the gallery, especially with singers present to absorb it. It came as a surprise when the pipes were replaced — the operation took place during a cleaning — to find that the

OPERATION PHOENIX

Mixtures had an unpleasantly screaming effect: and then I remembered that we had increased the pressures when the roofs were installed! Reduction to the original restored the balance, and all was well. (Plate XVIII showing the finished organ, can be compared with the similar view of the old organ shown in Plate VI.)

PLATE XVIII *Brompton Oratory, choir gallery and organ.*

CHAPTER TEN

In the Doldrums (Royal Festival Hall)

True to their undertakings, Harrisons' erected some of the Great, Swell and Pedal soundboards and fluework in their works during the late summer of 1951, and they even had part of the Swell shutter-front in operation. Through something like a coincidence, Dirk Flentrop was visiting me at the time and we went to Durham together, with Harrisons' approval, to hear the effect. Mr. Flentrop: "Mr. Harrison, why do you paper the inside of the Swell-box?" Mr. Harrison: "We do!" This was illuminating, certainly. But when we played 'the organ' from the console, the pipes sounded excruciatingly awful! The 'scrape' was there, of course; but worse still was the 'quinty', 'slow' start emitted by the Principal and Viola pipes. Mr. Flentrop observed only that these stops had not a nice singing tone, but he could not explain *why*: he reminded me of the importance of voicing all these pipes on 'full wind' (open feet) and keeping the speech 'quick'.

It was not to be wondered at that these criticisms were not excessively welcome at Durham.

With hindsight, a tracker action might well have minimised these speech difficulties, and generally produced a better response: the actual electro-pneumatic system was so quick as to choke the pipes or make them overblow, and this necessitated the slowing of the speech — hence the 'quinty' rather than 'octave-dominated' tone. If one tried to make the pipes quicker, by lowering the languids, they either became windy or overblew — simple consequences of my own (strictly executed but ill-advised) stipulations of 'low cut-up' and over-thick front-faces for the languids. Fortunately, Fred Howe did not attempt any further cutting-up at present, for the critical limit could easily have been passed. Wisely (though I did not appreciate that at the time), he left this operation until we were on the site in London.

However, it was a full year before any tonal regulation or finishing could be started in the hall itself: the question of the organ's appearance was deadlocked, through the conflicting interests of the Architects and Designers, the Acoustics Team, the Organ-builders and myself. Harrison naturally wanted to get on with the job, and when the idea of a front display (called by the Architect a "Frontispiece") was foundering — as early as 1950 — he proposed a total grille (which the Architects, etc, could design *ad lib* to their hearts' content) behind which the organ itself could be built according to "good organ-building practice", irrespective of its appearance which would now become an issue strictly secondary to the claims of practical efficiency and convenience of access for tuning and maintenance.

Liberated in this way, Harrisons' draughtsman decided on a two-storey structure for the Great and Positive divisions at least: the lower Great to contain all flue-stops from 16-feet to 4-feet, inclusive; the Lower Positive all from 8-feet to 2⅔ foot pitch, plus the Tierce; and in both divisions the upper soundboard contained all the Mixtures and other upper-work. In this instance the Architects and designers had been effectively outwitted, and there were some agonised enquiries from them, and even a final attempt to reinstate a central 'frontispiece' of 16-foot pipes — but events had moved too fast; soundboards were largely made, and any fundamental change would entail the scrapping of much executed work, with consequent delay and extra expense. The grille had come to stay — or so it seemed, until another breath-taking development supervened. The Leader of the Council, Isaac Hayward, hearing of the stalemate and the total-grille proposal, was incensed, and remarked with indignation, "We are paying for all these expensive pipes and we want to see them as a decorative feature of the Hall" — which put the situation back to 'Square One'. I myself still tried in vain to get the Pedal 16-foot Principal into a central front position: but this issue was closed forever.

But then the Deputy Architect, Dr. Martin, had a marvellous inspiration: he requested from Harrison a panoramic view of the pipework on the soundboards in the two-storey arrangement, and with incredible speed he designed a symbolic frontispiece of dummy pipes, wood and metal, to stand centrally in front of the organ proper. This quasi-Concordat was accepted gratefully on all sides, and there it stands in the hall for all to witness. (Plates XIX and XX) Various other large wooden design-features — such as a 3-foot continuous band of solid wood, running right round the stage area at podium height — were thereby supplanted or skeletonised: the large temporary sounding-board or reflector behind the orchestra was converted into a moveable folding screen: only the huge orchestral canopy remains as a tonal obstacle, but now raised to an agreed height where it would no longer seriously impede the organ's output. Thus by the autumn of 1952 we were almost ready for tonal regulation and 'finishing' to begin; but since the hall was now busily engaged, it was clear that this work would have to be done overnight, and the voicers and I agreed to do six nights' work per week in spells of three or four weeks running.

The console had not yet arrived, but a moveable test-keyboard was available, and one afternoon I heard (from the rear stalls) the sound of

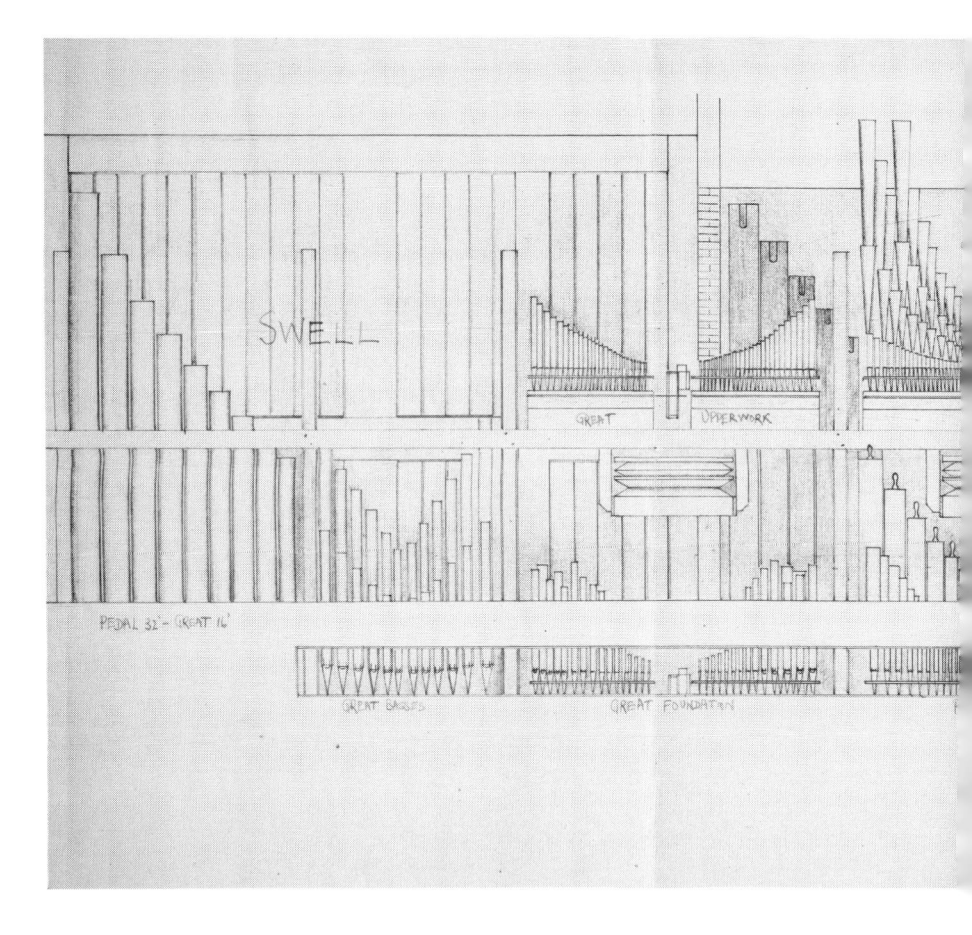

PLATE XIX *Royal Festival Hall, interior arrangement of organ.*

the Great Principal 8-feet being rough-tuned. *Hell's bells!* It sounded emasculated, remote, *feeble!* I rushed down into the organ chamber and was relieved to find that the wind-pressure had been set at only 3 inches, in accordance with an earlier-recorded decision. (My friend, Robert Noehren, had, during our frequent correspondence, represented to me the great merits of a low pressure accompanied by 'open foot' voicing — even down to 2 inches, as instanced by the small Rieger organ which he was using on the stage of the Hill Auditorium at Ann Arbor, and which successfully "shouted down" the large, enchambered Skinner organ, voiced on 5 inches pressure.) I got the wind-pressure up to 3½ inches at once — which was *better*, if not really adequate: the sound-absorption of the hall was incredible!

IN THE DOLDRUMS 167

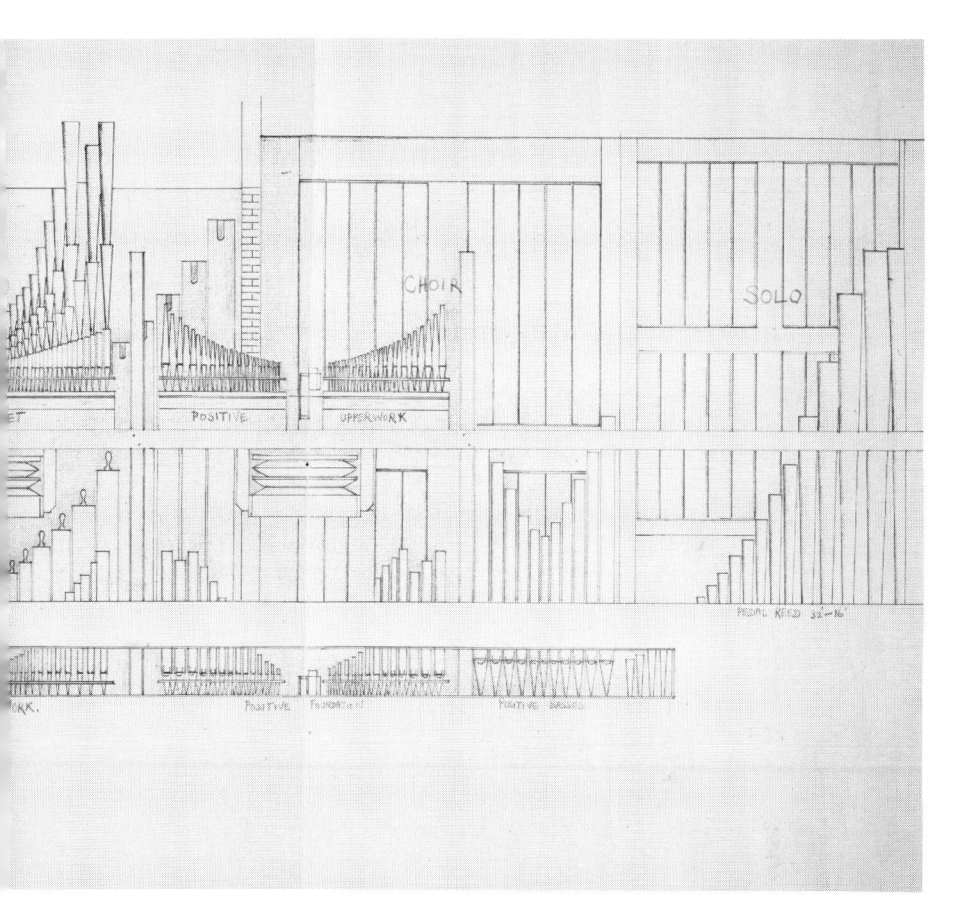

As we were about to embark on the tonal regulation, some characteristic remarks were forthcoming: Mr. Bob Wood (rather gruffly): "I hope you'll have some *nice soft stops!*", and his brother Harry Wood, whom I regarded as the electrical wizard, cooped up in a little corner of the organ, working out the most preposterous circuitry: "Will you start with the Swell? Mr. Arthur" — ie, Harrison — "always began with the Swell" — (presumably with the softest stop), an interesting sidelight on English organ-design and aesthetic around the turn of the century, when, as Germani shrewdly stated [34], the larger registers such as Great chorus or reed stops were only envisaged for use at exceptional climaxes — the whole organ being based on the Swell division, plus the Diapasons, etc, in due gradation.

When we actually began work on the first night, I made it my business (as I had previously warned Harrisons) to set middle C of the Great 8-foot Principal, on which *all* must depend. Leslie ("Bob") Rowland, assistant voicer, was at the keyboard, I was up in the stalls, Fred Howe inside the organ. I called out to the latter, "Is that a good note, Fred? Is it the best it will give?" Fred was furious: what on earth was I about? That wasn't the way to do the tonal regulation! Anyway, the point was eventually made: it didn't sound too bad; we set the other C's, with a struggle, including some other stops, especially, the Swell Quintadena 16-foot, or perhaps it was the Great 16-foot Gedacktpommer, a stop of complicated harmonic tonality. (I had already warned Harrisons that the aim was to secure from every pipe its optimum speech for its scale and construction, and that therefore its tonality or sonority could be expected to change from octave to octave — all C's being set at equal strength, measured by impact of addition, one to another.) The trouble was that in this stop, when two C's had been set, the addition of a third C could upset the relationship of the first two, necessitating a further modification. This also was too much for Fred! "You can't go on like this! *It isn't commercially possible!"* — a comment motivated, I am sure, by *Fear,* Fear of the unknown, perhaps. Anyway, he let himself be persuaded to carry on — with success, too. Later, when dealing with another stop, he said, "If your ears were any good, you wouldn't need to do all this balancing": and I rather cruelly replied, "It is the only way to ensure tonal clarity: your organ at ***" (mentioning one of which he was especially proud) "isn't clear at all — too top-heavy." Fred's indignation subsided and he carried on with the job, meek as a lamb.

As a diversion, when the console had arrived and been connected up to entire Great and Swell, and we were about to embark on the second round of regulation, with all the flue-pipes in and rough-tuned, I dropped into the hall in the afternoon. The screen was completed and in the open position. Screwing up my courage, I tried a large chord on Full Great to Mixtures ...! The resulting sound resembled a direct hit by an aerial bomb on a large farmyard. Some of the 'stage-hands' who were just leaving the hall sent up a rousing, derisive cheer! What a beginning! I shouted an angry rebuke, mainly because I felt that in consequence of all the 'whisperings', everybody on site was expecting the organ to turn out to be a monstrosity — and here was the apparent confirmation!

Gradually, as Fred, "Bob" and I worked on, the Great fluework began to sound civilised: Ernest Bean, the General Manager, visited us one evening and was entranced with the Great Rohrgedackt, especially when combined with the silvery tones of the Superoctave 2-feet — it *did* sound delicious; and Denis Vaughan, who was playing Double-Bass in Beecham's Royal Philharmonic Orchestra, and who played all the organ-parts for them, demonstrated how beautifully this

PLATE XX *Royal Festival Hall, the completed organ.*

Rohrgedackt would function with a Basso Continuo, played on his instrument. Things were looking up!

When we had set most of the Great and Swell and a Pedal stop (the rest still being in Durham), it was time for a real test. I was playing on the Compton (temporary) Electrone for the Beethoven *Missa Solemnis* with the London Philharmonic under Sir Adrian Boult, and I rather diffidently asked whether I might play some of the "Dona nobis pacem" from the *organ*-console. "Yes, that's all right!" I pulled out all the 16-, 8- and 4-foot stops on Great and Swell, and played my organ-part. (Was the organ *on*?!!!) As we finished the movement, Sir Adrian called out to me, "That all right? Couldn't hear a thing!" (Heavens! Neither could I! I flipped a note: yes, it *was* speaking — !) "Want to try again? Same place!" We tried again: no, the organ just wasn't there at all! I thanked Sir Adrian, and once again rushed into the organ. "Put the Great and Swell up to 3¾ inches, *please!*" Poor Harry Wood looked at me despairingly, but did as he was bid.

That night I had to face the voicers and spell out the bitter truth. My reputation sank very low indeed. However, Fred and "Bob" set to work, on the new pressure, as before. One of the difficulties arose from the size of the chest-borings for the pipes in the middle range: it was of little avail to enlarge the foot-holes of the pipes if the holes in the soundboard were smaller — an eventuality which I had not foreseen. A discreet amount of enlargement had to be made where possible; which meant removing pipes, but also running the risk of impaling the pallets on the drill, not to mention getting chips and shavings down among them, to be a potential source of ciphers in the future. But all this extra work was most painstakingly done, and after about two weeks we were ready for another test.

I persuaded (the late) Basil Cameron and the London Philharmonic to play the first three lines of the National Anthem, and asked James Dalton, at the console, *not to play the first line!* Breathless, I waited. *Deo gratias*, we were home this time, the organ clearly "made it", it was audible, even if not predominant. That was good enough, for there was at least as much more still to come. Everyone on the job felt relieved. (But "What a way to build an organ!" was the unspoken commentary behind the scenes: Harry Wood complained once, quietly, "Are we going forward or backward?")

Cuthbert Harrison imaginatively assisted our progress by supplying Fred Howe with a small voicing-machine (a miniature soundboard), which could be trunked up to any of the wind-reservoirs from a position in the Choir-lobby at the end of the organ-chamber. The C-pipes for any stop could then be set within the organ, and then brought out to the voicing-machine, on which all the intervening pipes could be brought into relation with them: and then all could be put back on the main soundboards for a final check. Fred was very expert and quick at this, and the work proceeded apace and with greater and increasing confidence and assurance. It was, for me, rather dispiriting to hear the lovely, full resonant tones of these pipes as they were voiced in a reverberant lobby, transformed into thin astringency when restored to the hall's ambience: that was our permanent handicap!

There was occasional 'light relief', as, for instance, when (in a fit of panic) I borrowed a treble-C pipe from the No. 3 Diapason at the Royal Albert Hall, and got Fred to blow it, by mouth, at its own pressure of somewhere near 5 inches, in the Festival Hall organ-chamber. There, it made a tearing, rough sound reverberating through the room! Or when one of the four 'Haskelled' (acoustically shortened) pipes of the 32-foot Principal was sounded without its interior tube in place, and thus nearly an octave too high, with a monstrous increase of scale and output: Fred's comment, "Sounds like a real organ ...!"

Or another time, when I saw the newly-arrived pipes of the Positive Gedackt, with slightly nicked languids (contrary to instructions): after a couple of weeks' all-night work, this was too much for my nerves, and I sent them all straight back to Durham! (Poor Mr. Wood!) That night, Fred threatened to walk out: but his innate goodness of heart was prevailed on, and he stayed and carried on, after I had apologised for not even trying the pipes in the organ. They were returned to London immediately, and actually this stop turned out to be one of the nicest in the whole instrument.

And then, when we came to the (Grand) Cornet, V ranks, of Dom Bédos scale, on the Great, with middle C compass, we found that middle C had been connected to bottom C of the keyboard, so that there was no treble at all — another 'monstrosity', no doubt! However, the correction was made, and because of its very wide scale and prominent position in front of the Great reeds in the centre of the upper storey, it sang out in unmistakably authoritative tones even in spite of its 'creamy' flavour and fullness.

An important final change was made empirically on the Great Gedackt-flute 4-feet, which turned out to be almost a duplicate tonally of the Gemshorn 4-feet. By leaving the mouths extra low, it was found possible to convert this redundant register into a sparkling wide-scale Quintadena 4-feet, most useful in solo combinations (for example, contrasted with the Larigot of the Positive) and adding some piquancy to the Great flue-ensemble.

CHAPTER ELEVEN

Fruition and an Assessment

Figure 23 presents in graphical form the diameter-scales of all the flue-pipes for the Royal Festival Hall, as recommended to the builders: the voicers had access to these diagrams as well as a written detailed commentary on the character of each stop as so delineated. Eventually all was regulated (according to what I will term "The Gottfried method") and tuned.

Then the reeds arrived from Durham, accompanied by Louis Eugène-Rochesson who had voiced them there, and who now put them into their places in the organ, with assistance from Harrisons' men. He, too, found the little voicing-machine of great service for putting the final touches on the pipes; and once again I was disappointed to hear the effect of the hall's ambience: the splendid virile tone of the trumpets, for instance, as heard in the reverberant lobby, was almost thinned down to 'comb and paper' sonority when they were moved into the organ.

At this time we had been hearing a good deal from the Continent about the importance of a resonating organ-case (which some authorities likened functionally to the sound-box of a violin or 'cello). With these theories I felt myself instinctively to be in full agreement, but my mooted proposal to install enclosing casework over and around the Great and Positive divisions was viewed sceptically by the organ-builders, and indeed strongly resisted by the Acoustics Consultant, Mr. Bagenal, on the ground that it would produce a 'boxiness' in the tone, and that for projection purposes the main orchestral canopy would suffice — not a surprising reaction from one who referred to "Organ" [sic], meaning thereby a kind of generally diffused, pervading, enveloping sound-effect! Fortunately Dr. Martin agreed to accept the principle but only subject to a satisfactory test with a mock-up reflector. This was successfully achieved by suspending a sheet of ply-wood over *one side* of the upper Great and comparing its effect with the other side. Eventually a compromise was reached in the form of two small, elegant canopies, permanently installed over the Great and Positive, invisibly supported by the upright members of the organ framework — actually an improvement visually; the 'floating' effect contributed a desirable 'lightness' to the whole front of the organ.

FRUITION AND AN ASSESSMENT 173

Figure 23

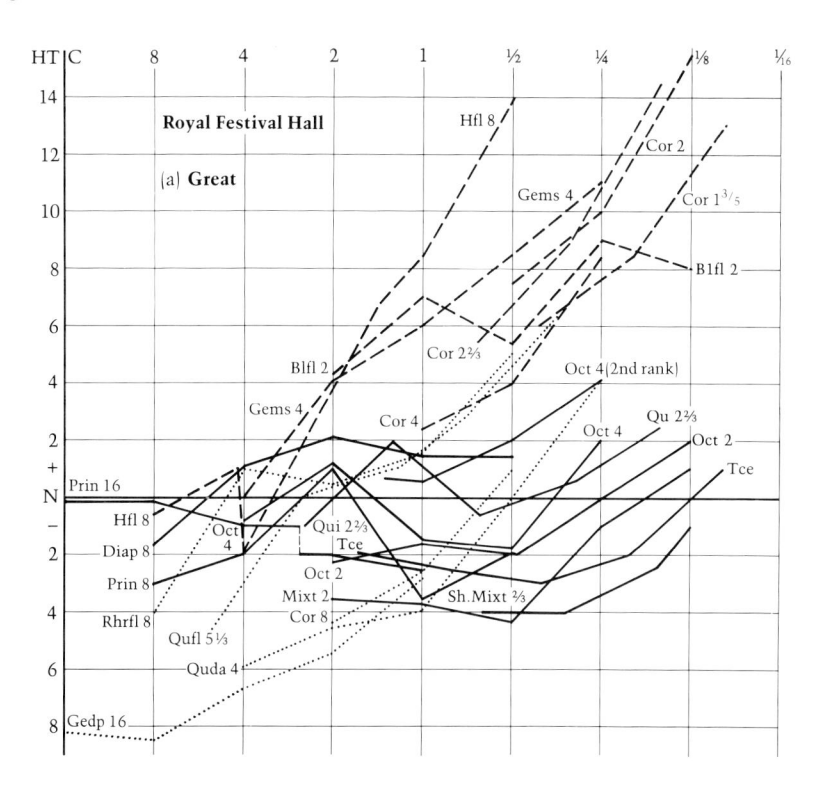

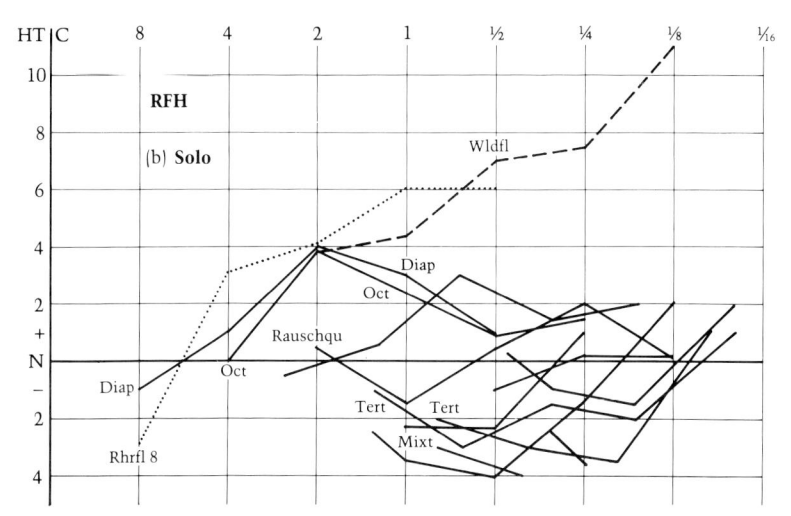

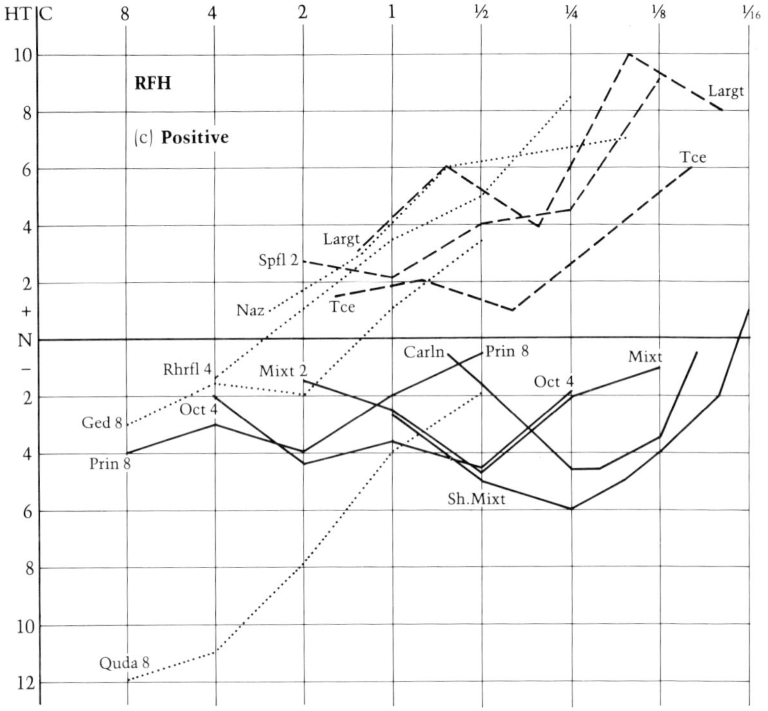
HT
C
8
4
2
1
½
¼
⅛
1/16
10
8
6
4
2
+
N
–
2
4
6
8
10
12
RFH
(c) Positive
Largt
Tce
Spfl 2
Naz
Carln
Prin 8
Mixt
Oct 4
Rhrfl 4
Mixt 2
Ged 8
Oct 4
Prin 8
Sh.Mixt
Quda 8

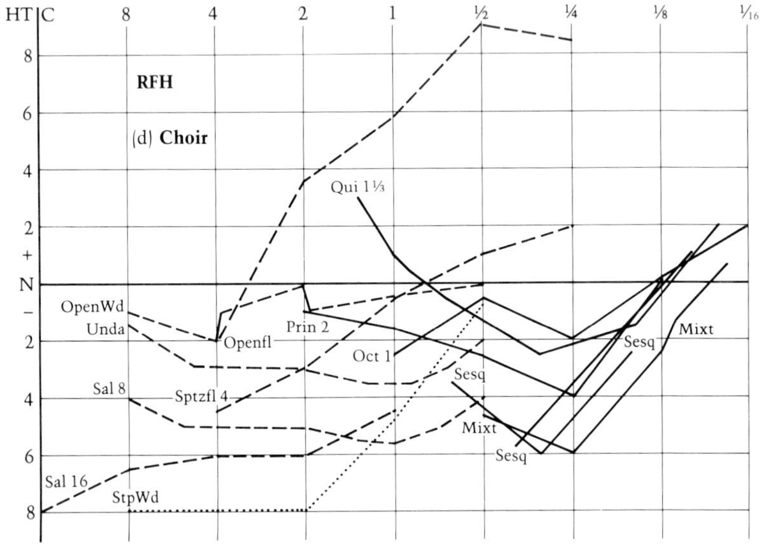
HT
C
8
4
2
1
½
¼
⅛
1/16
8
6
4
2
+
N
–
2
4
6
8
RFH
(d) Choir
Qui 1⅓
OpenWd
Unda
Openfl
Prin 2
Mixt
Sesq
Oct 1
Sesq
Sal 8
Sptzfl 4
Mixt
Sesq
Sal 16
StpWd

FRUITION AND AN ASSESSMENT

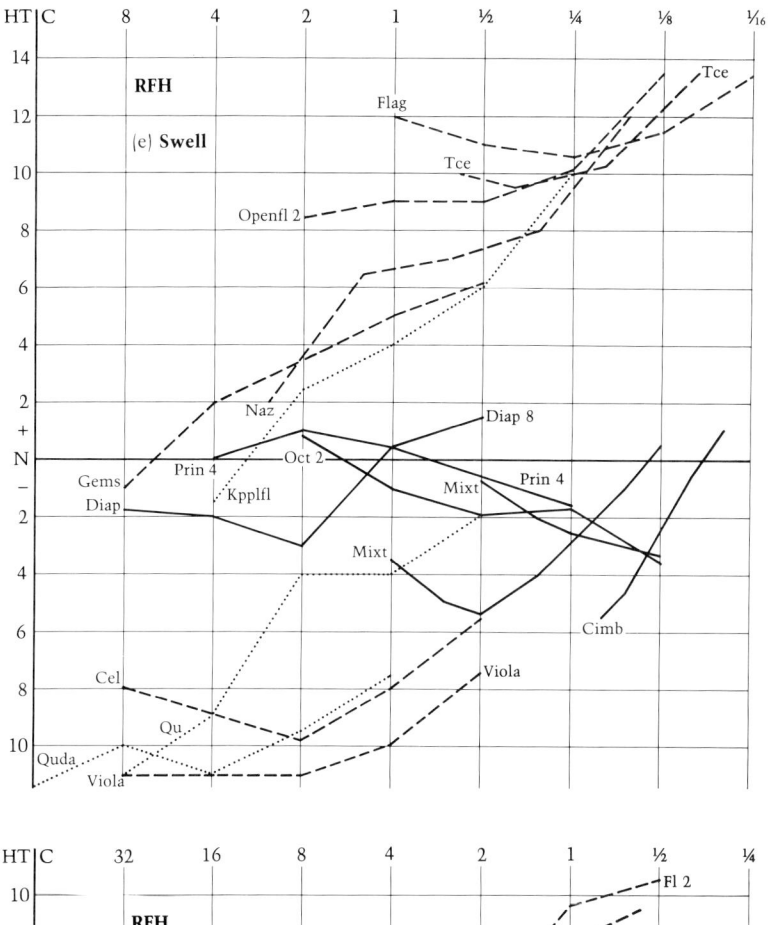

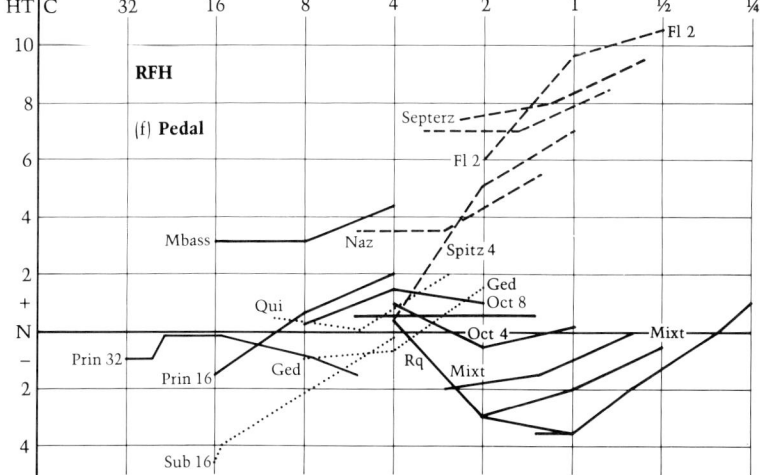

175

Was the sound of these choruses actually clarified? Sometimes "Yes", sometimes "No": it depended on the player and the stops chosen; and I recall how in Peter Hurford's initial recital in the early years, a Bach Prelude and/or Fugue sounded anything but clear, played on a skeletonised chorus consisting of only one stop for each pitch, 8-feet, 4-feet, 2⅔-feet, 2-feet, and two mixtures, on the Great; you could not hear which 'voice' was on top! It was only in 1975 that I obtained at last the necessary permission to extend the 'casework' down the sides of the Great and Positive — again as the result of a conclusive test. I borrowed two large flush-doors from the hall's maintenance department, and persuaded some professional friends to move them into position, and out, at the ends of the lower Positive, while identical musical fragments were played from the console. Other friends were posted to listen from various parts of the hall. They all reported that the placing of the doors had an audible effect, which they could not exactly describe, but seemed to put the music better "in focus". Eventually a whole set of lateral reflectors was made and installed by Harrisons', both at the higher and lower levels of Great and Positive, and supported by a substantial steel frame. Again working empirically, I found that one or two panels were better omitted from the lower Great: firstly, because one of them tended to obstruct the Swell Trumpets; and secondly, because the omission of one on the other side ensured a greater 'spread' for the impressive foundation-tone of this division. Retaining the tight enclosure of the Positive *in toto* increased its tonal precision, with an appropriately enhanced contrast with the other divisions, especially its 'opposite number', the Great. The general increase in contrapuntal clarity afforded by this simple device was most satisfactory, granted that the playing organist knew how to use its effect! Sloppy playing still sounded sloppy: why should it be otherwise? The same would be true of a magnificent piano!

To revert to the organ as first heard: many were the shocks experienced by those who expected "delicate Baroquery" on the opening night. Surprisingly perhaps, the most generous praise that night came from Fred Howe himself — that was *real* generosity. But of course one was not looking for that kind of personal tribute. Many people denigrated the French reeds: I myself chuckled inwardly at the thought that at the precise moment when the 16-foot Bombarde was revoiced out of all recognition in the former Lewis organ at Southwark Cathedral, a new one was taking its place less than a mile upstream! It was very interesting to note how often people's criticism was based on prejudice. When (as in the case of George Thalben-Ball's highly effective performance a few days later of the Reubke Sonata, which was the talk of the town for weeks) the audience and the critics were pleased, they *admired only the player*! When they were displeased, they *blamed the organ*! They could just as logically have put these judgements into reverse: in fact, Sir Thomas Beecham said publicly that we had a magnificent instrument in the hands of a player who understood how to play it. This was proved during later years: played haphazardly without proper forethought and preparation, it can sound as bad as any other organ, perhaps worse than many.

But at its inauguration, it *was* too loud — I had panicked over the wind-pressures, and after a few weeks' trial, I had them reduced by something like ⅛ inch to the present level, which allowed the pipes some small margin of 'tolerance' in their speech, where they *had* been 'driven' to an audible limit.

In 1963 two of the large Pedal flue-stops, the 32-foot and the Majorbass 16-foot were increased in scale by one pipe, for greater ease of speech: this was an improvement in the case of the latter stop, but the 32-foot Principal has never been successful in the way one had hoped, judging from the excellent performance of a similar register in the old organ at Leeds Town Hall by Gray and Davison. A 32-foot stop of this kind *needs* to be on the organ-front and in a more favourable acoustic ambience in order to achieve its full effect. On the other hand a great improvement was achieved by replacing the English-type shallots of the 32-foot octave of the Bombarde with the authentic French type (unobtainable in 1952): the pressure of this (extended) rank was also reduced to that of the main Great, Swell and Pedal, viz, 3⅝ inches, thus reducing the sharp-toned 'drive' but increasing the roundness. In 1975 a very substantial sounding-board was installed over these pipes, so as to intercept the exaggerated reflection off the very thin plaster ceiling of accessory sounds of high-frequency which in parts of the hall had a very offensive effect: this measure also (in lieu of real casework) increased the roundness and general musicality of this important but critical stop, as heard in the *tutti*.

Was the Royal Festival Hall organ intended by me to set a new fashion? No, it was not. It was in all respects a "one off", and everybody concerned with its building contributed to that result in that spirit, down to the last detail of the tonal finishing: and although I was involved sporadically in other, later, organ-building transactions employing the same firm, there was never, nor could there be, the same extraordinary degree of whole-hearted co-operation and devoted team-work which accompanied every phase of the building of this truly monumental instrument.

A similar relationship did manifest itself occasionally, with other organ-builders: first, of course, at the Oratory (J. W. Walker & Sons); and there was the final completion of the Buckfast Abbey organ, in both cases with Walter Goodey and Dennis Thurlow as the voicers.

In the case of Buckfast, it will be recalled that a number of unsatisfactory features of that scheme had been left unresolved in 1952-3: ten years later the opportunity arrived for rectifying them, and the programme of improvements was motivated largely by the fruits of experience gained both at the Oratory and the Royal Festival Hall. It consisted of (a) redisposition of all the lower (unenclosed) sections, and (b) reorganising the Pedal division as far as was practicable — clearing away whatever worthless material still remained, and improving what was retained, with one or two discreet but vital additions.

Under heading (a), in addition to rebuilding and improving the key-actions, the soundboards of Great and Positive were turned round through 180 degrees, so that the Mixtures and upperwork went to the rear (in the choir aisle) and the Principals came to the front (over the choir stalls). An exception was the Great Cymbal which had to remain second from the choir front, but this stop was revoiced with the cut-ups raised a little so as to remove the 'sting' from the tone. The former inferior and partly dummy 'show pipes' on the aisle front of the Great were scrapped, and an agreeable front-prospect of new pipes for the bass octave of the 8-foot was installed at each side of the framing arch. The 16-foot Principal pipes (Great and Pedal), standing in the centre bay of the choir aisle, were stripped of their cream paint, remade and polished in their natural lustre, to form a presentable aisle front, behind and below the Positive, under which was now found a place for the Pedal Bombarde and its extensions, so that the latter no longer needed a choking baffle to hold them in check. The rest of the Pedal fluework was now confined to the westernmost bay (under the Echo), from which position its few stops amply dominated the nave. The Great reeds and Flute 8-feet now found their proper places behind the rest of the Great, in the easternmost bay of the choir aisle. Token acoustic casework was installed, between the actual pipework and the choir aisle, excepting only the Pedal 16-foot Principal, which stands behind the reflector belonging to the Positive. Plate XXI gives a good idea of the final arrangement. Some of the former pipework, moved to the Echo division, was now replaced by better material, including a new Echo Dulciana 8-feet, with suitably fluty intonation to contrast with the rather 'reedy' Salicional.

On a much grander scale, the same builders produced for me (under the benign auspices of the genial organist, George McPhee) a monumental reconstruction of the large organ in Paisley Abbey (Renfrew, Scotland), in which lay embedded a fair amount of Cavaillé-Coll pipework from the (smaller) organ which the latter firm built for the ancient nave in 1872; the choir being in ruins. (This organ was very much like the one cited in Chapter Two, built for the French Church in London.) When the choir was restored, the authorities decided that a much larger organ would be needed to fill the vastly increased volume of the church, and a large Romantic, quasi-orchestral instrument was built within a tall, narrow chamber in the angle of the choir and the south transept. Most of the former pipes were retained, but their sound was mostly modified out of all recognition. (Fortunately they were left structurally intact, and it was not difficult

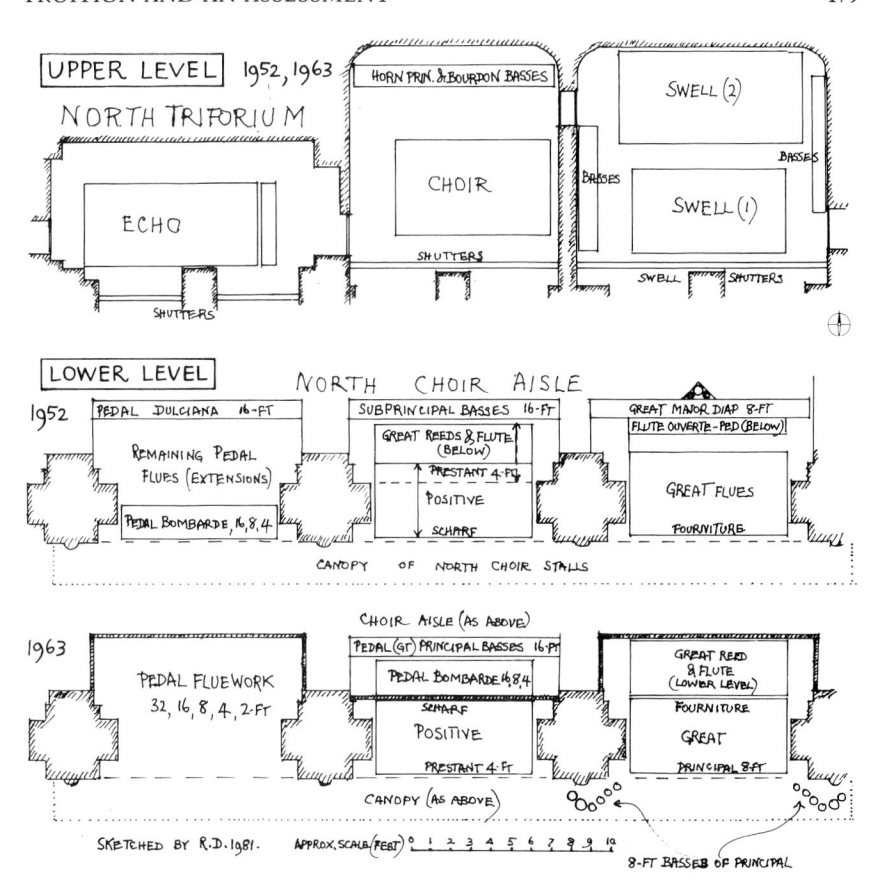

PLATE XXI *Buckfast Abbey, plan of the upper and lower levels of the organ showing the situation in 1952 and the final arrangement in 1963.*

to restore them to their original state and voice, to form the nucleus of a completely new design.)

That such a new design was sheer vandalism of a fine vintage organ might have been arguable — at Malvern Priory in 1976 I did take such a view, and strongly resisted any attempt to modernise or reconstruct the fine Rushworth organ of a similar vintage. But at Paisley there was a major disability: despite the use of wind-pressures of from 4 to 20 inches, the organ simply did not 'carry' down the nave.

Since the 1928 slider-soundboards had been lavishly constructed of excellent materials, they were all immediately re-usable, and the problem was simply to secure the projection of the sound into all parts of this large cruciform building, and to this end, to build up a new,

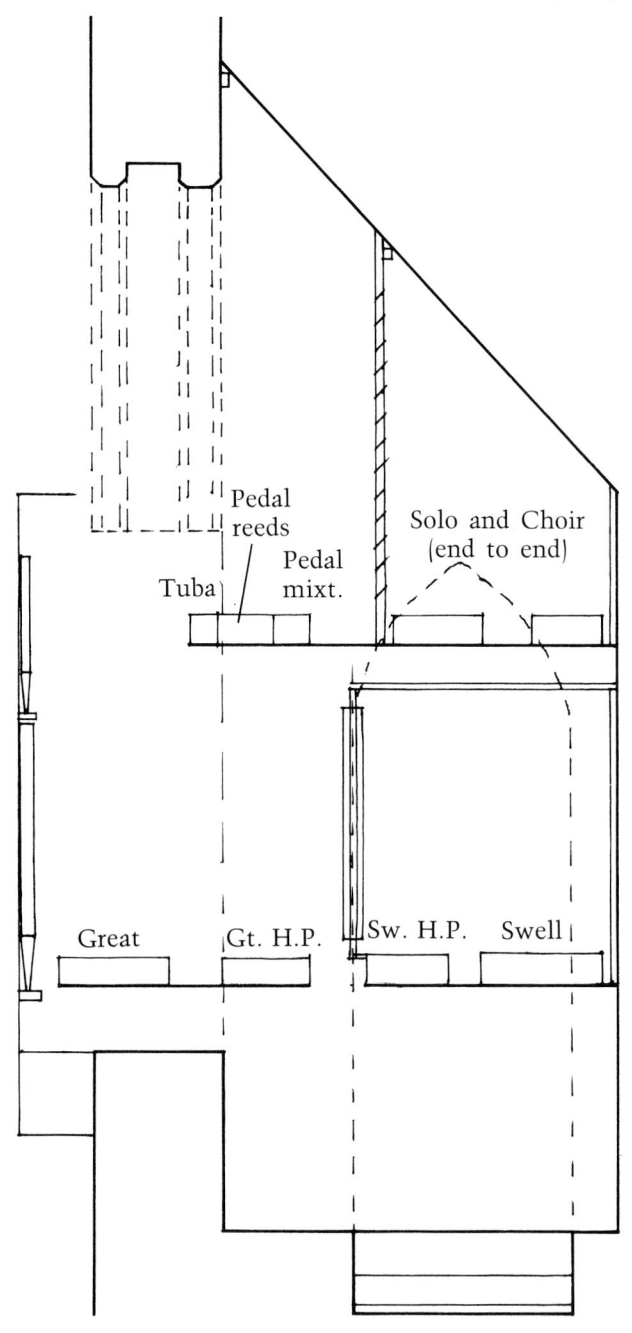

PLATE XXII *Paisley Abbey, section through the organ, 1928.*

clasically conceived specification of stops on the existing soundboards, re-sited. (Plates XXII-III give some idea of the 1928 disposition.)

A great advantage was gained by the removal of large wooden pipes which completely blocked the tall gothic arch connecting the organ-chamber with the south transept. These pipes (the Cavaillé-Coll Contrebasse 16-feet and most of its later 32-foot extension) were largely re-arranged across the eastern wall of the chamber, facing west: from which position they were for the first time completely audible, right down the nave! Apart from opening up the Pedal division, this arch was also useful as a frame for a new Bombarde division (4th manual) which also for the first time enabled a large, singing congregation in the nave and transepts to be adequately accompanied and supported: all this being achieved *without* the use of extraordinary wind-pressures.

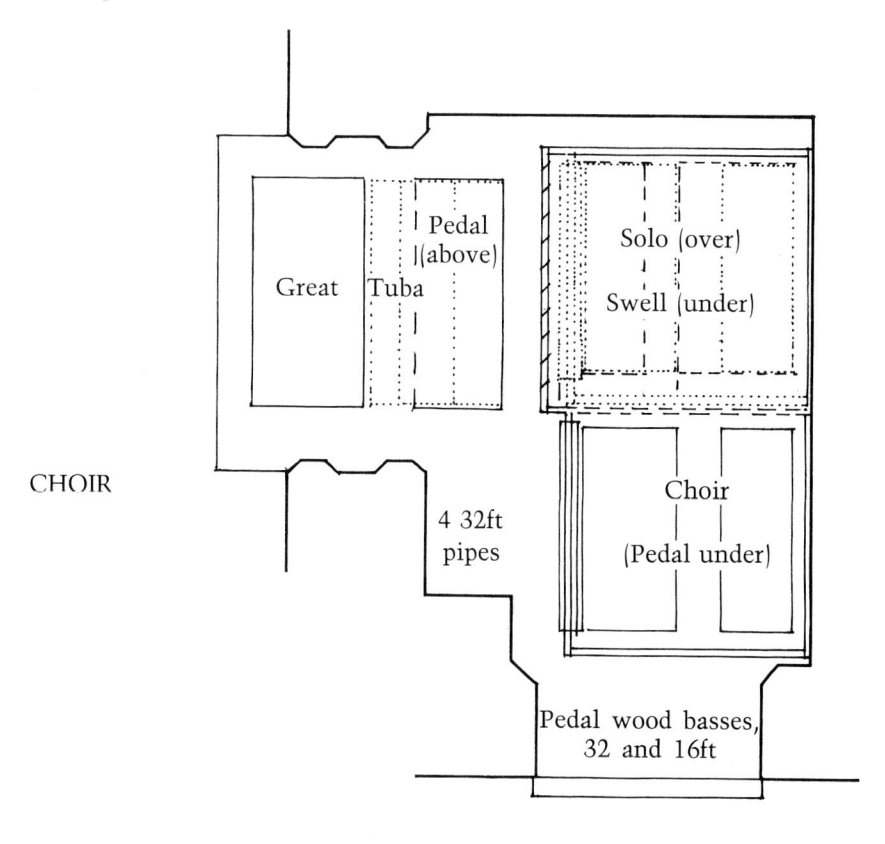

PLATE XXIII *Paisley Abbey, plan of the organ, 1928.*

There was only one regrettable incident, for which I myself must shoulder the responsibility: the carved oak 'case' (actually only a façade) which as an upward continuation of the choir-stalls graced and almost filled the arch from the chamber into the choir, was *sacrosanct* — the work of the locally revered architect of the choir itself, Sir Robert Lorimer. In 1928, when it was new, it was filled with an appallingly cheap display of *dummy* zinc pipes — with all the 'scaling' visually wrong — fat short pipes and long thin ones! The pipes of the Cavaillé 'Montre', made of high-grade tin and beautifully moulded, stood inside, round a corner! My aim was to put this Montre into Lorimer's case; but alas! the Cavaillé case-design had been made in 'soaring' nineteenth-century gothic, and the longest pipes had the longest feet. A quick trial of 8-foot C showed that it would protrude from the top of the woodwork in a most ungainly fashion: on the other hand, if remade with the foot-lengths varying inversely with the body-length, these pipes would fit in admirably. This meant "the melting-pot" for the longest ones, but the scales and the grade of metal were retained, and I felt that this piece of deliberate vandalism, regrettable though it might be in principle, was justified in the end-result (see Plates XXIV and XXV).

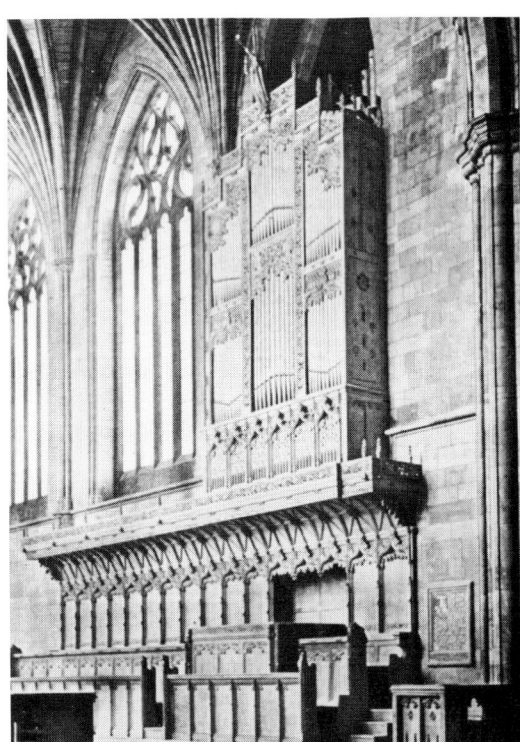

PLATE XXIV *Paisley Abbey, organ-case by Sir Robert Lorimer, 1928.*

PLATE XXV *Paisley Abbey, restored organ-case with partly re-cast Cavaillé-Coll Montre in prospect.*

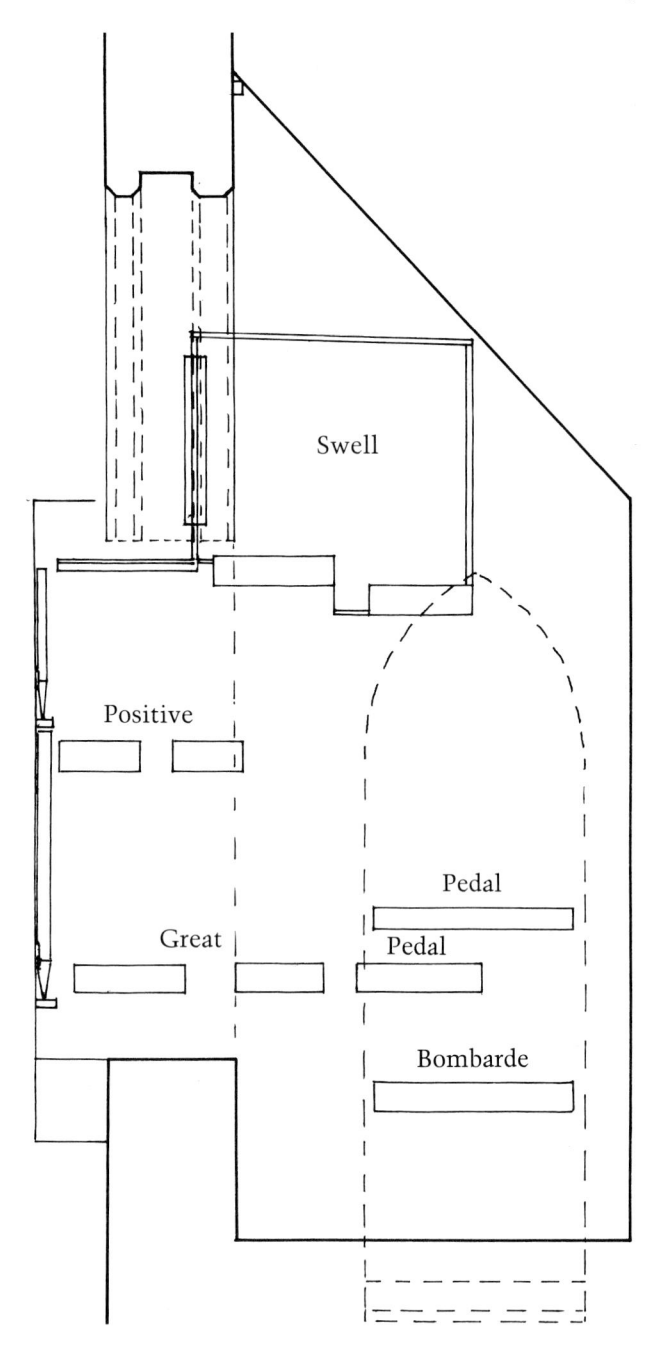

PLATE XXVI *Paisley Abbey, section through the organ, 1968.*

The key-actions were converted to 'outside' electro-pneumatic, whereby the wind-pressures for the pipes could be brought down to a reasonable, musical level, 4 inches now being the highest, and that only for the Pedal division. The new 'open-foot' voicing was in general supervised by Walter Goodey, actually executed by Dennis Thurlow, with assistance (for the reeds) from Arthur Jones and the younger, scrupulously careful Michael Butler. The interior planning in this cramped location presented many difficult problems, but the draughtsman at that time, Arthur Button, was as obstinate as I was, and *would not give up* until all was resolved to satisfaction: result — everything fitted like a glove when the organ was put in: the organ-builders on site were delighted! (Plates XXVI and XXVII)

The history and final development of the full specification is given below. One point of interest is the development of the tierce-flavoured

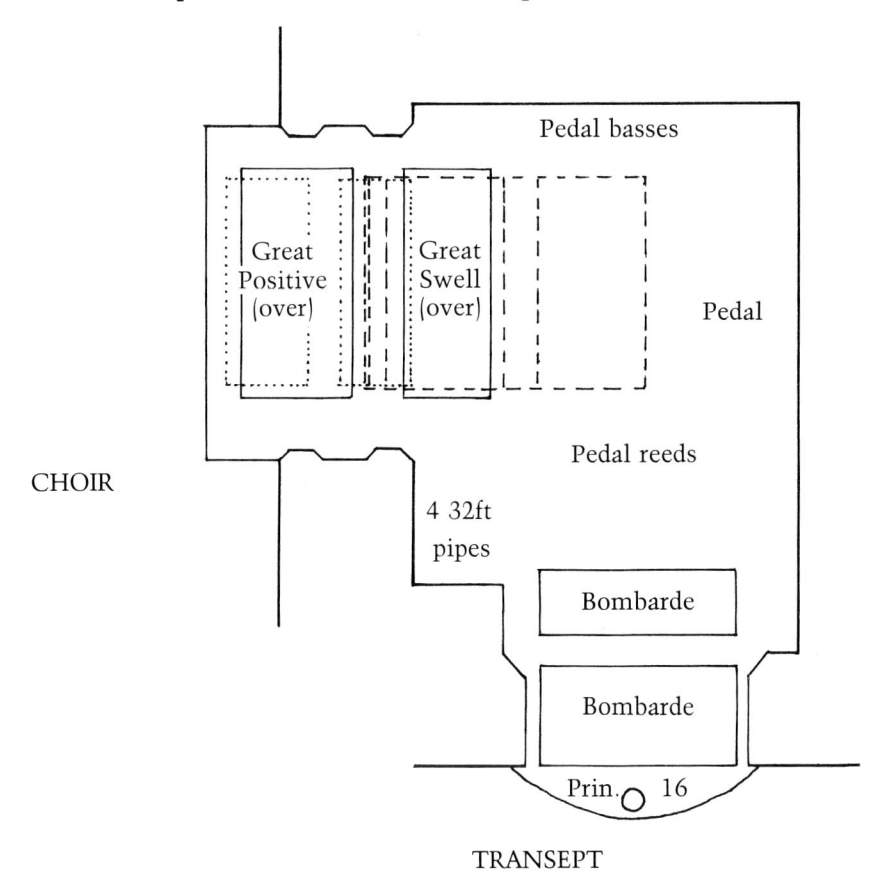

PLATE XXVII *Paisley Abbey, plan of the organ, 1968.*

mutations, rather in Dutch-baroque style. The Cornet IV on the Great is in fact a Dutch type and scale, except that it draws its fundamental from the separate 8-foot Bourdon (Cavaillé): the one on the Bombarde division is the Dom Bédos *'Grand Cornet'* of much larger scale and fat, hearty sonority, going down to tenor g, whereas the Great goes only to middle C. Both of these are balanced adequately with the *'Cornet décomposé'* in the Swell (wide-scale) and the narrow-scale Sesquialtera combination in the Positive.

The Positive division, above the main Great and in front of (while below) the large Swell-box, has its own impressive front array, taken from the tin pipes of the (Cavaillé) Salicional 8-feet and the new Principal 4-feet, also made of tin.

The transept-front consists of a plain pipe-display utilising the larger pipes of the (old, revoiced) Principal 16-feet, now shared by the Bombarde and Pedal divisions (see Plate XXVIII).

Apart from the ornamental casework in the arch into the choir, acoustical reflectors were put in behind the Bombarde, Great and Positive soundboards, to ensure the maximum tonal projection from the chamber: the re-siting of the Pedal has been mentioned already; its 'tone-cabinet' was in fact the chamber itself, looking west. In the event, enough Pedal tone seeped out round the other divisions for there to be no feeling of inadequacy from the choir side, where the console is now placed.

SPECIFICATIONS

1872 CAVAILLÉ-COLL

	GRAND ORGUE			RECIT EXPRESSIF	
(a)	Bourdon	16	(m)	Flûte traversière	8
(b)	Principal (Montre)	8	(n)	Bourdon	8
(c)	Flûte harmonique	8	(o)	Viole de gambe	8
(d)	Bourdon	8	(p)	Voix céleste (tc)	8
(e)	Salicional	8	(q)	Flûte octaviante	4
(f)	Prestant	4	(r)	Trompette	8
(g)	Octave	4	(s)	Basson-Hautbois	8
(h)	Doublette	2	(t)	Voix humaine	8
(i)	Pleinjeu III-VI				
(j)	Basson	16		PEDALE	
(k)	Trompette	8	(u)	Contrebasse (wood)	16
(l)	Clairon	4	(v)	Soubasse	16
			(w)	Violoncelle	8
(Figure 24 gives the scale-plan.)			(x)	Bombarde	16

PLATE XXVIII *Paisley Abbey organ showing the transept-front, 1968.*

188   BAROQUE TRICKS

Figure 24

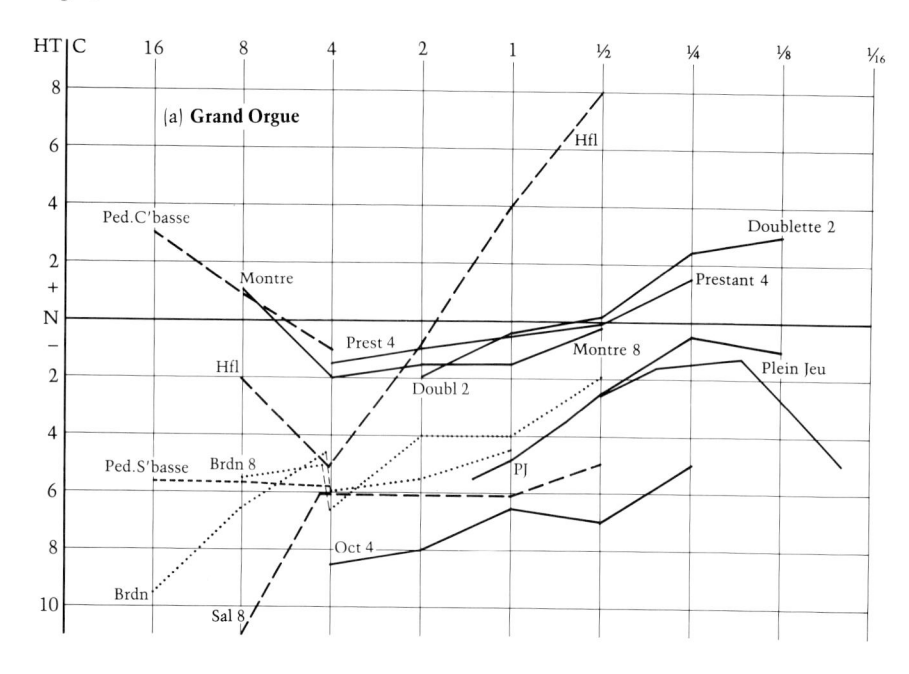

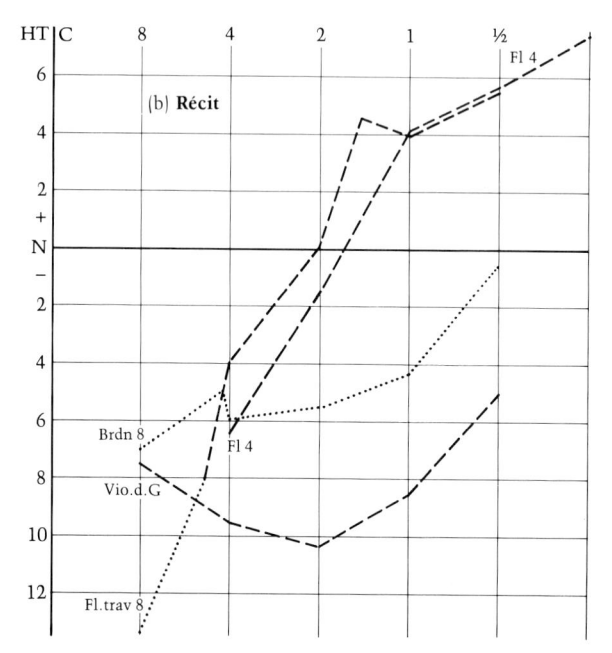

1928 HILL, NORMAN & BEARD
(Letters in brackets refer to the 1872 specification)

GREAT
	1	Double Open Diapason	16
	2	Large Open Diapason HP	8
	3	Open Diapason	8
(b)	4	Geigen Diapason	8
	5	Clarabella	8
	6	Principal	4
	7	Harmonic flute HP	4
	8	Twelfth (stopped)	2⅔
	9	Fifteenth	2
	10	Mixture 17, 19, 21, 22.	IV
(x)	11	Contra Tromba HP	16
	12	Tromba HP	8
	13	Tromba Clarion HP	4

SWELL
	14	Lieblich Bourdon	16
	15	Geigen Diap. HP (wood bass)	8
	16	Lieblich Gedackt	8
(n)	17	Bourdon HP	8
(o)	18	Viole de gambe	8
(p)	19	Voix célestes (tc)	8
(f)	20	Octave	4
	21	Lieblich flöte	4
	22	Flageolet	2
(i)	23	Pleinjeu [*sic*]	VI
	24	Waldhorn HP	16
	25	Cornopean HP	8
(s)	26	Hautbois d'amour [*sic*]	8
(l)	27	Clarion HP	4

CHOIR (enclosed)
(a)	28	Contra Flute	16
(e)	29	Salicional	8
(m)	30	Flûte traversière	8
	31	Dulciana	8
	32	Unda maris (tc)	8
(g)	33	Salicet	4
(q)	34	Flûte octaviante	4
	35	Nazard	2⅔
(h)	36	Doublette	2
	37	Tierce	1³⁄₅
	38	Bass Clarinet	16
(r)	39	Trompette	8
(t)	40	Voix humaine	8

SOLO (enclosed)
	41	Contra gamba	16
(c)	42	Flûte harmonique	8
(d)	43	Bourdon	8
	44	Viole d'orchestre	8
	45	Voix célestes (tc)	8
	46	Concert flute	4
	47	Octave viole	4
	48	Piccolo harmonique	2
(j)	49	Bassoon	16
	50	Corno di bassetto	8
	51	Orchestral oboe	8
(k)	52	Trompette	8
		(unenclosed)	
	53	Tuba magna HP	8

PEDAL
	54	Double Open Diap. (ext 56)	32
	55	Open Diapason 1 (wood)	16
(u)	56	Open Diapason 2 (wood)	16
	57	Contrebasse [*sic!!*] (metal)	16
(v)	58	Soubasse	16
	59	Contra Viole	16
	60	Octave (ext 55)	8
(w)	61	Violoncello	8
	62	Bass Flute (ext 58)	8
	63	Gedact (ext 58)	4
	64	Mixture 10, 12, 15.	
		(string pipes)	III
	65	Trombone HP	16
	66	Clarion (ext 65) HP	8

HP – High Pressure

= Great No. 1

= Solo No. 41

WIND-PRESSURES:
Great: 4 inches; (HP 12 inches)
Swell: 6 inches; (HP 10 inches)
Choir: 5 inches
Solo: 6 inches; (HP 20 inches)
Pedal: 4 inches; (HP 15 inches)

Figure 25 gives the scale-plan of most important stops.

Figure 25

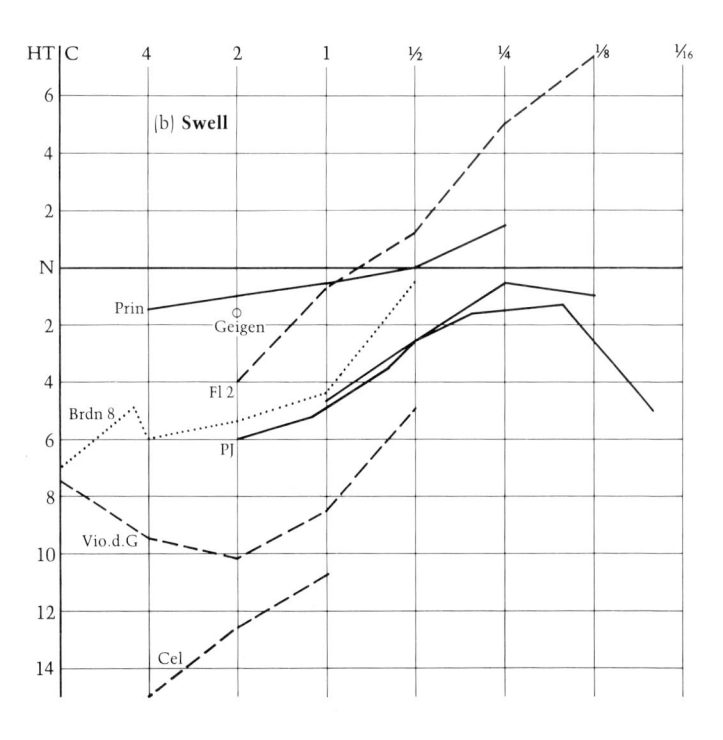

Paisley Abbey, 1928   (a) **Great**

(b) **Swell**

FRUITION AND AN ASSESSMENT

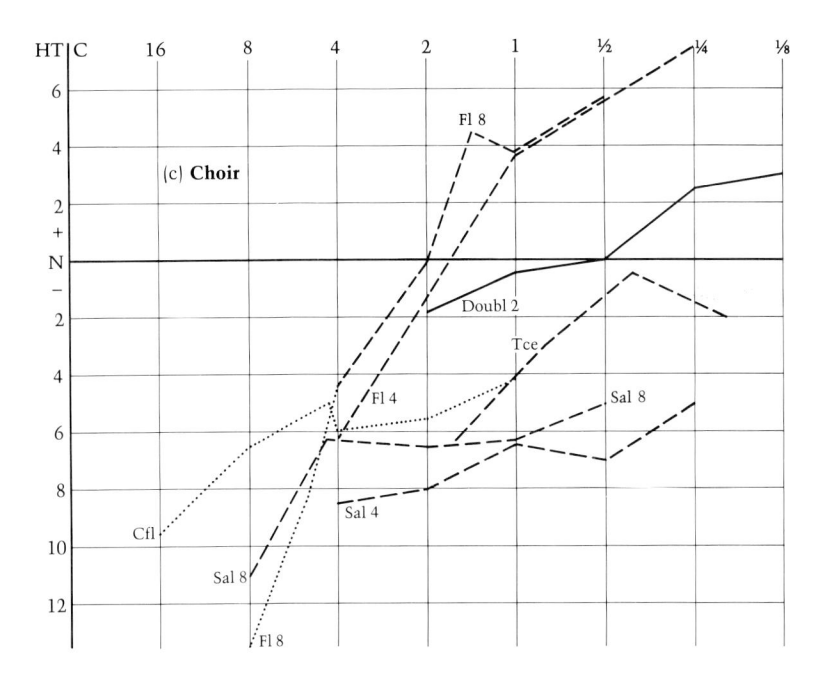

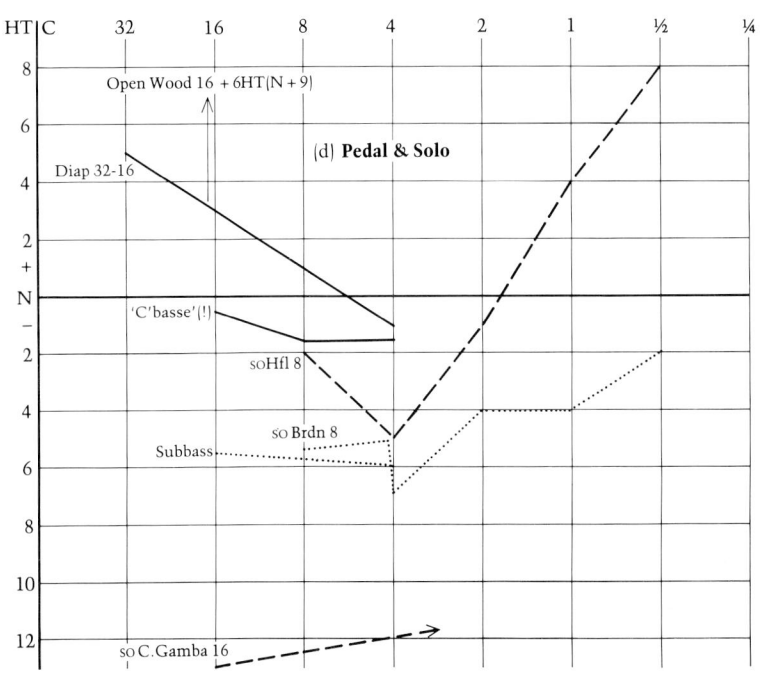

(c) Choir

(d) Pedal & Solo

1968 WALKER (DOWNES)
(Italic numbers in brackets refer to 1928 specification: all other stops are new.)

		Man I: POSITIVE *(unenclosed, upper case in chancel)*	
(29)	1	Salicional (front)[35]	8
(32)	2	Unda maris (tc, scale increased)	8
(30)	3	Traverse Flute[35]	8
(17)	4	Bourdon	8
	5	Principal (front)	4
	6	Chimney Flute	4
	7	Nazard (chimneys)	2⅔
	8	Doublette	2
	9	Wald Flute (conical)	2
	10	Larigot	1⅓
	11	Sesquialtera II	1⅓/2⅔
	12	Mixture IV	⅔
(50)	13	Cremona (revoiced)	8
		Tremulant	

		Man II: GREAT *(bottom of chancel case)*	
(28)	14	Bourdon	16
(4)	15	Montre (front)	8
	16	Spitzflute (wide)	8
(43)	17	Bourdon	8
(20)	18	Prestant	4
	19	Stopped Flute	4
	20	Quint	2⅔
(36)	21	Octave	2
	22	Blockflute	2
	23	Cornet (middle C) IV	4
	24	Mixture IV-VI	1⅓
(49)	25	Bassoon (opened up)	16
(52)	26	Trumpet (revoiced)	8

		PEDAL *(central position)*	
(54)	52	Contrebasse (ext)	32
(56)	53	Contrebasse (middle scale increased)	16
(1)	54	Principal (transept front)	16
(58)	55	Sub Bass	16
(41)	56	Salicional (revoiced)	16
	57	Octave (metal)	8
	58	Gedackt (metal)	8
(2)	59	Choralbass (revoiced)	4
	60	Open Flute	2

		Man III: SWELL *(top of chancel arch)*	
	27	Chimney Flute (wide)	8
(18)	28	Gambe	8
(19)	29	Voix céleste (tc)	8
	30	Principal (wide)	4
(34)	31	Flute octave (converted, non-harmonic)[36]	4
	32	Nazard (conical)	2⅔
	33	Gemshorn	2
	34	Tierce	1³/₅
(23)	35	Pleinjeu (enlarged) IV-VI	2
	36	Cimbel (with tierce) III	²/₅
(38)	37	Corno di Bassetto (opened up)	16
(26)	38	Hautboy (opened up)	8
(40)	39	Voix humaine (revoiced)	8
(39)	40	Trumpet (revoiced)	8
(27)	41	Clarion (revoiced)	4
		Tremulant	

		Man IV: BOMBARDE *(unenclosed, transept)*	
(1)	42	Principal (front)	16
(3)	43	Octave (revoiced)	8
(42)	44	Harmonic Flute	8
(6)	45	Prestant	4
(9)	46	Quartane II	2⅔
	47	Pleinjeu VI	1⅓
	48	Cornet (tg) V	8
(11)	49	Bombarde (revoiced)[37]	16
(12)	50	Trumpet (revoiced, new shallots)	8
(13)	51	Clarion (revoiced, new shallots)	4

FRUITION AND AN ASSESSMENT

	61	Mixture VI	2⅔
(65)	62	Bombarde (new shallots)	16
(24)	63	Bassoon (revoiced)	16
(53)	64	Trumpet No. 1 (new shallots)	8
(25)	65	Trumpet No. 2 (new shallots)	8
	66	Shawm	4

Approximate wind-pressures:
Great: 3½ inches (89 mm)
Swell: 3¾ inches (95 mm)
Positive: 2¾ inches (70 mm)
Bombarde: 3¾ inches (95 mm)
Pedal: 4 inches (102 mm)

Unison couplers throughout

Figure 26 shows the scale-plan of the present organ.

Figure 26

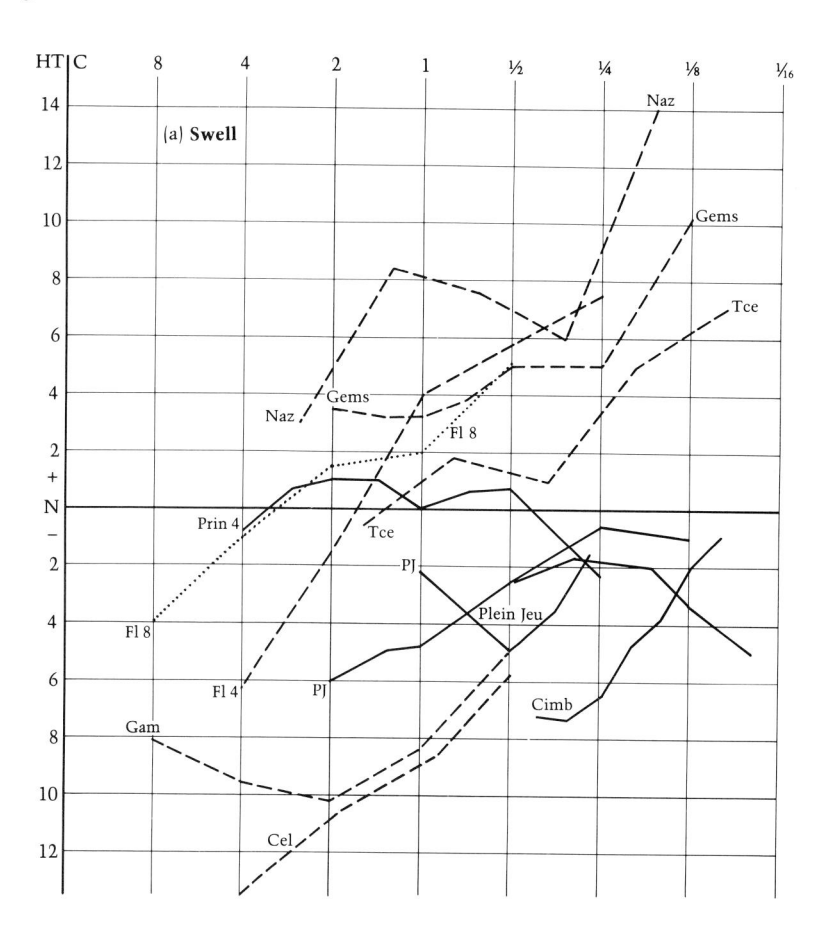

(a) **Swell**

(b) **Great**

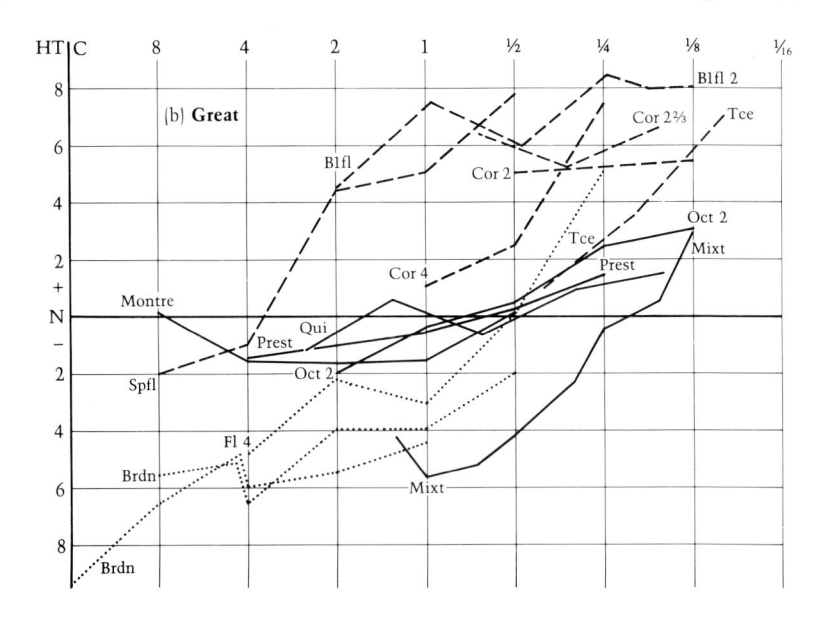

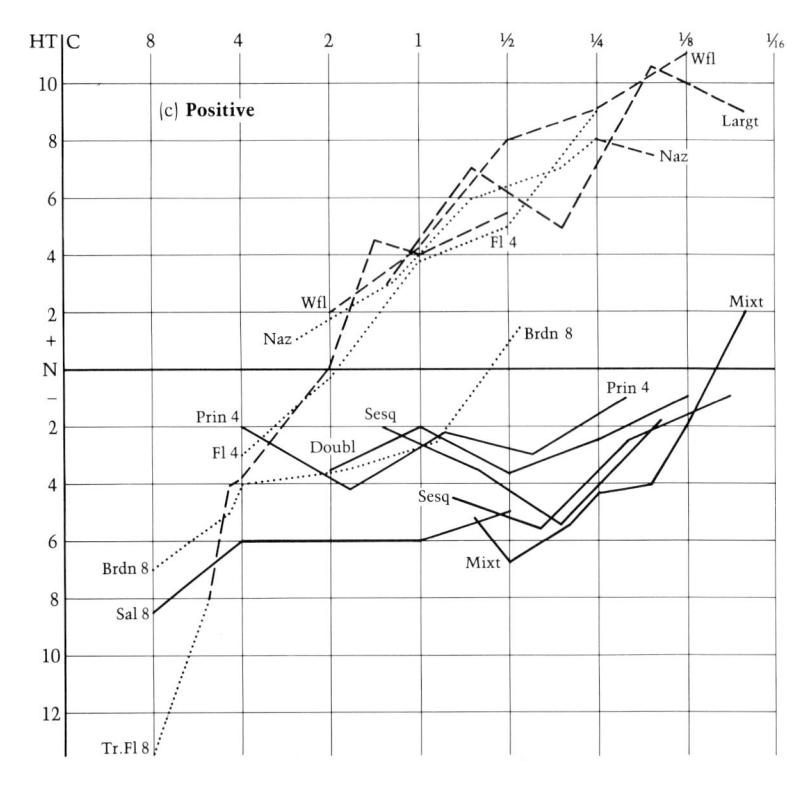

(c) **Positive**

FRUITION AND AN ASSESSMENT 195

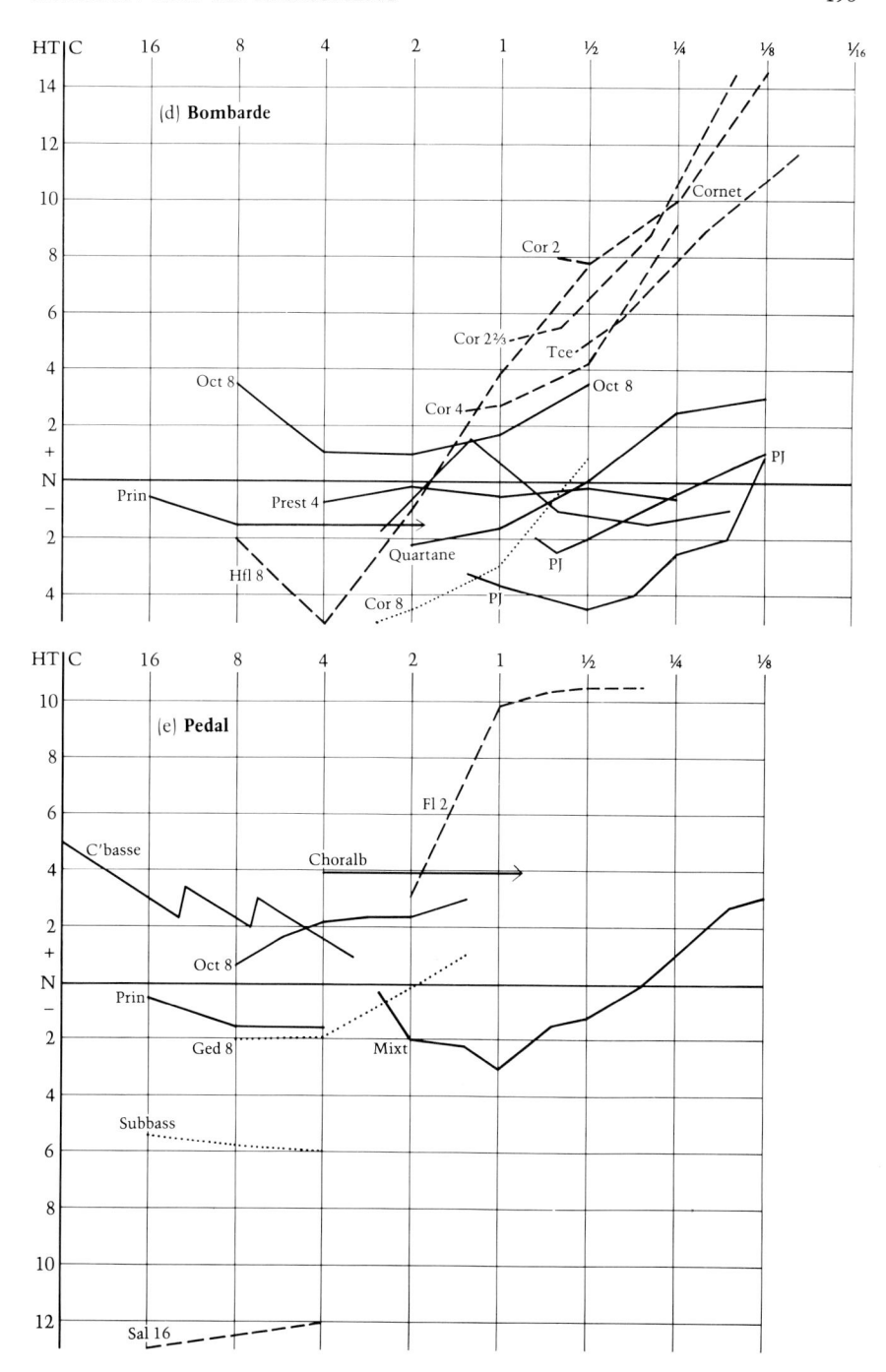

MIXTURE DISPOSITION

Positive	Sesquialtera II	C	1⅓	⁴/₅				
		c	2⅔	1³/₅				
	Mixture IV	C	⅔	½	⅓	¼		
		c	1	⅔	½	⅓		
		gs	1⅓	1	⅔	½		
		e¹	2	1⅓	1	⅔		
		c²	2⅔	2	1⅓	1		
		gs²	4	2⅔	2	1⅓		
		e³	4	2⅔	2⅔	2		
Great	Cornet IV	c¹	4	2⅔	2	1³/₅	throughout	
	Mixture IV-VI	C	1⅓	1	⅔	½		
		c	2	1⅓	1	1	⅔	
		c¹	2⅔	2	2	1⅓	1	1
		f¹	4	2⅔	2	2	1⅓	1
		c²	4	4	2⅔	2	2	1⅓
		a²	4	4	2⅔	2⅔	2	2
Swell	Pleinjeu IV-VI	C	2	1⅓	1	⅔		
		c	2⅔	2	2	1⅓	1	
		c¹	4	2⅔	2	2	1⅓	1
		c²	5⅓	4	2⅔	2	1⅓	1
	Cimbel III	C	²/₅	⅓	¼			
		Fs	½	²/₅	⅓			
		c	⅔	½	²/₅			
		fs	⁴/₅	⅔	½			
		c¹	1	⁴/₅	⅔			
		fs¹	1⅓	1	⁴/₅			
		c²	1³/₅	1⅓	1			
		fs²	2	1³/₅	1⅓			
		c³	2⅔	2	1³/₅			
		fs³	3¹/₅	2⅔	2			
Bombarde	Quartane II	C	2⅔	2		throughout		
	Pleinjeu VI	C	1⅓	1	⅔	½	½	⅓
		c	2	1⅓	1	1	⅔	½
		f	2⅔	2	1⅓	1	1	⅔
		c¹	4	2⅔	2	2	1⅓	1
		f¹	4	4	2⅔	2	2	1⅓
		c²	4	4	2⅔	2⅔	2	2
	Cornet V	g	8	4	2⅔	2	1³/₅	throughout
Pedal	Mixture VI	C	2⅔	2	1⅓	1	⅔	½
		cs¹	4	2⅔	2	1⅓	1	⅔

Neither this organ nor that in the Royal Festival Hall can be labelled "eclectic" with any degree of accuracy: both are tightly integrated entities, and each in its way is a "one off", as I said earlier. That the latter is "unprogenitive", as Dr Peter Williams has it, does not worry me in the least: so was Weingarten; so was Notre-Damc, Paris; so were the St George's Hall, Liverpool, Ottobeuren, etc: but that does not prevent their being fine organs!

But something like a fatal essay in eclecticism did occur at St Mary's Parish Church, Chigwell, Essex. Walker was the builder here, too: the date was 1963.

The former organ was a small, most undistinguished 2-manual tracker instrument, buried in a chamber on the North side of Bodley's superbly proportioned new chancel. (He built a new nave also, flanking and communicating with the ancient small village church which *ipso facto* became a South side aisle and Lady Chapel.) The organ-chamber and vestry were housed in a wing built out on the North side; there was no North aisle for the nave.

Aided and abetted by the then organist, John Auton, who was also Director of Music in nearby Chigwell School, and Conductor of the Chigwell Choral Society, locally famous for its very ambitious performances — I conceived the idea of a *multum in parvo* organ of two manuals and 27 speaking-stops, strategically planned for maximum tonal projection down the nave; in the present situation the organ lost 50 per cent of its volume as one stepped out of the organ-chamber door into the chancel! This was not a little due to the additional handicap of a lofty ceiling in the chamber, much higher than the chancel arch which also was considerably obstructed by 8-foot pipes at its apex. The only solution to the problem, as far as I could see, was to requisition the existing site of the console for a *Brustwerk*-type Swell (with grilles behind the North choir-stalls) arranged directly under the Great, which itself would be properly encased: the Pedal organ, considerably enlarged, was to go behind the Great, on the same level except for the two 16-foot flue stops which would stand on the floor on the West side of the chamber, facing East — the whole being covered by a new, stoutly constructed, false ceiling, fixed at the level of the apex of the arch into the chancel. As a result of all this, the console *had* to go across the chancel, and the action had to be altered to electro-pneumatic, except for the Swell-louvre control, which was ingeniously retained on a mechanical system despite the fact that excavation was impossible!

Since there was absolutely no other possible site for an organ I had no regrets or scruples of conscience about anything just described. Rather did they spring later from more basic considerations.

SPECIFICATIONS

HILL, 1899

GREAT		SWELL	
Open Diapason	8	Bourdon	16
Stopped Diapason (wood)	8	Open Diapason	8
Dulciana (leathered)	8	Hohlflute (stopped bass)	8
Principal	4	Salicional	8
Harmonic Flute	4	Principal	4
Twelfth	2⅔	Flautino	2
Fifteenth	2	Mixture [19, 22: 12, 15]	II
Trumpet	8	Cornopean	8
		Oboe	8
PEDAL			
Open Diapason	16	3 unison couplers.	
Bourdon	16	tracker manuals, pneumatic pedal	

(The scaling and voicing of all the fluework was conventional and in every way undistinguished: the Great and Pedal diapasons were rather wide, all the flute stops were meagre, excepting only the treble of the Great harmonic flute, which, however, then followed the Töpfer normal.)

WALKER (DOWNES), 1963 (see Plate XXIX)

GREAT (old soundboard)		SWELL (new)	
Open Diapason (front)	8	Gedackt (metal)	8
Rohrflute (chimneys)	8	Salicional	8
Octave	4	Céleste (from A)	8
Stopped Flute	4	Venetian Flute	4
Nazard (conical)	2⅔	Spitzflute	2
Fifteenth	2	Larigot	1⅓
Mixture III-V	1	Sesquialtera II	1⅓/2⅔
Trumpet (French shallots)	8	Cimbel II	⅓
Tremulant		Cremona	8
		Tremulant	
PEDAL (old Swell chest)			
Octave (metal)	8	3 unison couplers	
Gedackt (metal)	8		
Quintadena	4	Wind-pressures:	
Spitzflute	4	Great and Swell: ± 2½ inches	
Open Flute	2	Pedal: 4 inches	
Fagotto	16		
Trumpet	8		
Shawm	4		
(old Pedal chest)			
Principal Bass (old)	16		
Bourdon (old)	16		

FRUITION AND AN ASSESSMENT 199

PLATE XXIX *St. Mary's Parish Church, Chigwell, Essex.*

It will be evident that this organ was planned so as to be able to cope with the *entire* repertoire — I even made a test tape-recording of some of Vierne's *Third Symphony* (1st movement and *Adagio*). But it also subsequently fell to my lot to accompany the Choral Society's performances of Dvorak's *Stabat Mater*, Haydn's *Creation*, and even Elgar's *The Apostles* and *The Kingdom*! — (no orchestra in any of these!). Well, to be honest — given the village church ambience, and a flat, cruel acoustic — all these performances were in fact caricatures (as far as the accompaniment was concerned), and in spite of their obvious sincerity, they *sounded* like caricatures: it was a survival, or revival, of the old fallacy of the studio-, teaching- or practice-organ, replete with colourful stops, discreetly voiced — the exact opposite of, say, the philosophy underlying the recently installed Marcussen organ in St. Mary's Church, Nottingham (already referred to), so honestly and frugally planned, sited, and tonally projected, that a single Gedackt, as heard in the nave, has the 'presence' of the old Walker Tuba! These are surely extremes which are 'unprogenitive', and neither to be copied in future. The scale-plan of the Chigwell organ is given in Figure 27.

Figure 27

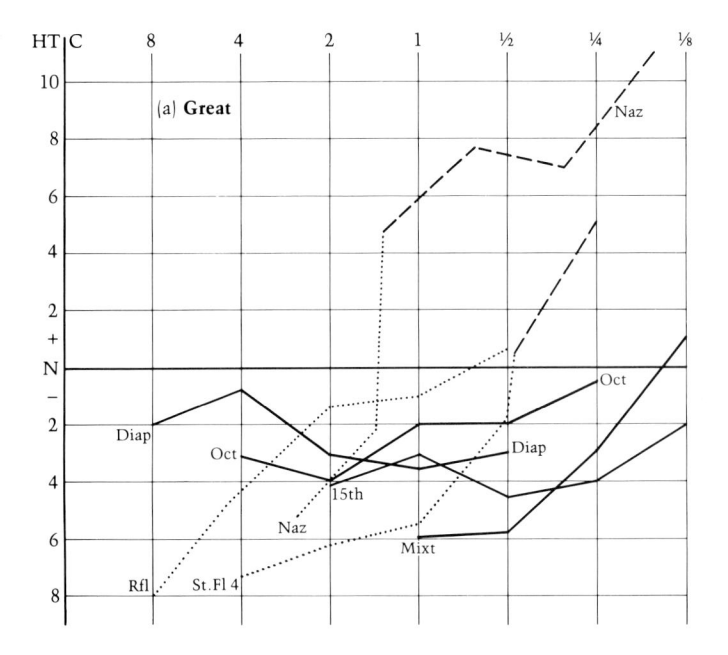

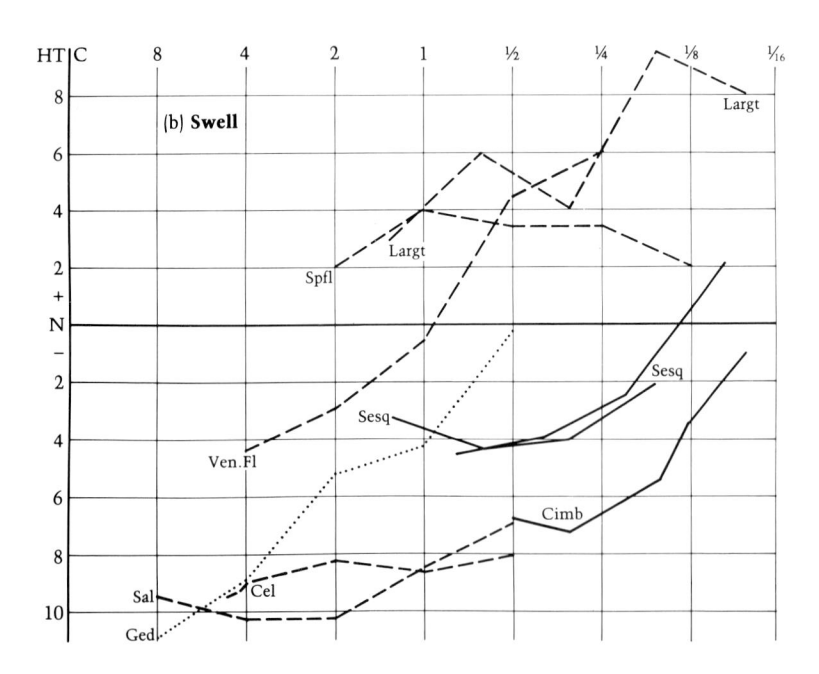

(c) **Pedal**

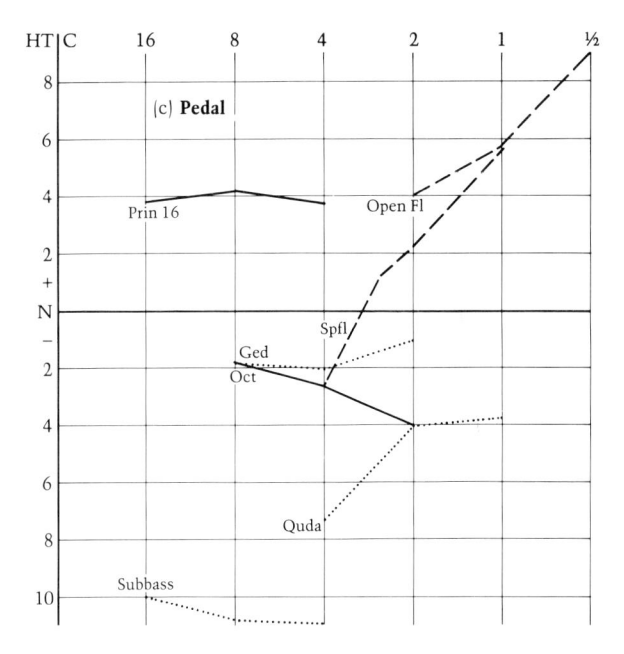

[chart showing pedal stops: Prin 16, Open Fl, Spfl, Ged, Oct, Quda, Subbass across pitches 16, 8, 4, 2, 1, ½]

There was one feature of the Chigwell organ which did prove its worth — the casework. Just after we had finished the tonal regulation and final tuning, I wandered off down the church while the organist was playing, but was horrified to observe the old complete 'fade-out' as I got down into the nave! I rushed back, to find that the voicer, in the course of removing some tools, had taken out the back-board of the Great case: as soon as he replaced it, all was well — the organ 'carried' well, right down to the West end.

With such a *multum in parvo* scheme I found it necessary, from the classical point of view, to ensure the greatest possible adaptability of all the resources on a trio-sonata basis: the important balances were therefore checked and secured, so that the right-hand tonal pinnacle would always be the more brilliant, though of *equal loudness* compared with the left-hand on the other manual (see Table I). A corollary would naturally be the equal power (by added impact) of narrow and wide scaled stops of similar pitch — the wide making their mark on the narrow by way of fullness, the narrow on the wide by way of sharpness: and this relationship to apply as between stops of different scale in the same division or in other divisions. Thus, at Chigwell (allowing for the Swell Salicional to be something of a special case *vis à vis* the Great Diapason), Diapason = Rohrflute = Gedackt; Octave = Stopped flute 4-feet = Venetian Flute; Fifteenth = Spitzflute 2-feet; Nazard = Larigot (the latter a fraction softer, as being of higher relative pitch from the unison).

That this was sound policy was confirmed recently (1974) in an article written in the Klais firm's Information Leaflet: it was followed out in great detail in the organs at St. Albans Cathedral and the Fairfield Hall, Croydon, in both of which I made the specifications and fixed the scales (though over the voicing and finishing I had only a limited amount of control, and therefore only a limited responsibility for the effect).

At St. Albans, where there was considerable spatial separation of all divisions, involving a difference of acoustic ambience between the choir-screen area (Positive) and the triforium level (Great and Swell), a most important unifying principle was the ample scaling of the wide-open flutes — Pedal 16-feet, Great 8-feet, Swell 4-feet, Positive 2-feet. In the *pleno* of each separate division, and its relationship to the others, this was the source of equal carrying-power. It was particularly so in the Positive, nestling down in the Eastern structure of the choir-screen and acoustically open towards both East and West — its flat roof acting as a tonal reflector in both directions: the Principal-chorus proper was of distinctly narrower scale than that of the other three divisions (see Figure 28), and hence the 2-foot Waldflute was conceived as a vital ingredient in its plenum — a fact which has not always been perceptibly grasped by such players as habitually plan their registration visually or theoretically rather than aurally!

At Fairfield Hall I planned the inter-manual relationship as noted in Table II. This was checked and verified aurally on site, and the wind-pressures were adjusted accurately to this end — very unpopular procedure with a rule-of-thumb organ-builder or voicer, but none the less musically essential. I am talking about variations of pressure of ⅛ inch or so: one ⅛ inch too low could verge on a thin insufficiency. So far as I had this adjustment in hand, I was satisfied that the optimum solution of this problem had been reached in the final sonority and tonal balance of this organ.

Problems of balance and tone-projection came up again at Gloucester Cathedral. Fortunately the rebuilding in 1971 went to the one firm that from the beginning had shown particular interest in the restoration to speech (and pristine beauty) of Thomas Harris's East and West diapasons, mostly silenced since the day when Father Willis ingeniously (but unworthily) turned the whole organ round through 90 degrees within the old case. The only front-pipes he left speaking were the large ones in the corner-towers, but their backs were then cut down as much as five semitones to produce a monster-scale! Luckily, in accordance with his normal procedure, he did not actually *shorten* the internal pipes belonging to these diapasons and 4-foot principals — he *slotted* them: and because the scale-increase thereby gained (about 3 semitones) would have endangered steady speech (even with his enhanced wind-pressures), he evidently left the cut-up of their mouths mostly alone. Since it became plain during our investigations that the

FRUITION AND AN ASSESSMENT 203

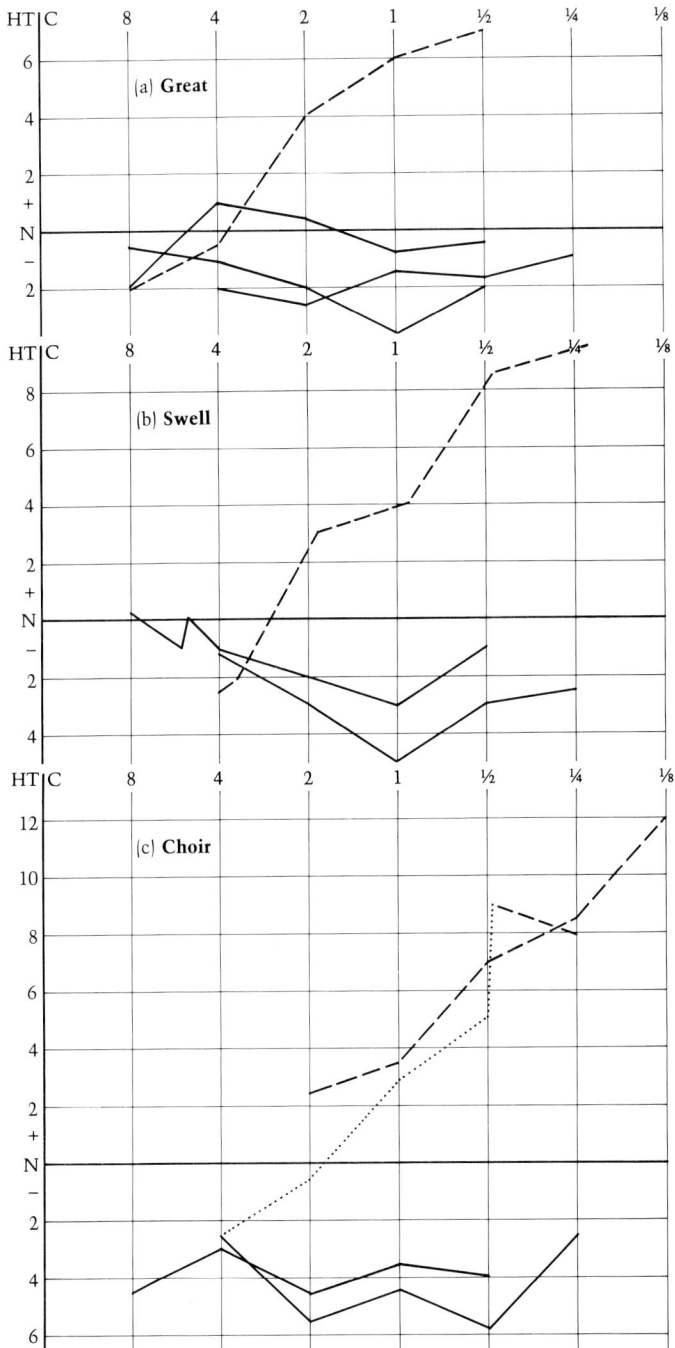

Figure 28

original pitch of this organ had been almost exactly the present International Normal (a' - 440), restoration was a simple matter — the slots were filled up, and a beautiful singing tone resulted, markedly different from Willis's fluty sonority on heavier wind. (Willis had raised the pitch by one semitone in accordance with late nineteenth-century standards.)

But if Father Willis's last rebuild, even in 1899, had remained intact, there would have been a compelling case for leaving it alone: but changes *had* been made both in specification and the voicing in a new rebuild in 1920 — moreover, the case (by now a mere roofless screen) had been cut in two and then successively deepened from its original 50 inches to more than 12 feet, so that as left in 1921, its West front was actually perched on top of the stone coping of the choir-screen! Of course the sides were broken: Willis had put the bass of his 16-foot Double Diapason across the South face in an unsightly projecting row above his new console; but the North face was devoid even of this pretence of elegance — from 1921 a row of Double Dulciana pipes stood there with merely patched-up woodwork (the trebles were continued within what remained of the Chair Organ case). By and large, these basses were only invisible, or partly so, because Willis had filled up the neighbouring Norman arch at the North end of the screen with the 16-foot Bishop pedal pipes (open wood) brought up from the screen's interior and (somewhat boastfully) painted stone-grey. Their place was eventually taken by a 16-foot Pedal reed and a new enclosed Solo division. A 32-foot extension of these open wood pipes — although judged unsuitable by Father Willis a few years earlier — was also inserted in 1921; and since there was no room for these huge pipes anywhere near the organ, they were carted off into the North triforium of the choir, *East* of the crossing! Only the sensitively reverberant acoustics of this remarkable building created the illusion that their sound belonged to the distant organ at all!

Thus, there was plenty of clearing up to be done, and the first step was to get everything back into its proper position within the case, the only exceptions being the two wooden Pedal stops, *viz*, the large-scale (and thus shortened) open pipes added in 1831, and the Sub Bass. The former were now restored to their original position within the stone screen, where they are invisible: and thus the beautiful Norman arch on the North side has now been opened up again. (The 32-foot Open Wood was unceremoniously thrown out for the irrelevancy it was.) The West front of the case was also withdrawn to a practical minimum depth of 10 feet 5 inches so as to stand clear of the carved stone parapet: the sides were properly restored and suitably adorned by a re-arrangement of six of Willis's 16-foot metal basses, appropriately decorated and now conveniently relegated exclusively to the Pedal division, along with most of the large original case-pipes. Finally, the fractured cornices of the towers were repaired and joined up most tastefully (under the supervision of Herbert Norman Esq), and the whole, including the priceless Chair Organ case, has been roofed over with solid timber.

There were certain interlocked dilemmas then to be faced, and the most serious concerned the actual treatment of the Harris pipework.

In the first place, the unique decoration of these pipes (even more impressive than the Thamar pipes now at Framlingham) gave its restoration a high priority, only to be entrusted to a specialist picture-restoring firm: and such was the fragility both of the metal and the paint thereon encrusted with layers of varnish and other 'patching', that these pipes could only be permitted the journey to the studio and back — an additional trip to the organ-works was out of the question! But first, since successive organ-builders had scrambled their order in the case, the important work of identification had to be undertaken — mostly by Mr. John Norman — before they could be removed *en masse*. When their proper locations had been re-established they were all given a new numbering: and thus I was able to measure the scales as they stood upright against a wall in the studio. Nothing could be done to them, tonally speaking, until they were back in the organ, apart from trial of a test-pipe — and I personally took a tenor a-sharp or b-pipe of the East Diapason, carefully wrapped up (and in John Whitworth's car) from Surbiton to Hornsey so that it could be put on its wind, on a voicing-machine. The foot-hole (and the corresponding hole in the pipe-block in the case) was *small*, but even then it became evident that its wind-pressure would have to be very low — perhaps of the order of 2½ inches, or even less. The languid was rather roughly, albeit sparsely, nicked. On the other hand, a preliminary test which I had made some months earlier with a tenor g-sharp pipe (out of the East front) on the soundboard *in the organ* before dismantling, had clearly demonstrated that for the instrument's present function and position on the screen, a wind-pressure of $3^{5/8}$ inches was absolutely *de rigueur*, so to speak!

It must not be forgotten that the Gloucester organ, as built by Harris, stood in the arch of the South transept, facing North, and was obviously never intended at that time to serve the whole vast building. Nevertheless the Dean and Chapter ruled in 1969 that there must be *one* organ only, to serve for everything — choir services, nave services, and the Three Choirs Festival. Clearly, the only solution would be an adequately planned 3-manual organ "looking two ways", with a 4-manual console.

As far as the Great (and even the Pedal division) was concerned, this conception presented in general terms no great difficulty: the East and West diapasons would provide the foundation for the former, with an appropriate chorus-structure for each side and reeds in the centre between them — and the entire pipework running again from North to South, and of course the front pipes 'conveyed' from the soundboards on to a pipe-block. The Pedal pipes could then be divided into C and C-sharp sides, the pipes running East-West within the sides of the case, taking in the larger basses in the corner towers as well as the six now to be displayed on the North and South faces. So far, so good, ignoring for the moment the dilemma of the wind-pressures.

On the East side, the old Chair case (roofed over anew) could house a new Choir division, pressing into service most, if not all, of the painted front pipes as the (original) 4-foot Principal — unfortunately the smaller gilded pipes turned out to be original solid wood dummies!

On the West, the issue was an open option, there being only some panelling of later date above the top of the stone traceried parapet and nothing at all below: there would just be sufficient headroom for a (4-foot) West-Positive, corresponding to the East Chair division, but tucked *under* the West Great and with no visible pipes.

The placing of the Swell division was then the dominant problem. Historically, the records produced no clue as to its position or design in Father Willis's rebuild of 1847 — his first important *opus*. Its compass was known to have been extended for the first time down to C (8-feet), but his citation of a "double Venetian front" is exasperatingly vague. Its pipes *must* at that time have run from North to South, and since the height of the case was insufficient to permit a second storey, the Swell-box must surely have been sited West of the Great. Did it have, literally, Venetian shutters in front *and* behind? If so, the Western output of the Great must have been somewhat impeded, even if the organ was roofless already: and how then was the West diapason winded? The console was certainly on the East (behind the Chair Organ), as a well-known picture of S. S. Wesley proves — and indeed some of the woodwork of the drawstop jambs survived *in situ* for many years.

The swinging round to 90 degrees with a South-side console came in response to the needs of congregational services in the nave — a fashionable movement which was responsible for a similar redisposition of the organs at Exeter and (eventually in principle) St. Paul's in London. Here at Gloucester, the ends of the re-positioned Swell-box completely cut off access to the Northern half of the Great (Harris) front pipes, East and West, thus silencing the whole stops below middle C. What to do?

Clearly a new Swell within the case must have an open aspect on both East and West sides, with vertical louvres under separate East-West control: and the only practicable site available would be *under* the Great, with the box so shaped as to command the open space on each side of the Chair case (on the East) and the West-Positive (on the West). The opening or destruction of certain old panels immediately below the East Great impost was strictly forbidden by the antiquarians, who, however, consented to the raising of the whole Great case by 16 inches. Despite the somewhat theoretical scruples of individuals like Susi Jeans (who seemed unwilling to acknowledge the over-riding value of a great integral restoration which was being accomplished), I had no guilty feelings whatever on this score, for nothing definite was known about the exact relation of Great and Chair in their original position in the South transept; moreover, even the screen on which the organ now stands is not the original one from the eighteenth century: and the squat, dumpy effect of the late nineteenth-century, lopsided arrangement lacked elegance with a vengeance! The antiquarians, who were often hard enough to satisfy, unanimously gave their blessing to this slight modification, and the present appearance of the organ case from either East or West is unquestionably majestic and dignified (see plate XXX, p.210).

As to the practical application: the case (like the original one at Worcester) was distinguished by its corners' resting on four round pillars with carved capitals — the usual 'waisting in' being replaced by open arches. The latter had been clumsily filled up with pieces of cloth-covered timber, but by the new, recessed grille-work, skilfully designed by Mr. Herbert Norman, their identity was re-established. I disposed the new Swell with its foundation-stops (flue and reed) in C and C-sharp sides, looking out East and West directly behind these grilles: the upper-work and the short-length Vox humana were arranged on a small central soundboard, elevated between the two halves.

All was well, when (after massive reconstruction and repair of the case) the Swell pipes began to appear: but on the arrival of the 8-foot conical Salicional — the softest stop in the new organ — the fabulous *diminuendo* to *pp*, cited by Father Willis, simply refused to happen! I tried reducing the wind-pressure, which made for a slight improvement, but the 'open' output from the other stops was then unacceptably enfeebled. I blamed the organ-builders for not making the shutters thick enough; but it was made clear to me that to thicken them now would inevitably restrict the output when they were fully open, ie, at a 90 degree angle.

I then had an inspiration, which although initially resisted, proved to be right. It was this: the Swell box measured 16 feet in width, nearly 6 feet in height (above the rack-boards) and slightly more than 5 feet deep. Especially in view of waste space around the small central soundboard, it would be arguable that its internal volume was excessive, and thus, with closed shutters, over-reverberant, especially since both sets of shutters had been faced internally with sheet metal to make them more reflective. (I recalled a similar early disability at the Royal Festival Hall, where the Swell-box is *enormous*, and where the failure to achieve a real *pianissimo* was only cured by actually thickening the shutters: but in that instance the Swell *front* was so enormous too — something like 240 square feet in area — that this slight reduction in shutter-opening was trivial; also, by contrary, the hall was so 'dry' that I always thought that an effective *crescendo* was inhibited thereby. But, again paradoxically, the hard concrete wall in the back of all the boxes there afforded a fine reflecting surface capable of enhancing low-frequency reverberation in the whole neighbourhood when the boxes were open, thus improving the generally dry acoustic properties of this otherwise superb hall.)

Anyway, something *had* to be done at Gloucester, and I persuaded the voicer to fix a sheet of hardboard, East-West, between the South Swell soundboard and the middle section. The result was sensational; but it carried one disadvantage for the player: the console being South of the organ-case, the North end of the Swell now sounded distinctly more remote — the C-sharp whole-tone scale sounded louder than the one on C-natural. However, most organists are quite accustomed to "flying blind", once they know their instrument, and the effect in the body of the building must always be the touchstone. In the nave and choir at Gloucester there was a notable improvement, and the one-sided effect was not perceptible at all. So two large, solid baffles were introduced and fixed permanently.

But now there was another, consequent problem. As heard from the West, the Swell Mixtures were now too prominent, lacking the screening effect of the Chair case on the East. (The Swell 8-foot flue-stops were on the West side of the box too.) The answer to this was not so difficult: removal of the lowest section of the baffles (adjacent to the mouths of the tenor and bass ranges of these stops) put everything right. (It will be recalled that a similar eventual removal of lowest sections of side-baffles benefited the broad sonority of the lower Great at the Festival Hall, some four years later.)

But to revert to the most serious, embarrassing dilemma — that involved in the voicing of the front diapasons. Here I shall have to face a charge of vandalism on two counts: firstly, as found, the two diapasons were of *identical*, very narrow scale. In view of the authorities' express musical requirements, there was no merit in preserving this scale for the West Great which would have to dominate the large nave: I therefore had no compunction about increasing the scale by two pipes (only one in the bass) simply by raising their pitch by two semitones. It was then feasible to borrow the lowest 20 pipes of this stop *at 16-foot pitch only*, on to the Pedals, using all the large tower-pipes not needed for the East Diapason, and sounding their original notes, or at least within a semitone of them in one or two cases. This carried us down to FF-sharp, the rest being supplied by the 6 Willis pipes now ranged in the elegant side arches in the North and South faces of the upper case.

But it was always my intention to retain the East Diapason and Principal intact, as a monument to the original builder, and a unique example of their period. The scale relationship of these two was extremely interesting in that (like at least one important Italian

FRUITION AND AN ASSESSMENT 209

example — S Petronio, Bologna[38]) — the Octave was throughout of wider scale than the Unison (see Figure 29).

It was when we finally put these Diapason pipes on their wind, in the case, that we came face to face with the grim truth: they just *would not* speak a decent note! The voicer was Philip G. Prosser (whose initials are among those which adorn the six North and South pipes): he was a perfectionist, and already uneasy because we had encountered an unexplained fluctuation in the wind-system of the Great fluework.

We slogged on for a couple of days. Reducing the wind-pressure did not really help, and the feet of these old pipes could not be knocked up so as to reduce the volume — the pipes were too fragile to survive such rough treatment, especially since the feet were not shaped: there were no 'toes', the end of the pipe was just pushed into the hole in the casework, which it fitted exactly.

Meantime we were behind schedule, for preparations for the Three Choirs Festival (at Gloucester in 1971) were pressing on, and our opportunities for voicing and tuning would soon be drastically cut and finally suspended altogether.

On the third day Philip and I came to the conclusion that the mouths of some of these pipes would *have* to be raised — there was absolutely no other way out of the difficulty, and I felt obliged to inform not only

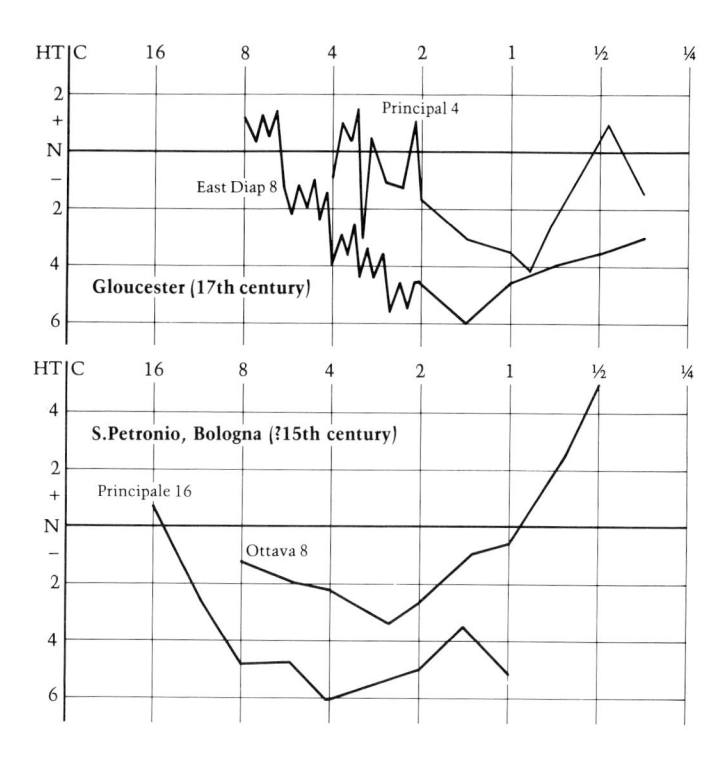

Figure 29

John Norman but also the Dean, who gave me his unqualified support. Of course it was an irrevocable step, and I felt that I could never look my musical antiquarian colleagues in the face again, even if the expedient were completely successful. Other people were busying themselves offering plenty of unsolicited, unacceptable advice on other facets of the work, but they left the Great problem severely alone, and concentrated rather on such things as the divided Swell, metaphorically tearing it to shreds!

There was just no escape: we took the step and cut up one upper lip: the pipe immediately spoke perfectly! This was our answer, and the other 16 or so on the East case-front were treated in this way as far as required. Table III gives the complete data.

PLATE XXX *Gloucester Cathedral organ 1971.*

Whatever may be said theoretically, there was no gainsaying the fact that we now had two excellent 8-foot diapasons, two 4-foot Principals and a Twelfth and Fifteenth from the seventeenth century and strongly resembling the same stops at Framlingham. The new material was integrated with this tonal framework and included a Spitzflute 8-feet and a Chimney Flute 8-feet, both of generously wide scale, a considerable number and enhanced variety of 8-foot and 4-foot stops, and a complete, if skeletonised, Principal-chorus and wide-chorus in every division. The general ensemble, as finished, was virile, colourful, varied, well-focussed and impressive yet clarified: the fullness of the 16-foot giant-scaled wooden Pedal pipes (renamed Flute 16-feet) completely compensating the lack of a 32-foot register.

The key-action of the rebuilt organ was direct-electric, applied to slider-soundboards, partly old and partly new: it was adopted after a comparative trial against a conventional electro-pneumatic unit, and it emerged from this trial as phenomenally superior. I have never known a more responsive key-action, short of tracker itself. (It is the only organ on which I have been able to give a completely clear account of Dupré's B major Prelude and Fugue!) For me, though, this was the end of electrics — such progress having been made already by those few builders who had had the courage to make "the Great Renunciation" and henceforth build only tracker organs. My final adventures have been concerned exclusively in this field, purely mechanical in the case of smaller organs; electrically assisted as far as stop-actions and combinations went, in a larger instrument.

The majority of people were delighted with the sound of the new organ, at the 1971 and 1974 Festivals: only a few deplored (for sentimental, nostalgic reasons) the destruction of the vague, disembodied blandness of the previous rebuild with its honking Tuba, large woolly Great Diapason and booming 32-feet, albeit with the remains of a fine dominating Willis Swell organ! Viewed musically and even historically, there really could be no doubt at all as to the general superiority of the new instrument. My final task was that of persuading the incumbent, excellent Organists to use *single stops* for choir-accompaniment, in preference to the conventionally established, hackneyed "Swell to 2-feet with 16-foot reed" — a sound which possessed more bulk than formerly and was out of proportion with the relatively slender choral forces at a weekday Evensong. It was surely noteworthy that at a critical stage of the tonal finishing, the wind-pressure of the Chair division was actually set so that the Stopped Diapason exactly matched the voice of a representative soloist, man or boy, from the Cathedral choir. (I made a similar adjustment to the voice of John Whitworth (distinguished counter-tenor) at the Fairfield Hall, Croydon, with the Choir Stopped 8-feet, which however was also enclosed and thus more flexible in a more brittle acoustic ambience.)

CHAPTER TWELVE

The Way Forward

Despite the splendid performance of a really well-designed electric key-action, which I also met in the organ I designed in the old cases at St John's Cathedral in Valetta, Malta, built by the illustrious firm of Mascioni (Cuvio, Varese), the time had arrived for a whole-hearted return to the tracker system, incorporating the many engineering improvements which had taken place both in Europe, America and Canada. In a sense, the rebuild at Gloucester had been subjected to this influence, since conversion to tracker with the console in its old place behind the Chair Organ would not be at all difficult with the soundboards in their new positions: links and sightlines with the nave could now be achieved by television.

I had enjoyed an exercise of this kind already, in redesigning a 3-manual tracker organ by Henry Jones of Fulham, a Victorian builder who was favoured for a time by Sir Arthur Sullivan (under whose direction he built a large organ for the Westminster Aquarium). This organ is located in Holy Trinity Church, Castelnau (Barnes) — West London suburb. The restoration was done by John Budgen and the firm of Bishop and Son. As we found the organ, its key-actions were its best feature. The list of stops was as follows:

GREAT		SWELL		CHOIR	
Bourdon	16	Liebl. Bourdon (tc)	16	Viole d'orchestre	8
Open Diapason (zinc front)	8	Open Diapason (tc)	8	Lieblich Gedackt	8
		Stopped Diapason	8	Dulciana	8
Rohrflute [sic] (open wood treble!)	8	Salicional (tc)	8	Flute	4
		Vox angelica (tc)	8	Clarinet	8
Gamba (tc) (very scratchy)	8	Gemshorn	4		
		Piccolo	2	PEDAL (pneumatic)	
Principal	4	Cornopean	8	Open Diapason (wood)	16
Harmonic flute (lowest octave grooved)	4	Oboe	8		
				Sub Bass	16
Mixture II	1⅓	6 unison couplers		Lieblich Bourdon (separate)	16
		Tremulant			

Dr George Thalben-Ball was organist of this church for a year or two, around 1914, and I think it may have been during his tenure that the Bourdon 16-feet was added to the Great. Its pipes stood second from the front of the soundboard, and next to the Mixture which it 'robbed' furiously, making the ranks go considerably out of tune.

The action of all three manuals was constructed on the 'village organ' principle — the lowest octave 'in sides' but running on chromatically from tenor c up. The touch was light enough to play *bravura* passages in Bach easily with all manuals coupled!

After a good deal of thought — the pipework in general being so undistinguished — I produced the following solution, which was artistically carried through by John Budgen with great care, resulting in a very musical ensemble for such a small instrument. All my usual tonal balancing was employed, the scale-plan was carefully integrated, and the reeds were opened up and cleared of impediments so as to speak quickly, freely and roundly. Final specification:

GREAT
Open Diapason	8	(improved)
Chimney Flute	8	(new metal treble, with chimneys)
Principal	4	(scale increased by 1 pipe)
Harmonic Flute	4	(bass octave grooved)
Quint	2⅔	(old Gamba cut down, with new stopped bass)
Superoctave	2	(new)
Mixture II	1	(revised: C 22, 26: c 19, 22: c' 15, 19: c" 12, 15)

SWELL
Open Diapason (tc)	8
Stopped Diapason	8
Salicional (tc)	8
Voix céleste (tc)	8
Gemshorn	4
Stopped flute (new)	4
(good second-hand pipes)	
Piccolo	2
Cornopean	8
Oboe	8

Wind-pressure: 3¼ inches
Couplers and tremulant as before

CHOIR
Lieblich Gedackt	8
Dulciana	8
Geigenprincipal (new)	4
(second-hand pipes)	
Flute	4
Clarinet	8

PEDAL
Open Diapason (wood)	16
Sub Bass	16
Open Flute	8
(old Lieblich, with stoppers removed)	

The next, more significant, move, with the same firm (following on from further tracker restorations at Ayot St. Lawrence (1-manual) and Wardour Castle (2-manual, *ex* Samuel Green and Dicker of Exeter)) was the designing and building of a new completely mechanical organ for the Great Hall of Lancaster University. After much long-drawn-out correspondence, John Budgen and I were allowed to agree on the following scheme:

GREAT		SWELL (above Great, as "Crown-positive")	
Open Diapason	8 (front, to F sharp)		
Chimney Flute	8 (wood bass oct)	Gedackt	8
Octave	4	Koppelflute	4
Stopped Flute	4	Nazard (stopped)	2⅔
Gemshorn	2 (conical)	Principal	2
Sesqualtera	II ("tertian" bass)	Cimbel II	½
Mixture III	1	Cremona	8

PEDAL (in side towers,
  C and C-sharp)
Sub Bass   16 (wood, on front)
Spitzflute   8 (lowest 6 on front, also serving
Octave   4   as bass for Great Diapason)
Trumpet   8

Unison couplers; tremulants
Wind-pressure: 2¾ inches   Scale-plan: see Figure 30

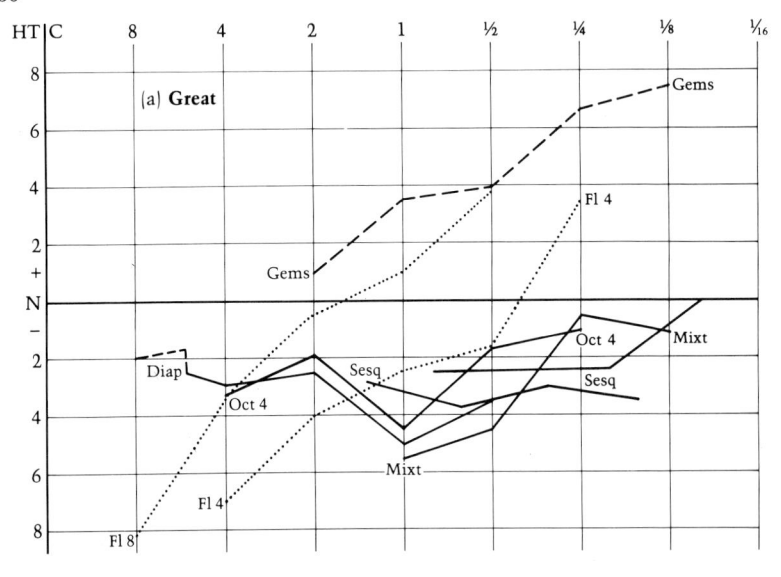

Figure 30

THE WAY FORWARD   215

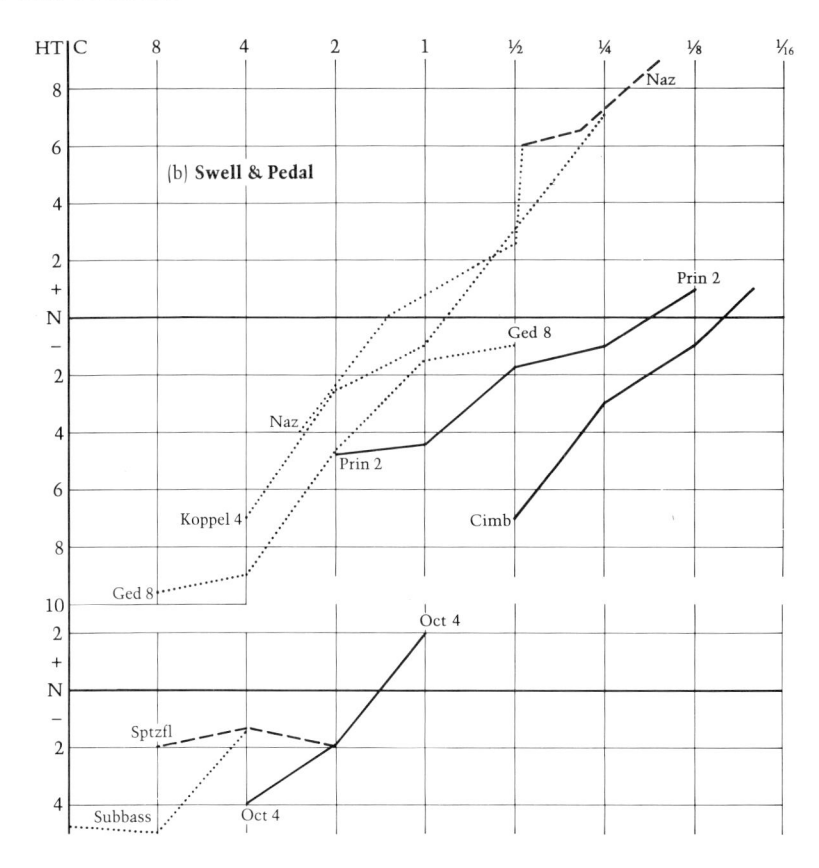

(b) **Swell & Pedal**

This organ was voiced 'on full wind', without nicking, and the pipes are cone-tuned. John made no secret of his dependence on me during all the preliminary voicing, when the flue-pipes sounded very 'raw'; and the pitch was kept flat so as to have some margin of regulation. When we got the pipes into the organ, and gradually brought them to pitch, all troubles disappeared: "the ice was broken", first by the Swell Gedackt — as the bodies were shortened and the mouths cut fractionally higher, one by one, a lovely full, smooth tone (with a characteristic 'attack') gradually replaced the 'quinty', scratchy notes first produced. This result encouraged John to continue thus with all the other stops. We finally checked the reeds for adequate tube-length (by the usual 'doubling' test); and a very musical instrument came out of all this. At its inauguration it was subjected to a quite absurd test (for a small organ) of having to match up to a full symphony orchestra in Saint-Saens' Third Symphony — which was broadcast! Oddly enough, it came through very well, both as heard in the hall and (less effectively) 'on the air'. A subsequent broadcast of a Bach Trio-sonata showed this organ very favourably in a different, more appropriate context.

Thus when I was invited to consult with the Cardiff City Council regarding the inclusion of an organ in the scheme of their new concert hall ('St David's Hall'), due to be finished in 1982, I had no hesitation in recommending the engagement of an organ-builder who had made 'the Great Renunciation' and was personally committed to building fine tracker organs exclusively.

The first step was to obtain a good siting from the Architects, who — as is not unusual — had been misled already in various directions (especially towards the concept of an enchambered organ in some cramped, wholly inadequate space). Remembering what a very personal matter the designing and laying out of a good *tracker* mechanism can be nowadays, I did not go further than stipulating that the organ (if built) must be free-standing, right in the hall, and of adequate size. I felt that it would be rash to go into detail at this stage. Intent, therefore, on 'starting on the right foot' and 'with both feet on the ground', I got permission to engage an organ-builder in whom I had confidence to make a feasibility-study for an organ of the size I felt this hall required, on the best siting the Architects could provide. The auditorium was planned to seat some 2,000 persons, with provision for a choir of some 350. I had a rough idea of a possible list of stops, about 50 to 55, distributed over three manuals and Pedal — the largest for which there was likely to be sufficient room. To suit the general architectural plan, the organ would have to be sited to one side of the stage, behind some of the chorus-seats: and since the console would almost certainly have to be *attached*, important considerations such as sight-lines, distance from the Conductor, etc, had to be borne in mind. Another essential consideration was the projection of sound of all parts of the instrument into the centre of the (basically oval) auditorium: thus, angles were important, even more than in Fairfield Hall, Croydon, where I had successfully worked them out with match-boxes (representing the organ-cases) on a ⅛ inch-scale plan!

The organ-builder, Peter Collins, made the feasibility-study for me, and as this looked extremely promising — entirely practical as well as refreshingly imaginative — he was eventually engaged to build the organ. The agreed specification of stops is as follows — basically similar to my own previous designs, though obviously the exact layout, the scales of the various stops, even the probable wind-pressures required, needed careful consideration and mutual discussion.

SPECIFICATION

3 manuals, C to a''', 58 notes   Pedals, C to g', 32 notes

Man I: POSITIVE (unenclosed)		Man III: SWELL	
Traverse Flute	8	Quintadena	16
(conical, part front)		Diapason	8
Gedackt	8	Chimney Flute (wide)	8
Quintadena	8	Viola ('Viole de Gambe')	8
Principal (front pipes	4	Celeste (from F sharp)	8
slightly conical)		Octave	4
Chimney Flute	4	Open Flute (wide)	4
Octave	2	Nazard (conical)	2⅔
Wald Flute (conical)	2	Gemshorn (conical)	2
Nazard (slightly conical)	1⅓	Tierce	1³/₅
Sesquialtera II	1⅓/2⅔	Mixture V-VI	2
Scharf IV-V	1	Cimbel III	²/₅
Dulzian (wood)	16	Harmonic Trumpet	8
Cremona	8	Hautboy	8
Tremulant		Vox humana	8
		Harmonic Clarion	4
Man II: GREAT		Tremulant	
Bourdon (metal)	16		
Principal (front)	8	PEDAL	
Spitz Flute (wide, conical)	8	Principal (Part front)	16
Bourdon	8	Major Bass (Open wood)	16
Octave	4	Sub Bass (wood)	16
Stopped Flute	4	Quint (stopped metal)	10⅔
('Gedacktpommer')		Octave (metal)	8
Block Flute	2	* Gedackt (metal)	8
Rauschquint II	2⅔	* Choral Bass (wide)	4
Tertian II	1⅓/1³/₅	* Open Flute ('Nachthorn')	2
Mixture IV-VI	1⅓	* Mixture IV	2⅔
Cornet (from g) V	8	Fagotto (wood)	32
Fagotto	16	(½ length to Gs:	
Trumpet	8	full length from A)	
Tremulant		Bombarde	16
		Trumpet	8
6 unison couplers:		* Shawm	4
also Man I octave to Pedal		* Cornett	2

Key-actions, mechanical-tracker   Tremulant to stops marked*
Stop-actions, electromagnetic
Combination-actions, adjustable by solid-state electronics
Balanced Swell and General-crescendo pedals
Organ-case of ash, console in rosewood

The success of this project will remain to be seen: a modern concert hall, with planned heating and ventilation, and above all, planned acoustics, can in the event produce many surprises. Nature cannot be 'pushed around' or guaranteed to behave according to human preconceptions, which can be full of snares for the maker of musical instruments, and indeed of *music*. The presence of a real, enclosing organ-case is one salutary element: there is no doubt that if piano, orchestra and song sound well in the new hall, this organ will have nothing to fear.

Many people may call the stop-list "antiquarian", "un-English", "Neo-baroque", etc: it is not necessarily any of these things. It does not flout musical history or the best traditions of British organ style: it *does* avoid some of the excesses of contemporary European design, for example, the exploitation of the more remote and very discordant harmonic intervals, usually anonymously indicated as "Oberton" — all the necessary brilliance can be obtained from sharply-voiced pipes giving the (acceptable) tierce at a high pitch, or even the quint, in Cimbel, Scharf and Tertian. Those well-intentioned connoisseurs who (in addition to their excellent activities of resuscitating, or at least, documenting, Victorian or earlier organs) are set on resurrecting a typical English stylistic model, are really placing an artificial restraint on what has emerged as a legitimate expansion of that style, perhaps partly under European or even American influence — nothing very new about that! I myself believe that we have nothing to lose, and much to gain, *musically*, from the enrichment of the rather frugal Victorian tonal palette with varied mutations, wide and narrow; integral chorus structures in all divisions; and reeds which 'latch in' with, rather than overwhelm, mildly-voiced flue-work in an organ whose main purpose is not to make a great *din*, but *music* — any music worthy of the name. The many features which can be culled from the Baroque Golden Age can, if well and imaginatively integrated, do nothing but enrich and beautify our nationally traditional style. The final product must, of course, be an instrument of character and clarity, as perfectly matched as possible to the ambience of its location, and possessing balanced, impressive and exciting (not to say *seductive*) tonal qualities. A great deal can be achieved just with the skilful planning of narrow- and wide-scale registers, which not only contrast effectively, but can also combine in the 'acoustic coupling' cited earlier: again, taking a leaf out of the Baroque book, the contrast of scale-*progressions* is at least equal in importance with the mere differentiation of scale-width. If all the scales go parallel (as is too often the case), the final result is *monotony*. This is a notable defect even in the monumental Schulze organ at Armley: whereas in a good Baroque organ the flutes can be seen, as well as heard, to end up with fat little 'tubs' in the treble, and the higher principals to run out almost like straws, at Armley they all go parallel; and thus, though the various

THE WAY FORWARD

stops all have a distinctive tone-colour, they all sound mysteriously alike! For all his occasional 'mass-produced' appearances, Cavaillé's scale-progressions were strongly characterised, and thus the sum of the 'Fonds 8-feet' in his organs had a rich, singing, mellow, composite 'diapason' sonority which was contrapuntally clear in itself. Figure 26 showed diagrammatically the original scale-progressions of the 1872 organ at Paisley Abbey, already mentioned: Figure 31 shows the progressions of some of the stops at Luçon, which he restored.

Figure 31

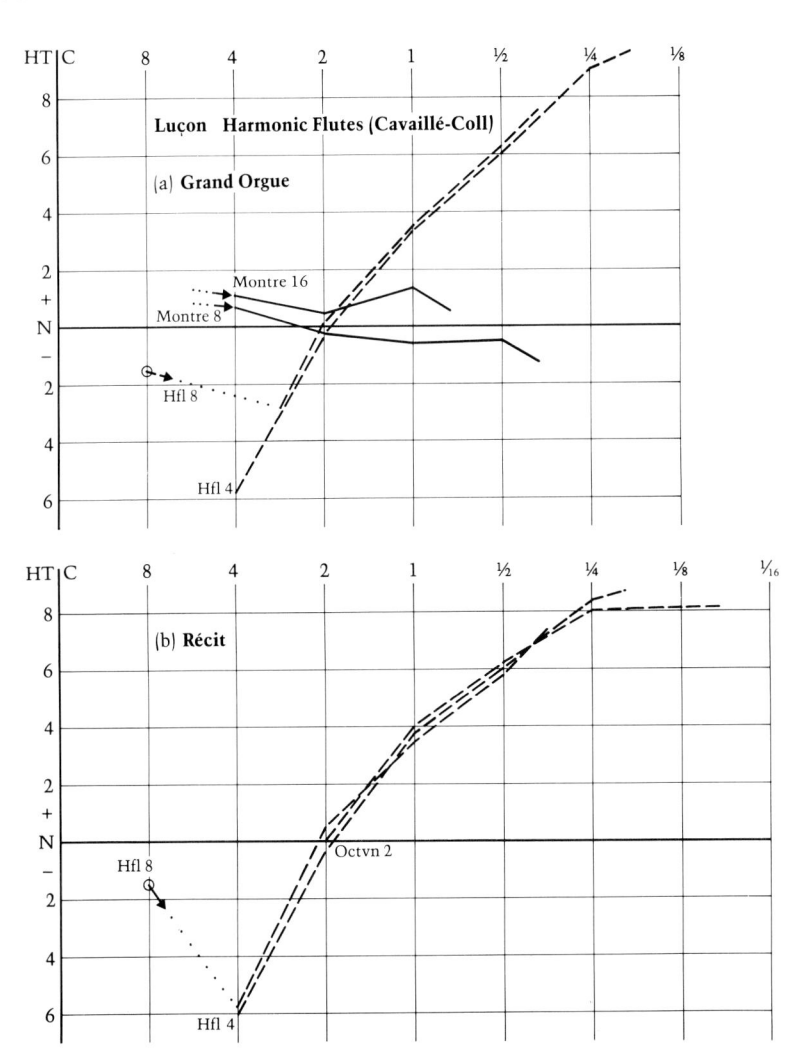

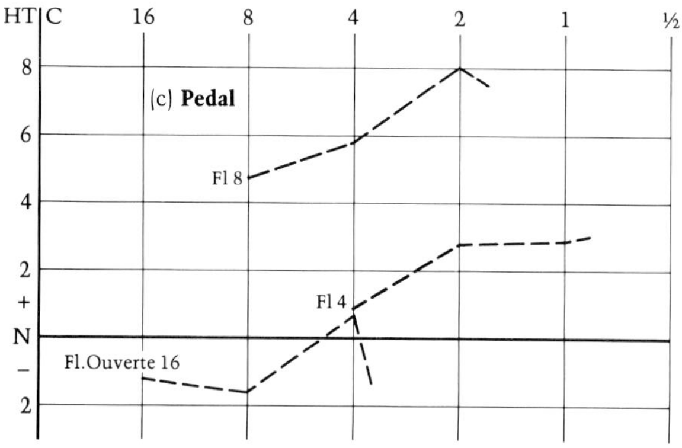
HT
C
16
8
4
2
1
½
8
6
4
2
+
N
–
2
(c) Pedal
Fl 8
Fl 4
Fl.Ouverte 16

However, a slavish copying of such things is of little value in itself: it is essential that the voicer understands them and knows what he is aiming at — above all things, EQUALITY, throughout the tonal range of each stop and *vis à vis* the other stops too.

Figure 32

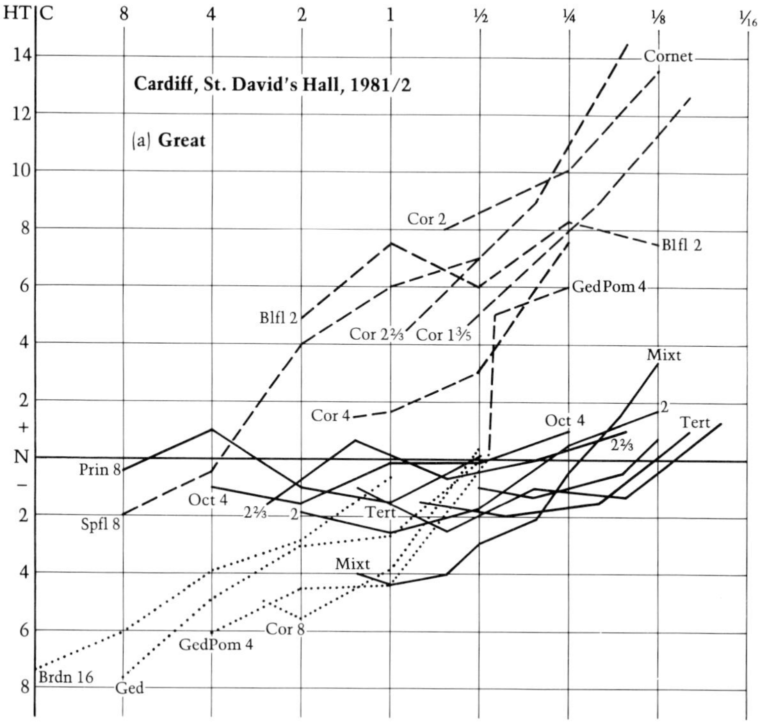
Cardiff, St. David's Hall, 1981/2
(a) Great
HT
C
8
4
2
1
½
¼
⅛
1/16
14
12
10
8
6
4
2
+
N
–
2
4
6
8
Cornet
Cor 2
Blfl 2
GedPom 4
Blfl 2
Cor 2⅔
Cor 1⅗
Mixt
Cor 4
Oct 4
2
Tert
2⅔
Prin 8
Oct 4
2⅔
2
Tert
Spfl 8
Mixt
Cor 8
GedPom 4
Brdn 16
Ged

THE WAY FORWARD

The theoretical scale-plan of the fluework) subject to strict practicality) is mapped out in Figure 32: the largest-reed scales will be those of the Swell Trumpet and Clarion, flared out at the bass end to compensate the lack of a 16-foot. Wind-pressures will probably be about 3⅝ inches for the Great, 2⅝ inches for the Positive, and 4 inches for Swell and Pedal — subject to adjustment on site, according to the acoustics. All the voicing will be on the 'open foot', 'full wind' system, the pipes un-nicked and cone-tuned. The reeds will lean partly towards English, partly towards French, and partly towards German style, according to their place and function. Trumpets *en chamade* were ruled out as a security risk, likely to invite mischievous vandalism: the Swell Trumpets will be the 'solo reeds'.

We shall see!

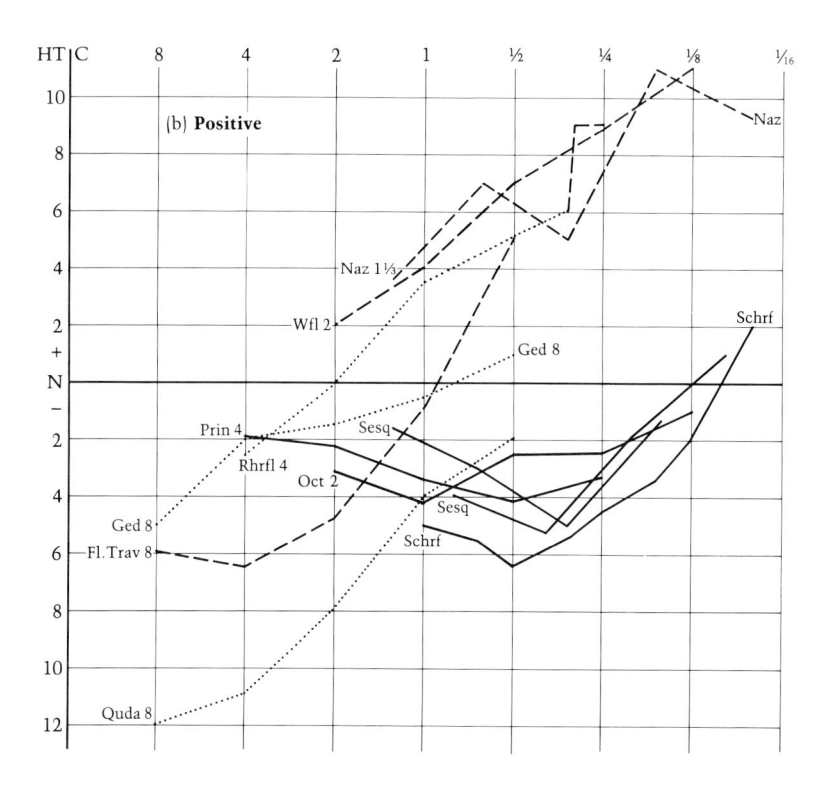

(b) **Positive**

(c) **Swell**

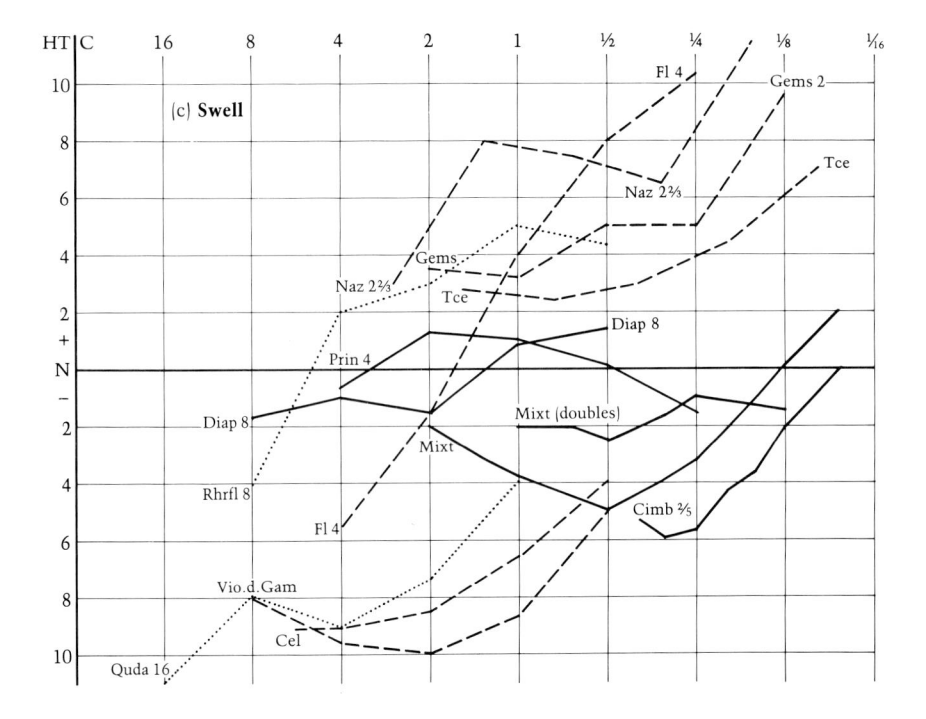

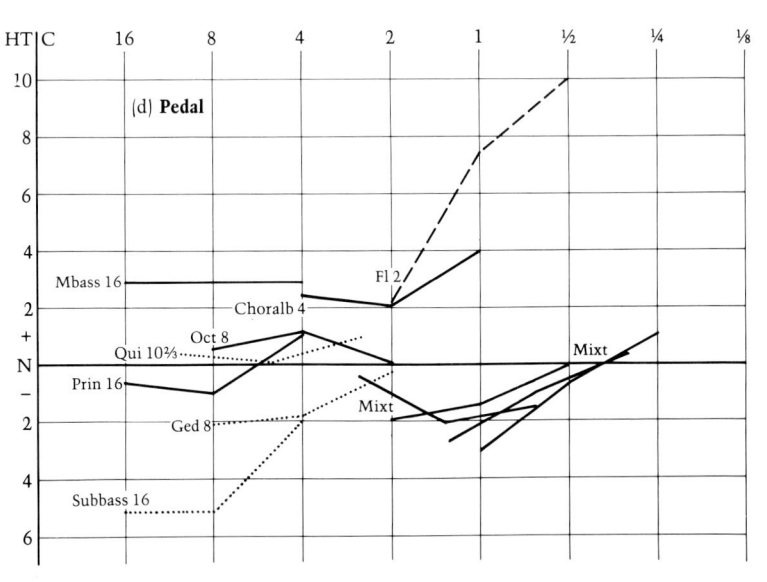

(d) **Pedal**

THE WAY FORWARD 223

PLATE XXXI *St. David's Hall, Cardiff, the new organ by Peter Collins completed during 1982 whilst this book was being prepared for publication. Photograph reproduced by kind permission of P. D. Collins.*
(Inserted by the Publisher)

NOTES IN THE TEXT

PREFACE
1. *Syntagma Musicum*, Tom II, Part 3, Chapter XIV *passim*
2. St. Alkmund's, Derby, Lewis 1888
3. St. Augustine's, Penarth, before the revoicing and reconstruction of subsequent years, during which the tonal character was considerably altered.

CHAPTER ONE
4. Bevington, 1855, 1870: the latter being the date of its installation in Derby where it was opened by W. T. Best on 29 March. It was awarded a First Class medal at the Paris Exhibition of 1855, according to F. W. Thornsby, *Dictionary of Organs and Organists*, London, 1912.
5. Thornsby, *op cit*
6. Kindly confirmed by Rodney Tomkins, BA FRCO (of Derby), from the "Scotchbrook Notebook", now in the possession of E. R. Stow Esq, Organist of the Queen's Hall Methodist Mission, Derby.
7. But actually by one Henry Booth (see Note 6).
8. Rodney Tomkins confirms Forster & Andrews, 1902, which Laurence Elvin fails to acknowledge in his book on this builder.
9. With one manual (new 'streamlined' model) dividing into treble and bass at e'/f'. It was the *de luxe* version with three undulants: Harpe Aeolienne 2-feet (bass), Harpe Aeolienne 8-feet (treble), Voix Céleste 16-feet (treble), as well as the usual (treble) Baryton 32-feet and Musette 16-feet.
10. Bourdon 16, Geigen 8, Lieblich flute 4, Harmonic Piccolo 2, Harmonics IV, Double Trumpet 16, Tremulant, Octave, Suboctave. At this early stage the (real) second 32-foot reed pipe (Bombarde) had not arrived on the scene: in addition to the Contra Tuba 32-feet [sic], a Contra Trombone 32-feet was also obtained from the bass of the Swell Double Trumpet, the lowest 12 notes being likewise quinted on themselves. The Dulcetone was out of action, and on the next visit of this organ to Derby, it had been replaced by a hefty Tuba Mirabilis 8-feet (worked by the same stop-knob) unenclosed.
11. Consult T. C. Lewis, *A protest against the modern development of unmusical tone*, (1897).
12. In all four organs the wind-pressures were raised later (and in two of them much louder 32-foot reeds were added) and the original balance was thereby lost.
13. Serlo Hall, Methuen, Mass.
14. This organ (after being despoiled of some of its contents) was largely rebuilt and completely revoiced by the Aeolian-Skinner Organ Company in 1947 under the auspices of the new Organ Institute who bought the hall and organ. Its effect is said to have been considerably altered. The original wide scales and even flute ranks in the Mixtures brought them near to Cornet sonority, an effect abhorrent to adherents of the then trendy Organ Reform.
15. A highly ingenious, efficient and responsive kind of electro-pneumatic action: the late Ernest M. Skinner claimed it as his invention.

BAROQUE TRICKS

16 The specification at this period will be recognised by all who possess Schoenberg's *'Variations on a Recitative'* in the Carl Weinrich edition (H. W. Gray, *Contemporary Organ Series*, New York). The foregoing notes on the balance of the various divisions of the organ will explain the apparent overweighting of the Choir Organ registration. The Princeton organ underwent considerable revision in later years, before the death of G. Donald Harrison, and is now reduced to a purer classical model.

CHAPTER TWO

17 As opposed to recordings, eg, those made by Louis Vierne at Notre-Dame, Paris.
18 Presumably by Bishop, around 1890.
19 The Catholic Church in Underwood Road, East London.
20 I found later that the pressure for these stops at the Oratory had been raised from 3¼ to 4¼ inches, along with the Great reeds which had the same wind-supply.
21 For the complete story of the evolution of the Buckfast organ, see Appendix A.
22 See Note 20 and *The Organ*, Vol VI, No 24, p 231.
23 The important question of how to maintain a *mechanical* connection from the console to the three sets of Swell-louvres was for the time being left unanswered: there was no possibility of running rods or trundles under the floor at the front of the gallery. (Whiffle-tree swell-engines are never sufficiently stable in their movements to meet strict musical requirements: anyone who is inclined to dispute this should go to Fairfield Hall, Croydon, where the 'wow' accompanying any sudden movement of the Swell-pedal can be seen as well as heard.) Davidson mooted Bowden cable, but with rueful memories of Pattman's organ, I turned it down.
24 Vol XIII (No 52), pp 203-214
25 The famous Schulze organ now in St. Bartholomew's Church, Armley, Leeds. (See Kenneth I. Johnstone, *The Armley Schulze Organ*, pub 1978, from the church.)

CHAPTER FOUR

26 The Notre-Dame organ was rebuilt (electrified) and its character was basically altered in the 1960s.

CHAPTER FIVE

27 ie, the 'Tender Specification' just quoted. Stop No. 1a was a Bourdon 16-feet restored to the Great division.
28 This was a dig at the contemporary Harrison 'Orchestral Trumpets' on heavy wind, as found in the organs of Newcastle City Hall and the Royal Albert Hall, London.

CHAPTER SIX

29 Especially in *Über die Orgelkunst*, Bärenreiter-Verlag, Kassel, 1934.
30 *L'Art du Facteur d'Orgues*, Part IV, Chapter 1
31 Cecil Clutton and Austin Niland, *The British Organ*, London, 1963, p 116 (lines 8-14)

CHAPTER NINE

32 Long and anxiously I debated the respective merits of the wide-scale Gemshorn 2-feet, or a half-length 16-foot reed. In the end, and under persuasion of Henry Washington, I rejected the latter, while having in mind the splendid Cornet sonority which the Gemshorn would help to provide. Only in Widor's famous Toccata does one miss the 16-foot tone in the middle episodes of this piece.
33 It was old Bevington and came from Ealing Town Hall (West London) where the old organ was demolished. Slightly increased in scale, it was given new tongues and French shallots.

CHAPTER TEN

34 F. Germani, *Method for the Organ*, Part IV, Book 1, (Rome, de Santis; English edition), pp 111-112. Compare also W. G. Alcock, *The Organ*, (Novello, London), p 20 f.

CHAPTER ELEVEN

35 The Salicional, as usual with Cavaillé, was a register of some substance, but with a sufficiently rich overtone development for it to be able to absorb completely the 2⅔ foot Nazard (*à cheminée*), thus producing a beautiful synthetic Quintadena, which can even be played in chords!

As we were regulating the (Cavaillé) 8-foot Traverse Flute, Dennis Thurlow said, "I can see no good in this stop." Admittedly it was pretty characterless as it had merely been put into the organ. I suddenly remembered Cavaillé's beautiful Harmonic Flutes, and how their basses usually had a Principal (or at least a Salicional) timbre. I pulled up the tenor C, to full strength — it still balanced the full, fluty treble, and the procedure worked: it became a beautiful 'Changing register', with horny bass and pure flute treble: everyone loved it!

36 The 4-foot Flûte Octaviante of the Swell was less tractable: the scale was good, but the harmonic portion was rather poor in quality. I decided to try an experiment: we cut the middle C pipe (1-foot) in half — it would be easy to make a new one, if it were spoiled. But in fact it succeeded: an impediment had been removed from its speech, and with its wide scale and full wind at the foot, it became a beautiful stop, and was all cut to simple (natural) length.

37 The pipes of this reed are of almost pure tin, and it turned out to be the most distinguished reed voice in the whole organ, once it was restored to its true French tone: it has breadth, richness and magnificent tonal opulence; it scarcely needed voicing at all, and its tuning is very stable. It is a real "voicers' joy".

38 Quoted in R. Lunelli, *Der Orgelbau in Italien* (Rheingold Verlag, 1956), p. 13, from information supplied by Prof. L. F. Tagliavini. The original scales of the Harris pipes at Gloucester were kindly supplied to the writer during the reconstruction of that organ in 1971 by Mr. H. John Norman (organ builder).

APPENDICES

Appendix A
The Organ in Buckfast Abbey

Begun in 1922 in the part-completed church, the organ was built piecemeal for some years by Hele & Co of Plymouth.

	1922-33	Two manuals, later increased to three	
GREAT		*CHOIR	
Bourdon	16	*Lieblich Gedeckt	8
Large Open Diapason	8	*Dulciana	8
Claribel Flute	8	*Lieblich Flote	4
Stopped Diapason	8		
Principal	4	PEDAL	
Harmonic Flute	4	Open Diapason (wood)	16
Fifteenth	2	*Open Diapason (metal)	16
Trumpet HP	8	Bourdon	16
		Octave (wood, ext)	8
SWELL		*Principal (ext)	8
Violin Diapason	8		
*Flauto Traverso	8		
Rohrflöte	8		
Salicional	8		
*Aeoline	8		
*Voix Céleste	8		
Gemshorn [sic]	4		
Flautina	2	Unison and octave couplers.	
Echo Cornet	III	Action, tubular pneumatic.	
Cornopean	8	*Interim additions	

About 1929 the console was detached and moved across to the south side of the monks' choir, the organ remaining on the north: the Swell was moved up into a new concrete chamber in the north triforium. The key-actions were *indirectly* electrified, the contacts being mounted on the pneumatic primary motors (the tubing having been cut down to minimum length) rather than on the keyboards: result, the more wind one used by addition of stops and couplers, the more (incredibly) sluggish this so-called electric action became!

In 1934 a nearby residence organ by the Aeolian Company was bought up and installed for the most part as a Solo division in a second chamber built in the centre bay of the triforium, west of the Swell. The scheme now stood as follows:

1934 – 39

Man I CHOIR		Man III SWELL	
(unenclosed)		*(enclosed, east triforium)*	
Lieblich Gedeckt	8	Gedeckt	16 (Aeolian)
Dulciana	8	Open Diapason	8
Lieblich Flöte	4	Violin Diapason	8
		Gedeckt (ext)	8 (Aeolian)
Man I SOLO		Flauto Traverso	8
(enclosed Aeolian)		Rohrflöte	8
Bell Diapson [*sic*]	8	Salicional	8
Hohlflöte	8	Aeoline	8
Gedeckt	8	Voix céleste	8
Viole	8	Gemshorn [*sic*]	4
Viole céleste	8	Gedeckt (ext)	4 (Aeolian)
Cone Gamba	8	Salicet	1
Vox Angelica	8	Echo Cornet	III
Quintatön	8	Contra Posaune (ext)	16
Principal (not Aeolian)	4	Cornopean	8
Octave Viole	4	Clarion (ext)	4
Concert Flute	4		
Flageolet	2	PEDAL	
Trumpet	8	Contra Bourdon (to EEEE)	32 (Aeolian)
Orchestral Oboe (Musette)	8	Open Diapason (wood)	16
Corno di Bassetto (free reed)	8	Open Diapason (metal)	16 (Great)
Clarinette (not Aeolian)	8	Violone (wood)	16 (Aeolian)
		Grand Bourdon (ext)	16 (Aeolian)
Man II GREAT		Sub Bass	16
Double Diap. (part Pedal)	16	Dulciana	16 (Aeolian)
Open Diapason I	8	Gedeckt	16 (Swell)
Open Diapason II (ext)	8	Octave (wood, ext)	8
Claribel Flute	8	Principal (ext)	8
Stopped Diapason	8	Viola (ext)	8 (Aeolian)
Principal	4	Gedeckt (ext)	8 (Swell)
Harmonic Flute	4	Gedeckt (ext)	4 (Swell)
Twelfth	2⅔	Trombone HP	16
Fifteenth	2	Fagotto	16 (Swell)
Trumpet HP	8	Trumpet (ext) HP	8
		Clarion (ext) HP	4

Octave couplers for Swell and Choir: other, unison couplers but *no* Solo to Great (!)
Key-actions still "pneumo-electro-pneumatic" (!)

1939 G Donald Harrison (Aeolian-Skinner, USA)/Downes scheme, engraved on the stop-keys of the new 4-manual console by J W Walker & Sons.

Man I BRUSTWERK
(choir aisle, east)

Quintade	16	(new)
Koppelflöte	8	(new)
Viola da Gamba	8	(old Solo Cone Gamba)
Vox Angelica	8	(old Solo)
Spitzflöte	4	(new)
Nassat	2⅔	(new)
Blockflöte	2	(new)
Terz	1⅗	(new)
Scharf	IV	(new)
Dulzian	16	(new)

Brustwerk on Man III

Man I POSITIV
(choir aisle, east or centre)

Quintade	8	(new)
Rohrflöte	4	(new)
Principal	2	(new)
Larigot	1⅓	(new)
Sifflöte	1	(new)
Sesquialtera II	2⅔	(new)
Zimbel	III	(new)
Krummhorn	8	(new)

Man II GREAT
(triforium centre)

Bordun	16	(new)
Principal	8	(new)
Spitzflöte	8	(new)
Bordun	8	(new)
Prestant	4	(new)
Flute Ouverte	4	(new)
Nazard	2⅔	(new)
Doublette	2	(new)
Tierce	1⅗	(new)
Cornet III	2⅔	(new)
Fourniture IV	2⅔	(new)
Cymbel IV	⅔	(new)
Bombarde	16	(new)
Trompette	8	(new)
Clairon	4	(new)
(last three stops in old French style)

Man III SWELL
(enclosed, triforium east)

Lieblich Gedeckt	16	(old Swell)
Diapason	8	(old Swell or Great)
Hohlflöte	8	(old Solo or Great)
Gedeckt	8	(old Solo)
Quintatön	8	(old Solo)
Viole de Gambe	8	(old Solo)
Violes Célestes	8	(old Solo)
Concert Flute	4	(old Solo)
Fugara	4	(old Solo Viole)
Flageolet	2	(old Solo)
Sesquialtera II	2⅔	(new)
Pleinjeu doux	VI	(new)
Fagot	16	(new)
Trompette	8	(old tubes?)
Basson-Hautbois	8	(new)
Clarinet	8	(old Solo)
Clairon	4	(new)

Man IV ECHO
(enclosed, triforium west)

Rohrflöte	8	(old Swell)
Flauto	8	(old Swell)
Salicional	8	(old Swell)
Céleste	8	(old Swell)
Dulciana	8	(old Choir)
Salicet	4	(old)
Lieblich Flöte	4	(old Choir)
Echo Mixture	III	(old Swell)

PEDAL *(choir aisle west)*

Principal	16	(old Pedal)	Sesquialtera II	5⅓	
(or Contrabass)			Mixture	IV	(new)
Bourdon	16	(old Aeolian)	Cymbel	III	(new)
Dulciana	16	(old Aeolian)	Bombarde	16	(old tubes?)
Echo Lieblich	16	(Swell)	(old French type)		
Violoncello	8	(new)	Trompette	8	(new)
Flötenbass	8	(new)	(old French type)		
Still Gedeckt (ext)	8	(Swell 16-feet)	Clairon	4	(new)
Choralbass	4	(new)	(old French Type)		
Rohrflöte	4	(new)	Rohr Schalmei	4	(new)
Nachthorn	2	(new)	Cornet	2	(new)

The outbreak of World War II made this scheme abortive.

1940-46
The interim disposition of the organ, wired up afresh to the new 4-manual console is described fully in Chapter Two. A mooted resumption and completion on less ambitious lines resulted in the Walker/Downes specification of January 1947 quoted in Chapter Two (page 65). An important revision after my first Dutch trip of August 1949 is shown in Chapter Eight (page 144).

1962-
The only subsequent change was the re-arrangement of the Great, Positive and Pedal soundboards with some consequent revoicing, and the recasting of the main Pedal division, as follows:

PEDAL *(in central and western bays of choir aisle)*

Sub Bass	32	(pressure reduced)
Principal	16	(Great)
Bourdon (ext)	16	
Gedeckt	16	(from Swell)
Flute Ouverte (conical)	8	(new)
Gedeckt (ext)	8	
Recorder	4	(new)
Gedeckt (ext)	4	
Nachthorn	2	
Bombarde	16	
Trumpet (ext)	8	
Clarion (ext)	4	
Clarinet	16	(from Swell)
Clarinet (ext)	8	
Clarinet (ext)	4	

The flue-scales of this division are shown in Figure 33. The apparent paucity of stops is compensated by their prominent position in the building, which puts them into aural balance with the manual divisions.

APPENDICES

Figure 33

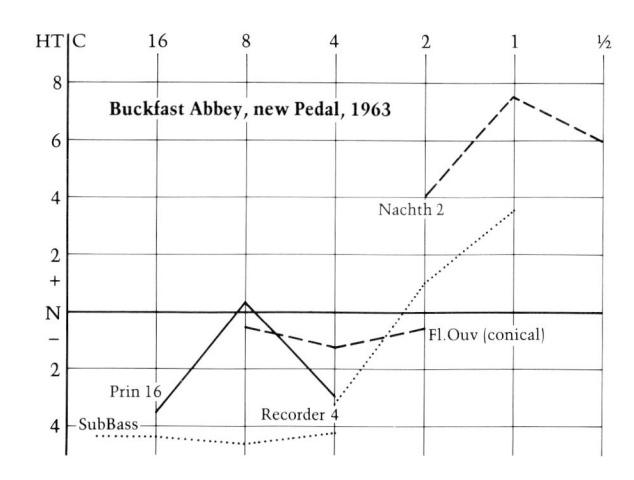

Buckfast Abbey, new Pedal, 1963

Appendix B
Alkmaar, St. Laurenskerk, grote orgel, flue-scales

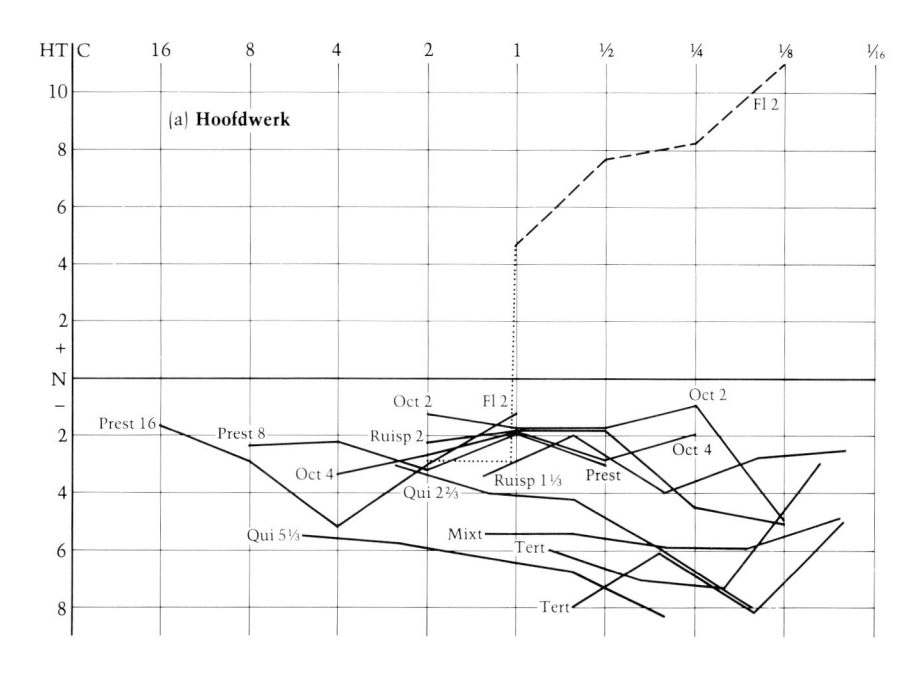

(a) **Hoofdwerk**

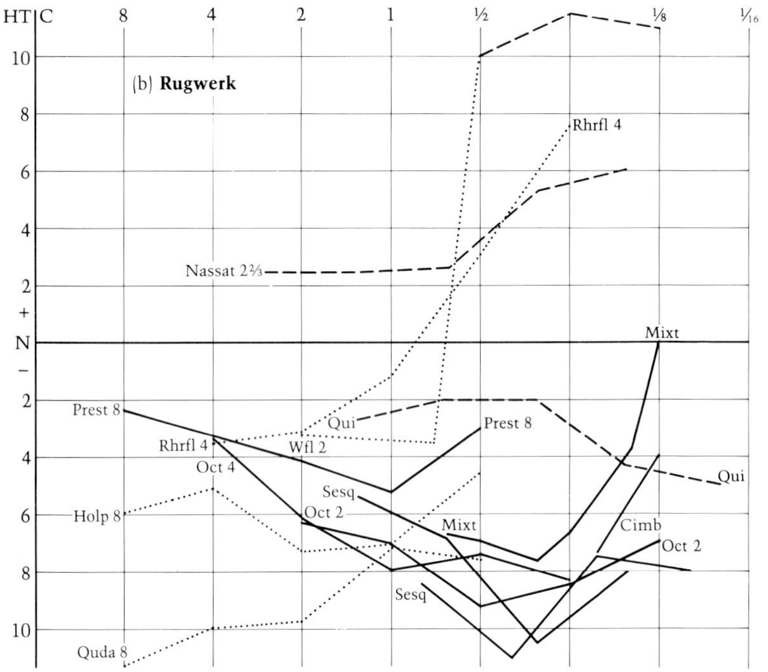
HT
C
8
4
2
1
½
⅛
1⁄16
10
8
6
4
2
+
N
–
2
4
6
8
10
(b) Rugwerk
Rhrfl 4
Nassat 2⅔
Mixt
Prest 8
Qui
Prest 8
Rhrfl 4
Wfl 2
Oct 4
Qui
Sesq
Holp 8
Oct 2
Mixt
Cimb
Oct 2
Sesq
Quda 8

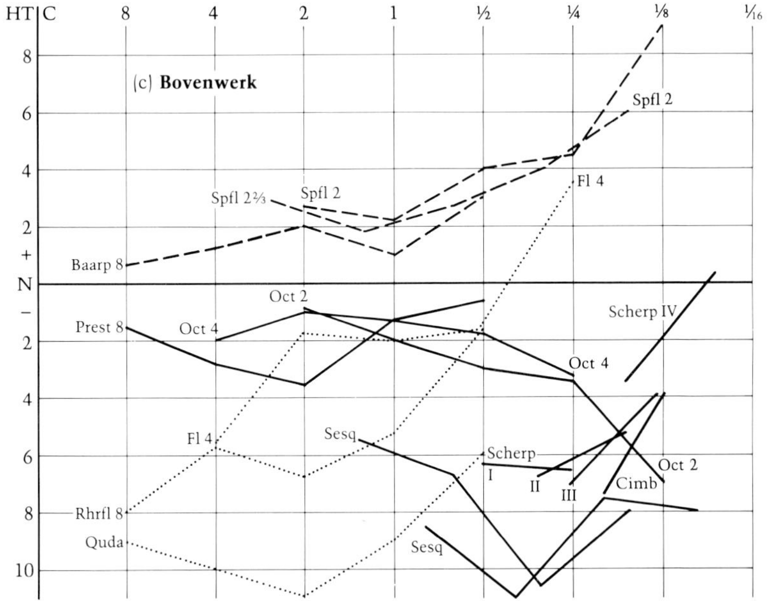
HT
C
8
4
2
1
½
¼
⅛
1⁄16
8
6
4
2
+
N
–
2
4
6
8
10
(c) Bovenwerk
Spfl 2
Fl 4
Spfl 2⅔
Spfl 2
Baarp 8
Oct 2
Scherp IV
Prest 8
Oct 4
Oct 4
Fl 4
Sesq
Scherp
I
II
III
Oct 2
Cimb
Rhrfl 8
Quda
Sesq

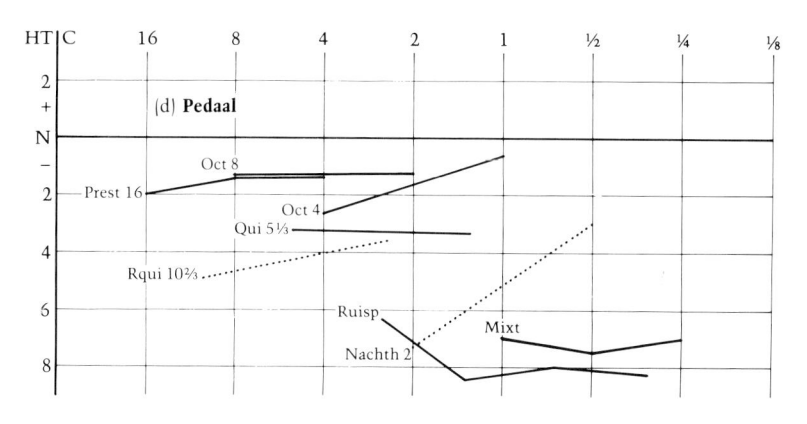

```
HT C     16        8         4         2         1        ½        ¼        ⅛
 2
 +           (d) Pedaal
 N
 -                      Oct 8
 2    Prest 16
                            Oct 4
                         Qui 5⅓
 4
         Rqui 10⅔
 6
                              Ruisp
                                              Mixt
                              Nachth 2
 8
```

Appendix C
Final Specification of the Royal Festival Hall Organ

HARRISON & HARRISON/DOWNES, 1949-53(-63-79)
4 manuals C to c^4, 61   Pedals C to g, 32
Unless otherwise stated, all pipes are of spotted metal (50% tin, 50% lead)

GREAT *(Man II, unenclosed)*		POSITIVE *(Man I, unenclosed; transferable to Man II)*	
1 Principal	16		
2 Gedacktpommer	16	21 Principal	8
3 Principal (tin)	8	22 Gedackt (30% tin)	8
4 Diapason	8	23 Quintadena	8
5 Harmonic Flute (12 wood)	8	24 Octave	4
6 Rohrgedackt	8	25 Rohrflute	4
7 Quintflute (stopped)	5⅓	26 Rohrnazard	2⅔
8 Octave I-II	4	27 Spitzflute (conical)	2
9 Gemshorn (conical)	4	28 Tierce	1⅗
10 Quintadena	4	29 Larigot	1⅓
11 Quint	2⅔	30 Mixture V	2
12 Superoctave	2	31 Sharp Mixture V	1
13 Blockflute	2	32 Carillon II-III	½
14 Tierce	1⅗	*(enclosed in Choir box:)*	
15 Mixture V	2	33 Trumpet	8
16 Sharp Mixture IV	⅔	34 Dulzian	8
17 Cornet V(c1)	8	– Tremulant	
18 Bombarde	16		
19 Trumpet	8		
20 Clarion	4		

CHOIR *(Man I, enclosed; transferable to Man IV)*

35	Salicional	16
36	Open Wood (oak)	8
37	Stopped Wood (oak)	8
38	Salicional (conical)	8
39	Unda Maris (conical)	8
40	Spitzoctave (conical)	4
41	Openflute (30% tin)	4
42	Principal	2
43	Quint	1⅓
44	Octave	1
45	Sesquialtera II	⅔
46	Mixture IV	½
47	Cromorne	8
48	Schalmei	4
-	Tremulant	

SOLO *(Man IV, enclosed)*

49	Diapason	8
50	Rohrflute	8
51	Octave	4
52	Waldflute (conical, 30% tin)	2
53	Rauschquint II	2⅔
54	Tertian II	1⅓
55	Mixture VI	1⅓
56	Basset Horn	16
57	Harmonic Trumpet	8
58	Harmonic Clarion	4
-	Tremulant	

SWELL *(Man III, enclosed)*

59	Quintadena	16
60	Diapason	8
61	Gemshorn (conical)	8
62	Quintadena	8
63	Viola	8
64	Celeste	8
65	Principal	4
66	Koppelflute	4
67	Nazard (conical)	2⅔
68	Octave	2
69	Openflute	2
70	Tierce (f)	1⅗
71	Flageolet	1
72	Mixture IV-VI	1
73	Cymbel (tin) III	⅕
74	Bombarde (12 half-length)	16
75	Trumpet	8
76	Hautboy	8
77	Vox Humana	8
78	Clarion	4
-	Tremulant	

PEDAL

79	Principal (12 zinc, 4 Haskelled)	32	(20 from Gt 1)
80	Majorbass (pine)	16	
81	Principal	16	
82	Sub Bass (stopped, pine)	16	
83	Salicional	16	(20 from Ch 35)
84	Quintadena	16	(20 from Sw 59)
85	Quintflute (stopped, 30% tin)	10⅔	
86	Octavebass	8	
87	Gedackt (stopped, 30% tin)	8	
88	Quintadena	8	(20 from Sw 59)
89	Nazard (conical, 30% tin)	5⅓	
90	Superoctave (tin)	4	
91	Spitzflute (conical, 30% tin)	4	
92	Openflute (30% tin)	2	
93	Septerz (30% tin) II	3⅕, 2²⁄₇	
94	Rauschquint II	5⅓	
95	Mixture V	2⅔	
96	Bombarde (12 zinc)	32	(20 from 97)
97	Bombarde	16	
98	Dulzian	16	(20 from Pos 34)
99	Trumpet	8	
100	Cromorne	8	(20 from Ch 47)
101	Clarion	4	
102	Schalmei	4	(20 from Ch 48)
103	Cornett	2	

Unision manual- and pedal-couplers
Swell Octave (16-, 8- and 4-foot stops only)
Great Suboctave

APPENDICES

WIND PRESSURES:

Great	main	92 mm
	upperwork and reeds	76 mm
Swell		92 mm
Positive		70 mm
Choir		81 mm
Solo		115 mm
Pedal	foundations	100 mm (Principal 32-feet 90 mm)
	main	92 mm
	Bombardes	92 mm
	other reeds and mixtures	76 mm

MIXTURE DISPOSITION

Great	Mixture V	C	2	1⅓	1	⅓	½
		c	2⅔	2	1⅓	1	⅔
		g	2⅔	2	1⅓	1	1
		c¹	4	2⅔	2	1⅓	1
		f¹	4	2⅔	2	2	1⅓
		c²	4	2⅔	2⅔	2	2
		cs³	4	4	2⅔	2⅔	2
	Sharp Mixture	C	⅔	½	⅓	¼	
		Gs	1	⅔	½	⅓	
		ds	1⅓	1	⅔	½	
		as	2	1⅓	1	⅔	
		f¹	2⅔	2	1⅓	1	
		c²	4	2⅔	2	1⅓	
		c³	4	4	2⅔	2	
	Cornet		8	4	2⅔	2	1⅗ throughout
Positive	Mixture V	C	2	1⅓	1	⅔	½
		fs	2⅔	2	1⅓	1	⅔
		c¹	4	2⅔	2	1⅓	1
		c²	4	2⅔	2	2	1⅓
		c³	4	2⅔	2⅔	2	2
	Sharp Mixture	C	1	⅔	½	⅓	¼
		A	1⅓	1	⅔	½	⅓
		fs	2	1⅓	1	⅔	½
		ds¹	2⅔	2	1⅓	1	⅔
		c²	2⅔	2	1⅓	1⅓	1
		a²	4	2⅔	2	1⅓	1⅓
		fs³	4	2⅔	2⅔	2⅔	2
	Carillon	C	½	⅕			
		G	1	½	⅖		
		g	2	1	⅘		
		g¹	4	2	1⅗		
		g²	8	4	1⅗		
		c³	8	4	3⅕		

Choir	Sesquialtera	C	2/3	2/5				
		c	1 1/3	4/5				
		c¹	2 2/3	1 3/5				
	Mixture	C	1/2	1/3	1/4	1/6		
		G	2/3	1/2	1/3	1/4		
		c	1	2/3	1/2	1/3		
		g	1 1/3	1	2/3	1/2		
		c¹	2	1 1/3	1	2/3		
		c²	2 2/3	2	1 1/3	1		
		c³	4	2 2/3	2	1 1/3		
Solo	Rauschquint		2 2/3,	2 throughout				
	Tertian	C	1 1/3	4/5				
		c	1 3/5	1 1/3				
	Mixture	C	1 1/3	1	1	2/3	1/2	1/3
		c	2	1 1/3	1	1	2/3	1/2
		g	2 2/3	2	1 1/3	1	1	2/3
		c¹	4	2 2/3	2	2	1 1/3	1
		g¹	4	2 2/3	2 2/3	2	2	1 1/3
		g²	4	4	2 2/3	2 2/3	2	2
		c³	5 1/3	4	4	2 2/3	2 2/3	2
Swell	Mixture	C	1	2/3	1/2	1/3		
		c	1 1/3	1	1	2/3	1/2	
		g	2	1 1/3	1	1	2/3	
		c¹	2 2/3	2	2	1 1/3	1 1/3	1
		g¹	4	2 2/3	2 2/3	2	2	1 1/3
		g²	4	4	2 2/3	2 2/3	2	2
	Cymbel	C	1/5	1/6	1/8			
		F	1/4	1/5	1/6			
		As	1/3	1/4	1/5			
		ds	2/5	1/3	1/4			
		g	1/2	2/5	1/3			
		b	2/3	1/2	2/5			
		ds¹	4/5	2/3	1/2			
		g¹	1	4/5	2/3			
		b¹	1 1/3	1	4/5			
		ds²	1 3/5	1 1/3	1			
		gs²	2	1 3/5	1 1/3			
		cs³	2 2/3	2	1 3/5			
		f³	3 1/5	2 2/3	2			
		a³	4	3 1/5	2 2/3			
Pedal	Rauschquint		5 1/3,	4 throughout				
	Septerz		3 1/5	2 2/7 throughout				
	Mixture	C	2 2/3	2	1 1/3	1	2/3	
		gs	2 2/3	2	1 1/3	1	1	

TABLE I
St Mary's, Chigwell – Planned Tonal Balances

L.H. GREAT		R.H. SWELL
Rohrflute 8	=	Gedackt 8
Diapason 8 or Flutes 8, 4	=	Gedackt 8, Flute 4
Flutes 8, 4	=	Salicional 8, Flute 4
Rohrflute 8, Octave 4	=	Gedackt 8, Flute 4, Spitzflute 2
Rohrflute 8, Octave 4, Nazard	=	Gedackt 8, Flute 4, Spitzflute 2, Larigot
Flutes 8, 4, 15th	=	Gedackt 8, Flute 4, Cimbel
etc.		

L.H. SWELL		R.H. GREAT
Gedackt 8, Salicional	=	Rohrflute 8
+ Flute 4	=	+ Flute 4
Gedackt 8 (Salicional 8), Spitzflute 2	=	Rohrflute 8 (Nazard), 15th
Gedackt 8, Flute 4, Cremona	=	Flutes 8, 4, Nazard
Gedackt 8, Flute 4, Spitzflute, Sesquialtera	=	Flutes 8, 4, Nazard, 15th
etc.		

TABLE II
Fairfield Hall, Croydon – Planned Tonal Balances (selected)

L.H.		R.H.
Swell Gedacktpommer 8	=	Great Rohrflute 8
Swell Spitzflute 8, Stopped Flute 4	=	Great Rohrflute 8, Spitzflute 4
Swell Spitzflute 8, Flute 4, Gemshorn 2	=	Great Rohrflute 8, Spitzflute 4, Rauschquint
Great Rohrflute 8, Blockflute 2	=	Swell Gedacktpommer 8, Gemshorn 2
Great Rohrflute 8, Blockflute 2	=	Choir Stopped 8, 15th
Great Rohrflute 8, Octave 4	=	Choir Stopped 8, Principal 4, Nazard 2⅔
Great Diapason 8, Spitzflute 4, Flute 2	=	Choir Stopped 8, Principal 4, 15th
Great Rohrflute 8, Octave 4, Rauschquint	=	Choir Stopped 8, Flute 4, 15th, Tertian
Great 8, 4, 2, Rauschquint	=	Choir 8, 4, 2, Mixture
Great 8, 4, 2, Rauschquint or Mixture	=	Swell 8 4, 2, Cimbel
etc		

TABLE III
Gloucester Cathedral – East Diapason
Modifications to cut-up of front pipes, made by Ralph Downes

Scale: original (?)
Present pressure: 3½ inches full
Foot control
All measurements in millimetres

Note		Circumference (outside)	Mouth	Original cut-up	New cut-up
bottom	F	372	86.5	24.5	25.7
	F♯	343	80.6	21.0	21.0
	G	342	80.0	20.0	20.5
	G♯	316	77.0	19.0	19.7
	A	315.5	74.5	19.5	21.0
	A♯	283	67.5	18.5	19.0
	B	284	66.5	18.5	20.5
tenor	c	245	58.0	17.0	17.5
	c♯	244	57.0	15.6	16.7
	d	226	53.5	15.0	16.0
	d♯	228	53.6	14.6	16.3
	e	201	46.0	12.5	13.0
	f	201	47.5	12.0	12.6
	f♯	185	45.5	12.5	13.4
	g	184	45.5	11.5	12.8
	g♯	160	42.0	9.5 *(?)	12.0
	a	160	37.5	10.5	11.3
	a♯	147	35.0	9.5	10.3
	b	148	34.5	11.0 ‡(?)	10.3

* probably a recording error: probably 10.5
‡ probably a recording error: probably 10.0

INDEX

(Abbreviation: ob = organ-builder)

Abend, F. (ob) 123ff, 126f, 145
Acoustic coupling 138, 218
Acoustics team (RFH) 77, 88, 97, 111, 137, 164
Adkins, J. H. (ob) 11, 18, 19
Aeolian Company 227f
Aeolian Skinner Company 32, 52, 66, 224 (note 14)
Alcock, W. G. 226 (note 34)
Alkmaar, St. Laurenskerk 113f, 130, 132, 139, 231ff
Allen, Sir Hugh 24
Amsterdam
   New Church 112f, 115
   Old Church 112f, 127, 135
Ann Arbor, Michigan 166
Aprahamian, Felix 77, 97
Architects' team (RFH) 97, 111, 123, 134, 164
Armley (Leeds), Schulze organ 64, 67, 104, 218, 225 (note 25)
Arnaut de Zwolle 67
Audsley, G. A. 69, 88
Austin, T. (ob) 124f, 135, 137
Auton, John 197
Ayot St. Lawrence 213

Bach, J. S. 13, 22, 23, 32, 34, 42, 43, 47, 48, 54, 55, 69, 103, 115f, 213, 216
Bach Choir (London) 73
Bach Choir (Oxford) 24
Badura-Skoda, Paul 8
Bätz, J. (ob), Utrecht 116
Bagenal, H. 77, 88, 106, 172
Balance (tonal) 201f, 237
Batholemay Bros. (ob), Philadelphia 29
"Baroque style" 72
Batiste, E. 13

Bean, Ernest (General Manager RFH) 168
Bédos de Celles, Dom F. (ob) 47, 58, 59, 63, 64, 67-70, 99, 123, 141, 171, 186
Beecham, Sir Thomas 176
Beethoven 2, 169
Benham, G. 56
Bennett, T. H. 14f
Bernau, St. Marie 126
Best, W. T. 13, 224 (note 4)
Bevington (ob) 13, 63, 224 (note 4), 225 (note 33)
Birmingham (Town Hall) 13, 28
Bishop, J. C. (ob) 204
Bishop & Son (ob) 212ff, 225 (note 18)
Bishop & Starr (ob) 39, 50, 63, 129
Bodley (architect) 197
Bologna, S. Petronio 209
Booth (ob) 17, 224 (note 7)
Boston, Massachusetts
   Music Hall 30, 34
   Symphony Hall 96
Boult, Sir Adrian (late) 169f
Brahms, J. 72
Brindley & Foster (ob) 74
de Brisay, A. C. D. 46
Bristol
   Colston Hall 138
   St. Mary Redcliffe 105
British Library 109
Bruckner, A. 73
"Bubble & Squeak" 43
Buckfast, St. Mary's Abbey 52-55, 64ff, 77, 106f, 108, 123, 129, 132, 135, 144-151, 177f, 179, 227-231
Budgen, John (ob) 212-215
Burke, Dom Gregory (late) 151
Butler, Michael (ob) 185
Button, Arthur 185

Cambridge King's College 23
Cameron, Basil (late) 170
van Campen (Architect) 15
Cappel (Schnitger organ) 130ff
Cardiff
   City Council 216
   St. David's Hall 216ff, 220ff
Casework, resonant 97, 130, 160f, 172, 176f, 201f, 205, 216
Cavaillé-Coll, A. (ob) 33ff, 45, 47f, 51f, 56, 61, 82, 87, 97, 103, 109, 127, 130, 178f, 181ff, 186, 219, 226 (note 35)
Chigwell, Essex
   Choral Society 197, 199
   St. Mary's Church 197-201, 237
Clare, Maurice 137
Clicquot (ob) 87, 109
Clutton, Cecil 8, 67, 133f, 225 (note 31)
Cocker, Norman 105
Collins, Peter (ob) 216
Collop, Albert (ob) 155, 160, 162
Columbia University, USA 96
Conacher, Peter (ob) 17
Cook, E. T. 22
Copenhagen
   Danish State Radio Hall 83, 96
Couperin, F. 47, 48, 56
Covell, William King 30
Croydon
   Fairfield Hall 202, 211, 216, 225 (note 23), 237
Cunningham, G. D. 28, 42

Dalton, James 170
Davidson, R. W. ("Kingsgate") (ob) 58-64, 67ff, 74, 76, 99, 106f, 225 (note 23)
Derby 9-20 (passim)
   All Saints Church (Cathedral) 9, 13-17, 20
   Choral Union 13
   Drill Hall 13
   Green Hill Wesleyan Church 17
   Hippodrome (variety theatre) 18
   King Street Wesleyan Church 17
   St. Alkmund's Church 7, 11f, 20f, 224 (note 2)
   St. Andrew's Church 17ff
   St. Werburgh's Church 17
   White Hall Super Cinema 18
D'Evry, E. 40

Dicker (of Exeter) (ob) 213
Dixon, Lt-Col. G. 58, 63, 136
Dolmetsch Family 58
Driebergen 115
Dubois, F. 13
Dupré, Marcel 22, 42, 45, 47, 211
Durham (Cathedral) 105
Dvořák, A. 199

Eagle, Fred (ob) 58, 135
Earlam, S. (ob) 53f
Eclecticism 79, 96, 133
Elgar, Sir Edward
   Apostles 199
   Cockaigne 103
   Enigma Variations 103, 133
   Kingdom 199
Elliott (ob) 13
Elvin, Laurence 224 (note 8)
Ely (Cathedral) 63
Erard, "Max" 19
Exeter (Cathedral) 7, 206

Festival of Britain, (1951) 79, 88
Flentrop, D. A. (ob) 113, 115ff, 125, 130, 135, 148, 164
Förster & Nicolaus (ob) 123
Forster & Andrews (ob) 17ff
Framlingham, St. Michael's 205, 211
Franck, César 13, 17, 45, 72, 103, 105
Freiburg, Organ Conference 68
"Frontispiece" (RFH) 123, 165

Gammons, Ed 45
Germani, Fernando 167, 226 (note 34)
Gibbs, James (Architect) 13
Gloucester (Cathedral) 202, 204-212, 226 (note 38), 238
   Three Choirs Festival 205, 209, 211
Goldsborough, Arnold 72
Goodey, Walter (ob) 99, 106, 135, 148ff, 160ff, 177, 185
Goodridge, Peter (Architect) 155
Gottfried, Anton (ob) 35ff, 67ff, 172
Gouda, St. Jan 127
Gray & Davison (ob) 13, 44, 177
Green, Samuel (ob) 213
Grieg, Edvard 18
de Grigny, Nicolas 47
Grison, Jules 13
Groton (School), USA 35, 96

INDEX

Guilain 47
Guilmant, A. 13

Haarlem 135
Hague, The
  New Church 112, 116
Handel, G. F. 73
Harris, Thomas (ob) 202, 205
Harris, Dr. (Sir) W. H. 24
Harrison, Arthur (ob) 136, 167
Harrison, Cuthbert (ob) 98, 106, 124, 129f, 132ff, 164
Harrison, G. Donald (ob) 28, 32-36, 45, 50-53, 56, 64, 72, 93, 96, 98, 103, 123, 127, 130, 225 (note 16), 229f
Harrison & Harrison Ltd. (ob) 23, 88, 98, 103, 111, 123, 130, 164f, 168, 172, 176, 233
Harrow (School) 138
Hartford, Conn USA
  Trinity College 33
Harvard (University) USA
  Germanic Museum 96
Haydn, Joseph ("*Creation*") 199
Hayward, (Sir) Isaac 115
Hele & Co. (ob) 227
Hibbert, Norman 17
Hill, Wm. (ob) 7, 14, 19, 23, 25, 63, 198
Hill, Norman & Beard (see also Norman & Beard) 189ff, 202
Hindemith, Paul 105
Hock, Susi (=Jeans) 43, 74
Hollins, Alfred 13
Howard, Michael 8, 58
Howe, Fred (ob) 135, 137f, 140, 150, 164, 168, 170f, 176
Hunt, Rev Noel Bonavia 23
Huré, Jean 109
Hurford, Peter 176

Ingram, Eustace (ob) 17
Ireland, John 13
Jeans, (Lady) Susi 43, 74, 109, 123f, 207
Johnstone, Dr. K. I. 225 (note 25)
Jones, Arthur (ob) 185
Jones, Geraint 125
Jones, Henry (ob) 212
Jones, Robert Hope (ob) 137
Jones, W. C. (ob) 46, 52ff, 56f, 135, 138

Keeton, Dr. Haydn 17

Klais (ob) 202
Klotz, Hans 109, 112, 125f
Kroonenberg, Cor 115

Lancaster (University) 214f
Leeds (Town Hall) 177
Lefébure-Wély 13
Lewis, T. C. (ob) 7, 11f, 20ff, 33, 44, 83, 97, 158, 176, 224 (note 11)
Ley, Henry G. 25
Leyden
  Marekerk 112
  Pieterskerk 112
Lichfield (Cathedral) 18
Liszt, F. 72
Liverpool (St. George's Hall) 197
London
  Alexandra Palace 44
  Barnes, Holy Trinity, Castelnau 212f
  Brompton Oratory 39-44, 46, 50ff, 56-64, 67-72, 73-77, 106f, 117, 123, 129, 135, 152-163, 177, 225 (note 20)
  Coliseum 18
  Crystal Palace 13
  County Council (later GLC) 77, 88, 134, 165
  Ealing (Town Hall) 225 (note 33)
  Notre-Dame de France 45f, 51f, 178
  Royal Albert Hall 22f, 73, 105, 136, 138, 170, 225 (note 28)
  Royal Festival Hall 7, 29, 45, 77-106 (passim), 109ff, 115, 117-123, 125, 126-129, 133f, 137, 141ff, 158, 164-177, 207f, 233ff
  St. Martin's in the Fields 13
  St. Paul's Cathedral 7, 22, 82, 105, 206
  Southwark Cathedral (St. Saviour's) 21f, 46, 176
  Underwood Road (E 1), St. Anne's Catholic Church 225 (note 19)
  West London Synagogue 105
  Westminster Abbey 73, 105
  Westminster Aquarium 212
  Westminster Cathedral 22f
London Philharmonic Orchestra 73, 77, 169f
Lorimer, Sir Robert (Architect) 182
Lott, John B. (Mus Bac) 18
Luçon 219f

Lunelli, Renato 226 (note 38)

McPhee, George 178
Mahrenholz, Christhard 74, 109
Malvern, Priory Church 179
Manchester
　Cathedral 134
　Holy Trinity, Hulme 22
Marchal, André 77, 85, 87, 97
Marcussen (ob) 83, 199
Martin, Dr. (Sir) Leslie 111, 165, 172
Mascioni, G. (ob) 212
Mendelssohn-Bartholdy, Felix 13
Messiaen, Olivier 105
Methuen, Massachusetts 30, 97, 224
　(note 13)
Michell & Thynne (ob) 96
Minay, William O. 23
Mittelkirchen 126, 132
Models (RFH organ) 111
Möller (ob) 30
Mustel, orgue 18f, 46

New York, St. Mary the Virgin 33
Newcastle-upon-Tyne (City Hall) 225
　(note 28)
Nicholson (ob) 61
Nicking (in flue-pipes) 116, 135f, 160, 162
Niland, Austin 225 (note 31)
Noehren, Robert 109, 112-116, 117, 166
Normal-scale 68-71
Norman & Beard (ob) 64, 123
Norman, H. John 205, 210, 226
　(note 38)
Norman, Herbert L. 205, 207
Nottingham 13
　Elite Cinema 21
　St. Mary's Church 20, 40, 199
　Trent Bridge Pavilion 19

Oratory, Birmingham 61
Oratory, London (see London, Brompton Oratory)
Oratory, Roman 42
Organ, The (quarterly) 56
Organ-case (see Casework, resonant)
Organ Music Society 77
Organ Reform
　America 32
　Germany 68

Organ stops (special references in text)
　Baarpijp 116, 141, 161
　Cornet (grand) 25, 171
　Diapason, "Bell" 13
　Diapason, "big" 18f, 22f
　Fourniture 67-71
　Geigenprincipal 20
　Italian Principal (sic) 141
　Quintadena 116, 141, 161, 171
　Reed, smooth or HP 18f, 22f
　Trumpet *en chamade* 221
Ottobeuren 197
Oxford
　Keble College 23, 25
　St. Peter's 24
　Sheldonian Theatre 24f

Paderewski, Ignaz 8
Page, Bernard 45
Paisley (Abbey) 178-197, 219
Paris
　La Madeleine 47
　Notre-Dame 42, 47f, 85, 87, 115, 197, 225 (notes 17, 26)
　Palais de Chaillot 83, 85
　Ste. Clotilde 109
　St. Eustache 85, 87
　St. Gervais 48f
　St. Sulpice 47f
Parry, C. H. H. 13
Pattman, G. T. 18f, 225 (note 23)
Peasgood, Osborne 73
Peer Gynt (Grieg) 18
Penarth, St. Augustine's Church 224
　(note 3)
Philadelphia, USA
　St. Luke's, Germantown 96
Pitman chest action 28, 33
Pius X (Pope) "Motu Proprio" 40
Plummer, F. Isherwood 12
Poitiers (Cathedral) 109
Praetorius, Michael 7, 224 (note 1)
Princeton, New Jersey, USA
　Plainsboro, Presbyterian Church 29f
　University Chapel 25-29, 30, 32f, 35-38, 42, 44, 96, 225 (note 16)
　University Choir 28, 33
　Westminster Choir College 30, 33, 35
Prosser, Philip G. (ob) 209f

Quoicka, Rudolf 109

INDEX

Raymar, Aubyn 25
Raymond, Chester A. (ob) 32, 35-38
Reflectors (sound) 123, 161f, 172, 176, 178, 186, 201, 208
Reger, Max 13, 72, 74, 105
Renunciation, "The Great" 211, 216
Reubke, J., Sonata 176
Rheinberger, Josef 13
Rieger (ob) 166
Robertson, F. E. (ob) 69
Rochesson, Louis-Eugène (ob) 46f, 61, 74ff, 83, 85, 87, 97, 107, 162, 172
Roosevelt (ob) 64
Rouen, St. Ouen 48
Rowland, Leslie ("Bob") (ob) 168
Rowntree, John 96
Rushworth (& Dreaper) (ob) 23, 25, 179

St. Albans (Cathedral) 8, 202
St. Martin, Léonce de 47, 85
St. Maximin 109
Saint-Saëns, C. 13, 18, 215
Salisbury (Cathedral) 22, 105
Salomé 13
Salt Lake City USA (Tabernacle) 96
Samson et Dalila 18
Scales (flue) 54, 59, 63f, 66-71, 75, 85, 99ff, 104f, 108, 116-120, 124ff, 129ff, 135, 138-142, 145ff, 188, 190f, 193ff, 200f, 202f, 208f, 214f, 216, 218-222, 231ff, 238
Schnitger, Arp (ob) 109, 112, 125f, 130ff, 138, 154
Schnitger, Franz Caspar (ob) 113, 139
Schoenberg, A. 225 (note 16)
Schulze, Edmund (ob) 22f, 63f, 67, 104, 218
Schumann, Robert 72
Schweitzer, Albert 23, 48
Searles, E. R. (ob) 30
Self, William 34
Sheffield (Albert Hall) 13
Silbermann, Andreas (ob) 107
Silbermann, Gottfried (ob) 32, 35, 96, 123, 130
Simon, Llewelyn (ob) 25
Skinner, Ernest M. (ob) 25, 224 (note 15)
Skinner Company (ob) 25, 28, 30
Smart, Henry 13
Smets, Paul 109, 138
Smith, "Father" (ob) 13, 44

Southwark (Cathedral) (see London)
Souvigny 109
Specifications
  Alkmaar, St. Laurenskerk (scales of fluework) 231ff
  Buckfast, St. Mary's Abbey 55, 64f, 144f, 227-231
  Cardiff, St. David's Hall 217
  Chigwell, St. Mary's Church 198
  Derby, All Saints' (Cathedral) 14
    St. Alkmund's (Lewis) 12
    St. Werburgh's 17
  Driebergen (Holland) 115
  London
    Barnes, Holy Trinity, Castelnau 212f
    Brompton Oratory 39f, 62, 153, 155
    Notre-Dame de France 45, 178
    Royal Festival Hall 79ff, 83ff, 90-96, 120ff, 128f, 133, 233ff
  Nottingham, St. Mary's 20
  Paisley Abbey 186, 189, 192f
  Princeton, New Jersey, USA (University Chapel) 26, 37f
    (Plainsboro Presbyterian Church) 29
  Worcester, Massachusetts USA All Saints' Church 34
Stanford, C. V. 13
Steinkirchen (Schnitger organ) 125, 132
Stevens (Architect) 11
Stow, E. R. 224 (note 6)
Strickland, William 44
Stringer (of Salop) (ob) 14
Sullivan, Sir Arthur 212
Sumner, W. L. (late) 96
Swansea, Brangwyn Hall 21

Tagliavini, Prof. L. F. 226 (note 8)
Tchaikovski, Overture 1812 103
Thalben-Ball, George 176, 213
Thamar, Thomas (ob) 205
Thompson-Allen, Aubrey (ob) 44
Thornsby, F. W. 224 (notes 4 and 5)
Thurlow, D. F. (ob) 58, 135, 149f, 161, 177, 185, 226 (note 35)
Times (newspaper), London 73
Töpfer, J. G. (ob) 67-70, 97, 99, 104, 108, 152
Tomkins, Rodney 224 (notes 6 and 8)

Trevor, C. H. 25, 40, 42, 61, 69
Tunks, F. (ob) 22
Tyne Dock, St. Mary's (Schulze Organ) 23, 63f, 67

Utrecht (Dom) 116

Valetta (Malta), S. Giovanni 212
Vente, Dr. M. A. 138
Verne, D. Batigan 63f
Vierne, Louis 23, 25, 42, 46, 47, 85, 105, 199, 225 (note 17)
Voicing
  "First Class" 136
  Flue-pipes (see also Nicking) 66, 116, 124f, 130, 132, 147ff, 152f, 160f, 164, 170f, 208ff, 215, 218-221
  "Modern" 20
  Reeds 58-61, 66, 74ff, 162, 172, 213, 215, 221

Walcha, Helmut 123, 130
Walcker, E. F. (ob) 30, 34, 35
Walker, J. W. & Sons (ob) 20, 40, 43-46, 50-53, 57f, 66, 77, 129, 135, 148, 177ff, 192ff, 197ff, 229f
Walker, Reginald (ob) 43, 56, 66, 106, 155
Walter, Bruno 73
Wardour Castle (Church) 213

Washington, Henry 42, 50, 51, 154, 225 (note 32)
Watters, Clarence 45
Webb, F. 88
Weingarten 197
Weinrich, Carl 30, 38, 225 (note 16)
Werkprinzip 113
Wesley, S. S. 13, 206
Westminster Choir College 30, 33, 35
White, Ernest (ob) 45
Whitelegg, Richard (ob) 30
Whitworth, John 205, 211
Wicks, Allan 8
Widor, C-M. 13, 45, 225 (note 32)
Williams, Edwin (Architect) 77, 83, 93, 137
Williams, Dr. Peter 197
Willis, "Father" (ob) 7, 22, 24, 44, 48, 82, 105, 130, 202, 204, 206f, 211
Willis, Henry II (ob) 17
Willis, Henry III (ob) 21, 23ff, 44, 109
Windchest design 66
Wolstenholme, Wm. 13
Wood, H. (ob) 167, 170f
Wood, R. (ob) 134, 167
Worcester (Cathedral) 207
Worcester, Massachusetts, USA All Saints' Church 33f

Yates, Roger (ob) 150